VICTORINE

FRANCES PARKINSON KEYES

Victorine

Julian Messner, Inc.

New York

Published by Julian Messner, Inc.
8 West 40 Street, New York 18

Published simultaneously in Canada
by The Copp Clark Publishing Co. Limited

PRINTED IN THE UNITED STATES OF AMERICA

Foreword

THE LOVE STORY OF PROSPER VILLAC AND VICTORINE LABRANCHE WAS not originally visualized as a book; it was planned as the third part of a three-generation novel. But when the author—namely myself—was well into the second part, two things became obvious to her: first, that by the time she was through with the love story of Claude Villac, Fleex Primeaux and Lavinia Winslow, the book would already be more than what publishers have a tiresome way of calling "comfortable trade length"; second, and far more important—for authors should not be too much concerned as to whether the trade is comfortable or not—she realized that any episode, however dramatic, would seem like an anticlimax after the discovery of Blue Camellia. The gilded youth of the 1920's simply did not belong in the same category as the pioneers of the 1880's or the reactionaries of the turn of the century.

What to do? Fictional characters have a way of coming very much alive, at least to their creator; you simply cannot casually kill them off, especially as the more alive they are to her, the more likely they are to seem alive to readers. The first fictional character to come alive, in the section dealing with the twenties, happened to be a dog—a huge Dalmatian named Levvy. Naturally, Levvy needed an owner and Victorine LaBranche came alive as such. Then she needed a father, and there was Moïse LaBranche. So much for the new figures on the scene. Prosper Villac, who was eight years old when difficulties about trade length began to arise, would soon be grown up; he seemed a logical suitor for Victorine. And then, there was his pretty little sister Anne Marie, who would be growing up, too, and entitled to a love story of her own. How was I to dispose of all these people? The beautiful little porcelain Dalmatian, which had been given me by a well-wisher for a mascot as soon as Levvy entered my life, and which, for a long time had appeared to regard me in an encouraging manner from his station on my desk, now began to gaze at me banefully. "I have been your faithful companion for several years," he seemed to be saying, with justifiable reproach, "are you about to send me to the pound?"

In my dilemma, I consulted, first my American and then my English publisher. "Of course I want the story of Victorine," Mrs. Messner said, almost testily. "My goodness, you've sent me several chapters, in rough draft, about her already! What do you expect me to do with them? Tear them up? You've got to put a whole book in the twenties, that's all." (She spoke as if a whole book were the merest trifle—publishers have a way of doing that, even when they know months—and maybe years—of intensive toil are ahead of an author.) Douglas Jerrold, my English publisher, was less casual, but even more demanding. "I am very much pleased with your *mise-en-scène*," he informed me. "However, I'd like it a little more bloodcurdling. Couldn't you have a murder in the rice fields?"

I strive to please. I did not unearth any murders in the rice fields of my *mise-en-scène* which, needless to say, is a real one and where, I am glad to report, crime does not seem to be rampant or even frequent. But I did discover the story of an accident, which occurred elsewhere in Louisiana and which might have happened in any rice-producing area. With this the bloodthirsty Englishman declared himself content and I went ahead.

The name of Dale Fontenot, which seemed to me suitable for the young man of fine principles and distinguished background who figures in my narrative, is used for a fictional character by special permission of the parents and widow of the real Lieutenant (j.g.) Dale Fontenot, U.S.N., who graduated from the United States Naval Academy in 1953 and was tragically killed in a plane crash, while in flight training, at Corpus Christi Air Base several years ago. My fictional character resembles him in personal attributes, but not in career. It is exactly the opposite in the case of my fictional character, Brent Winslow, whose *achievements* were actually those of Salmon Wright, "the Burbank of the rice industry," though there is no other resemblance between them. These achievements have been the inspiration for some of the material in this book, as they were for much of it in *Blue Camellia*; and Mr. Wright actually reigned as the first king of a Rice Carnival Day, with his daughter, Edith, now Mrs. Carl Kemmerly, as his queen. I am deeply indebted to Mrs. Kemmerly and to her sisters and brother, Mrs. Thomas A. Warner, Sr. (Lillian Wright), Mrs. Paul C. Hoffpauir (Rosemary Wright), and Mr. Salmon Wright, Jr., for their kind permission to make better known, in fictional form, the great debt which the entire rice industry owes to their father. The achievements of Henri Bendel, a native of Lafayette, were responsible for those attributed to Moïse La-Branche, though, as unfortunately, unlike my fictional figure, he never returned there, at least to my knowledge, in the years since I began spending my winters in Louisiana, I have not been able to dwell on his career with as much detail as that of Salmon Wright. Again, as a personality, Moïse LaBranche is entirely fictitious. Dale Fontenot is the only real name that has been used, except—as in *Blue Camellia*—in the case of well-known characters who are now part of history. This time, there are only four: Captain Robert Mouton, the scion of a great family and distinguished in his own right as an outstanding horticulturist, a gallant soldier and a successful politician; Georges Armand Martin, noteworthy alike as a physician and a jurist; W. W. Duson, one of Crowley's founding fathers and chief promoters and, for many years, editor of the Crowley *Signal*; his son, W. W. Duson, Jr.; and Huey Long, who needs no identification to any reader. In every other case, except these just mentioned, names, achievements and characteristics are all fictitious.

The editorials quoted from the Crowley *Signal* have actually appeared in it, though not on the dates attributed to them; I am indebted to Max Thomas, its present owner and publisher, who has been kindness and co-operation itself in connection with all my work in Louisiana, for permission to switch the dates to suit my purpose, and to him and the widow, sons and daughter of W. W. Duson—Mrs. W. W. Duson, Sr., W. W. Duson, Maxwell Duson, Henry C. Duson and Mrs. Mildred Duson Cossey—for permission to make a slight change in the one which was actually printed in 1929, with the caption, "An Annual Monument." For my purposes, it was necessary to use it as a tribute to a man who was still living and to call it "Perennial Gratitude." I have, at all times, had access to the files of the Crowley *Signal* and have drawn on them freely, especially those for 1926–27, which included the accounts of Rice Carnival Day.

For editorial advice, I am again greatly indebted to Hermann B. Deutsch, Associate Editor of the New Orleans *Item*, and Mary Alice Fontenot, who has served on the editorial staff of the Lafayette *Advertiser*, the Opelousas *Daily World* and the Eunice *News*. As far as Mr. Deutsch is concerned, I can only repeat what I said in the Foreword to

Blue Camellia: "His helpfulness has not been limited to the editorial field. He is an authority on a greater variety of subjects than almost anyone else I know, and it is no exaggeration to say that several chapters in this book could not possibly have been written by me, if I had not had his almost inexhaustible fund of information, much of it based on practical experience, on which to draw. I am glad to make this public acknowledgment of my great indebtedness." In his research, Mr. Deutsch has had the co-operation of Mr. Edgar V. Schafer, Jr. and Mr. Gordon T. Schafer, respectively president and vice president of the Universal Rice Milling Products Company and Mr. James P. Gaines, assistant to the president of the Rice Millers' Association, all of New Orleans. I did not have the privilege of meeting these gentlemen myself and, as there are apparently some local differences in the designation of rice mill equipment, past and present, I have adhered to the terms given me in and around Crowley, since that is where our fictional rice mill is located.

As far as Mary Alice Fontenot is concerned, her knowledge of local conditions in the rice country is based not only on lifelong residence and marriage to the manager of a rice mill, but to the fact that, by heredity, as well as environment, she is intimately allied to this section of Louisiana. Her almost infallible ear for the nuances of local speech, her familiarity with all forms of local usage, and her experience as a journalist and a reviewer have served to enlarge, still further, her usefulness to me. My gratitude to her is unbounded.

Much valuable and varied information has also been given me by the following persons: Rt. Rev. Albert J. Bacque, Pastor of St. John's Cathedral, Lafayette; Mr. George Sabatier, formerly manager of the Superior Rice Mill of Eunice and now a rice broker in that city; Mr. George Schlessinger of the Louisiana State Rice Milling Company, Inc. of Abbeville; Mr. J. Otto ("Chingie") Broussard, manager of the Edmundson-Duhe Rice Mill in Rayne and Mr. Edmond D'Aquin, Sr., manager of the rough rice department in the same mill; Mr. Vincent Riehl of Lafayette; Mr. Sidney Fontenot of Eunice; Miss Ann Schuffhausen, secretary to the manager of River Brand Rice Mill, Eunice; Mr. Frederick J. Nehrbass of Lafayette; Mrs. Carl Kemmerly of Baton Rouge; Mrs. Sigmund Katz of Covington; Miss Julia Hutchinson and Miss Pearl Landry, who are largely responsible for familiarizing me with the territory all the way between Lafayette and Cypremort Point; Miss Mario Mamalakis, Associate Professor and Circulation Librarian of Southwestern Louisiana Institute, Dr. Martin Samson of Crowley, Dr. Robert C. Kelleher of New Orleans and Dr. Nicholas Chetta of New Orleans.

(Incidentally, lest it should strike any reader as strange that anyone could be committed to an institution for the criminally insane with no investigation beyond the examination of the parish coroner, let me state that, at the time about which we are writing, such examination was all that was required in Louisiana.)

Much of the later work on *Victorine* has been done while I have been greatly handicapped by serious intermittent illnesses and constant painful physical disability because of lameness, which have kept me, for months, in the old slave quarters, which it seems especially appropriate to me, under the circumstances, to keep on calling by their original name. I doubt whether the book could have been finished on schedule time had it not been for the efficient and loyal co-operation of my secretary, Deanie Bullock. In fact, as far as I am concerned, her name should be coupled with that of Victorine as the real heroine of this story.

FRANCES PARKINSON KEYES

The early part of the work on *Victorine* was done at Compensation, the place acquired in Crowley on purpose to give me a writing center in my *mise-en-scène,* which I then thought would be used for only one book. I was the happy possessor of the house and grounds comprising this pleasant property for ten years, but sold it under the mistaken impression that my work in southwestern Louisiana was practically done; so *Blue Camellia* was finished and *Victorine* continued in near-by Lafayette, where I was fortunately able to rent a *pied-à-terre.* Less fortunately, this nice little house was sold over my head and the major part of the work on *Victorine* has been done in the slave quarters connected with Beauregard House in New Orleans, with a brief return to Lafayette and Crowley for the purpose of checking and rechecking in the interests of authenticity. The Town House Motel in Lafayette was my headquarters while this was being done.

F. P. K.

PART ONE

---

*Spring and
Summer, 1926*

The Gold Slippers

Chapter One

"WELL, THANKS A MILLION, CAPTAIN BOB. NO ONE BUT YOU COULD HAVE ferreted this out for me."

"*Il n'y a pas de quoi, cher,* and after all, it did not take much ferreting. You talk as if I were the hero of a *roman policier*—not just a small-town mayor whose hobby is horticulture."

"Lafayette isn't such a small town any more. And I seem to remember a piece in the paper that said you were equally at home in banking, education, politics—*and* your garden. At that, it didn't go into your war record."

"Oh, people are beginning to forget about the war—just as well, too! As for the rest, *des compliments, cher—rien que des compliments.*"

Prosper Villac laughed, but just why he could not have said. Perhaps it was because he was always amused at Bob Mouton's complete unconsciousness at switching from English to French and from French to English, when he was talking casually; it was something he always had done, and probably always would do, and it did not matter much in Lafayette, where almost everyone, except newcomers who did not count, was bilingual anyway. When he went over to Crowley on business, which he often had occasion to do, he sometimes had to stop and translate, because Crowley, with its more generally Anglo-Saxon background than any other place in the vicinity, was not predominantly bilingual. But, as it happened, Prosper Villac, who came from there, was very nearly so. His father Claude Villac had been an Acadian with a reasonably good education, and was fluent in both what was locally known as *français de l'Academie* and the more typical Cajun dialect. Prosper's mother Lavinia, who had been graduated with honors at the Academy

of the Sacred Heart in Grand Coteau, and taken special courses at the
then recently founded Sophie Newcomb College in New Orleans, spoke
French with a slight accent, but with complete grammatical precision.
She had seen to it that both Prosper and his younger sister Anne Marie
had been as thoroughly schooled as she was.

Perhaps it was on account of Anne Marie, and not on account of
Captain Bob's unusual though pleasant manner of speech that Prosper
was laughing now, with a sense of happy triumph. He had adored his
sister from the moment that the new baby, whose tiny head was haloed
with golden down, and who opened soft blue eyes to stare at him, had
been cautiously put into his arms by their father, who stood watchfully
by, because the three-year-old boy, who was usually up to some deviltry,
could not be trusted to handle an infant with knowledgeable or tender
care. But Prosper had given his father and everyone else a surprise; he
not only seemed to know by instinct exactly what to do for Anne Marie,
but he loved doing it; and he had gone on loving to do anything he could
for her ever since: he comforted her when she cried, helped to take care
of her when she was sick, taught her the first lessons she learned, petted
her in and out of season, and showered her with presents, whether there
was any special reason for a gift or not. It did not need to be Christmas or
Easter or her birthday; if he heard her express a wish, or guessed that she
had one that was unfulfilled, he hastened to see that it was granted if he
possibly could. He had begun by breaking open a piggy bank to buy her
a doll that bleated mah-mah if you turned a key; he had saved his allowance to give her a turquoise ring "matching her eyes" before it had
occurred to anyone else that she was old enough to have a ring—as indeed their mother said she was not. He had forestalled fashions in fancy
belt buckles, gold lockets and pearl beads when he became conscious that
girls liked such things; and now he had succeeded, thanks to Captain
Bob, in getting her a fine specimen of the so-called "Lost Camellia" for
which she had been hankering.

She had, apparently, inherited her passionate love of flowers from her
maternal grandmother, Mary Winslow, whose knowledge of them and
skill with them were bywords throughout the countryside and beyond it.
His mother regarded a well-ordered garden as an essential part of any
properly run establishment; but her feeling for one did not go beyond
this. It was Anne Marie who had kept digging and weeding and water-
ing, and refused to leave any of the work in her own special corner to the
capable old yard man, Sylvestre, if she could help it; and she trespassed
elsewhere on what he considered his preserve. Moreover, she was not

satisfied to have the spacious grounds encircled with golden day lilies, mauve azaleas, purple iris, pink crape myrtle and white chrysanthemums; various other blooms followed each other in quick succession, so that one or the other was sure to be blossoming throughout the year, like her roses. She wanted all sorts of exotic plants in her garden as well; and, as a matter of course, she wanted every known variety of camellia. The result was that the Villacs' flower garden was now far and away the largest and most beautiful in Crowley, which was saying a great deal; and when it seemed to Prosper and to their mother that there could not possibly be anything more Anne Marie would want to add, she had started talking about this Lost Camellia.

She had read about it in some book, one of those ponderous volumes about gardens into which she was continually sticking her pretty little nose, instead of confining her reading to light novels and very few of those, like most of the girls they knew. In this tome, whatever it was, Anne Marie had read about a camellia that had been imported into the United States early in the first wave of camellia popularity, and which had since been lost, to all intents and purposes, from collectors' knowledge. Even its original designation had somehow disappeared from view and, consequently, from commerce; so now there were only references to it, no available specimens; in the references it was called the Lost Camellia. . . .

"It can't really be lost," Anne Marie had insisted. "It *was* brought into the United States—the book says so. It must be *somewhere*."

"How many kinds of camellias have you got in the garden now?" Lavinia inquired, looking up from some equally weighty tome she was reading and which, Prosper guessed, though he could not see the title, was about rice, for she felt just the same way about this that Anne Marie did about camellias.

"Only sixty. And it wouldn't matter if I had six hundred, as long as there was one I had heard about that was lost. I'd want to find it."

"To change the subject for a moment, have you telephoned Dale Fontenot yet?"

"No, not yet."

"He really wants an answer about that picnic at Cypremort Point. You ought to be reasonable and give it to him. He has to make his plans."

"He's welcome to make all the plans he wants. He can have a picnic at Cypremort Point without me."

"You know that the whole idea of the picnic is to have you there."

"Yes, I know, Mother. But I keep telling Dale—"

That was Anne Marie all over. She kept telling Dale Fontenot, one of
the nicest fellows that ever lived, who had a fine sugar plantation, Sapphira, on Bayou Cypremort, that she hadn't made up her mind yet. She
kept saying the same thing to Didier Benoit, who was also one of the
nicest fellows that ever lived, and who didn't own a sugar plantation
himself, because his father was still living, but who, with his brother
Maurice, would be heir to Pecan Grove, just out of Lafayette on the
Broussard Road. She said the same thing to half a dozen other fellows,
too. It seemed to Prosper—and he thought it seemed the same way to
Lavinia—that every unattached man or boy, and some that were supposedly already firmly anchored, who looked at Anne Marie, wanted her
to make up her mind to marry him. What was worse, this had been going
on for years and years already. Here she was, nearly twenty-four, and she
hadn't even reached her teens when Prosper and Lavinia had been
obliged to start brushing boys off the porch. If she hadn't been the
sweet, feminine type she was—golden haired, pink cheeked, blue eyed,
with a disposition as lovely as her looks—people would inevitably have
started saying it was evident she really wanted to be an old maid. But it
was impossible to say that about Anne Marie. She was obviously made
to love and be loved. Only she couldn't make up her mind. . . .

Prosper started to tease her about this as she sat, a pink finger still
slipped in the book about camellias she had been reading, to mark the
place. Then he wished he hadn't.

"You haven't made up your mind yet, either, have you?" she asked
innocently. The innocence was not assumed; Prosper felt reasonably sure
of that. Gossip, however slightly tinged with malice, was somehow always silenced by Anne Marie's presence; it did not belong in the same
room with her. As for scandal, he doubted if she had ever connected it
with anyone she knew. But, as he stole a quick glance at his mother, he
saw that her mouth, normally a firm one, had tightened, which was
always a bad sign. If he had been pinned down, he would have admitted
she must have known that he had been going, with increasing frequency,
to the dance hall over August Scholtze's grocery store, to which August
had given the highfalutin title of Salle des Tuileries; but neither
Prosper's mother, nor anyone else, had pinned him down so far. He
eluded such pinning rather well. However, should anything of the kind
happen, he might also be cornered into admitting that the main reason
he went there was not to dance, but to see Titine, the amusing and
arresting girl who played the accordion, and who did not always remain
with the rest of the band, but wove her way among the merrymakers

when they were taking time off for a drink between dances. Sometimes she sang droll little Cajun songs, interspersed with still droller commentaries, as she wandered; and sometimes she stopped to chat for a moment or two with the patrons, at which times she was wittier still; and the way she laughed at her own sallies was very contagious. Besides, she was very good to look at, and the closer she came, the more alluring she appeared. Of course, August could not have an open bar because of that stupid Prohibition law; but there was one of sorts in a small space partitioned off behind the grocery store downstairs, and another behind the dance hall upstairs; and a few little tables were scattered in plain sight around a cleared space. It was the easiest thing in the world to secure setups and snacks, but Titine did not serve these. She always carried her accordion and it was distinctly understood that such pay as she received was for playing, and that August saw to that, as he did in the case of the other musicians. It was perhaps a little less distinctly understood that Titine was August's girl, but very few of his patrons would have been willing to take a chance on a misunderstanding about that, either. They were careful to keep their side of the badinage with Titine free from bawdiness, and though they welcomed her jovially when she stopped beside them, they never pointedly asked her to do so. She was equally discreet; she never stayed too long beside any one group, stopped too often in any one place, or leaned too close to anyone. She had not done so in Prosper's case. It was really almost as absurd to imagine that there was, or could be, anything between them, as to imagine that he and Paula Bennett, the sheriff's old maid cousin, were having an affair. To be sure, he and Paula were often alone at the Claudia Rice Mill, where he was the manager and she the secretary, when their respective duties kept them overtime; but he knew there had been gossip about that, also, and that his mother must have heard it; she was probably already dreaming up some way of seeing that at least two other employees of the rice mill would be kept overtime whenever Paula was. Lord, Paula must be ten years older than he was—well, five anyway, and she was the one woman of his acquaintance who, as far as he knew, had never had a suitor with either honorable or dishonorable intentions. It was a pity that matters of that sort could not be more evenly proportioned—the elderly aunt, Amanda Eaton, with whom Paula lived, never had to brush boys off their porch; and Anne Marie, on the other hand, had so many applicants for her favors that she could not make up her mind—at least not about men, only about camellias. If she had been thinking of Dale or Didier or any of the others, she wouldn't have been concentrating on some lost specimen; neither would she have been asking awkward questions, which made Lavinia Villac's mouth tighten; she would have been too much absorbed in rosy dreams. . . .

"No, I haven't made up my mind, either," Prosper said rather shortly, in answer to Anne Marie's question. "Why on earth should I want to get married and leave home when I've got a sister like you?" he went on, less shortly, and then added quickly, "and a mother like ours?"

"Well, why should I want to get married when I have a brother like you and a mother like ours?" Anne Marie responded sweetly. "Haven't I everything in the world I could ask for already?"

"You don't ask for things. That isn't your way. But sometimes you want them without asking for them. Right now, you want that Lost Camellia, don't you?"

"Well, rather."

"In which case I haven't the slightest doubt Prosper will find it for you," Lavinia said rather dryly. "Have you two any idea how late it is? Since, for a wonder, we're all home and by ourselves—no visit to the Tuileries tonight, I take it, and Dale and Didier both camping beside their telephones waiting for messages they won't get—suppose we go to bed early, just this once?"

So his mother did know about Titine, Prosper told himself, tossing with unaccustomed restlessness from one side of his bed to the other. Not, he repeated mentally, that there was really anything to know— worse luck! And Anne Marie wanted that Lost Camellia—wanted it bad —and her birthday was fast approaching. She certainly had a present coming to her from her brother. It was up to him to find that camellia, without any more dares from their mother, if he were to give her anything that would have much meaning to her.

His specialty, like his mother's, was not flowers, but rice, though he did not take his work at the smaller of the two family mills very seriously, and never would, as long as she actually managed the Claudia as well as the Monrovia, though, nominally, he was in charge of the former. He admired his sister's garden and sometimes, because he knew this would please her, offered to help her work in it; but, uncoached by her, the only varieties of camellias in it that he could have identified offhand were Alba Plena and Pink Perfection and Governor Mouton . . . Governor Mouton. . . .

No longer restless or drowsy, but delightfully alert, Prosper sat up in bed with an exclamation of pleasure, which he did not even attempt to smother. Governor Mouton was the one which had been named for an ancestor of Captain Bob's; and Captain Bob himself—now mayor of Lafayette, and one of the most versatile and agreeable men of Prosper's acquaintance—knew almost everything in the world there was to know about camellias. The next afternoon, without waiting for the Claudia to shut down, Prosper left poor Paula still chained to her typewriter, jumped into his dilapidated Oldsmobile and chugged away, thanking his lucky stars that there was less mud than usual at this season, and hardly noticing the great emerald green stretches of the rice fields through which his road passed.

He did not even stop at City Hall when he reached Lafayette. He figured that Captain Bob would have left by then for his nursery, and he was right. The mayor, obviously unoppressed by cares of office, was walking up and down between neat rows of shrubs when Prosper first caught sight of him, and had stopped to inspect the leaves of one small bush with loving care by the time his visitor joined him. Prosper, who at the moment had only one thing on his mind, cut his host's cordial greeting short.

"Captain Bob, did you ever hear of some flower called the Lost Camellia?"

"*Pourquoi pas?*"

"I didn't ask you why not. I asked you if you had."

Captain Bob straightened up and looked at his caller with an expression of injured dignity. He was a rather short man, his figure comfortably rounded by good Cajun food and his color pleasantly heightened by good homemade wine, which few right-minded citizens of Lafayette had seen fit to abolish from their daily fare by anything so unworthy of notice as the Volstead Act. He wore a small mustache and altogether was far more suggestive of a Gallic bourgeois than an upper-class American in his appearance. But, like the governor and the general who were among his progenitors, he could give an impression of importance whenever it suited him to do so. It suited him now.

"Of course I have heard of it. The merest amateur in horticulture has done so. *Et moi, je ne suis pas—*"

"Look, Captain Bob! You know my sister Anne Marie is almost as crazy about camellias as you are. She has read about this damn flower in some book, and she's hell-bent to have one in her garden. Besides, she has a birthday coming up—"

"*Et pourquoi tu n'a pas dit cela tout de suite?* Well, never mind why you didn't tell me right away instead of asking me such a question. Let

me inform you, my friend, that the beautiful specimen is not lost any
more; I found it myself, not so long ago."

"Where?"

"In St. Francisville. I recognized it at once, of course, from the descrip-
tions I had read of it—probably in the same book your sister read. Just
how it got to St. Francisville I am not sure yet. Perhaps no one is. But
that does not matter. I found it in a neglected old garden last winter.
C'est la même chose. Only it is not called the Lost Camellia in St.
Francisville. It is called Landrethii."

"Then if I went to St. Francisville I could buy a plant, perhaps?"

Captain Bob's eyes twinkled as he stroked his chin with a plump hand
adorned with a large seal ring. He had ceased to stand on his dignity.
He was his usual genial self again.

"Of course you may have a plant, but you do not need to go to St.
Francisville or to buy one. *Je me ferai le plaisir—*"

"You have a Lost Camellia or a Landrethii or whatever you choose to
call it right here?"

Captain Bob sighed in mock distress, while his eyes continued to
twinkle. "It has escaped your notice, perhaps, that I am doing everything
I can to beautify the city of Lafayette with proper landscape gardening,"
he said with mild sarcasm. "You are a nice boy, Prosper, but I have
never thought you were especially observant. *Bien sûr j'en ai; j'en ai
deux.* It will give me great pleasure to let you present one of these specimen plants to your sister with my compliments and your love. I should
like to add my love, too, but I have purposely refrained from permitting
myself to become enthralled in that quarter. Not that I do not appreciate
Anne Marie. But I am afraid of your mother. I know she would be
much too strict to suit me as a *belle-mère.* Well, now, let us locate those
Landrethiis. If I am not mistaken they are quite near by, in the second
row. *Un moment, mon vieux. . . .*"

He whistled shrilly and a strapping Negro gardener appeared in answer to the summons. Captain Bob pointed to a plant and spoke swiftly
in clipped gumbo French, after which the workman hastened away to
return with wheelbarrow, keen-edged shovel, sacking and nails. Under
the captain's supervision, he sliced away enough of the sandy soil around
the camellia's base to leave its roots encased in a ball of earth, which
was carefully wrapped in sacking, the latter being pinned securely with
a few nails.

"*Ça, c'est bon!*" declared Captain Bob. "Poleet will take it in the
wheelbarrow to your car, Prosper. It is to be planted sack and all, you

will of course inform Anne Marie." Then, after the plant had been stowed carefully in the back of the rickety Oldsmobile, he asked: "Is it still only in camellias, then, that your sister's interest is centered?"

"Looks that way."

"I hear that Dale Fontenot—*c'est un très bon parti, tu sais*—"

"I know. But Anne Marie says she can't make up her mind."

"And Didier Benoit—*aussi un joli garçon!*"

Prosper shrugged. Captain Bob grinned.

"Well, I shall have to see if I cannot conquer my fear of your very handsome, very cultured, but alarmingly efficient, mother. Perhaps that will be the only solution. *En attendant, au revoir, et bonne chance!*"

It was at this point that Prosper had taken his leave and gone his way, laughing, partly at Captain Bob and partly at himself. Briefly he toyed with the idea of going on to New Iberia and Jeanerette and thence to Cypremort, since the roads were in such unusually good condition. But he dismissed the tentative plan almost as soon as it occurred to him. Dale would welcome him warmly at Sapphira, he knew that; but much as he liked Dale, he did not feel exactly like having a visit with him just then. Dale, like Anne Marie, had every amiable quality; but also like her, he lacked a little of the hearty conviviality that had made the hour with Captain Bob so enjoyable, and at the moment Prosper was in the mood for something more, rather than less, exhilarating. Besides, Dale was certain to take advantage of such a call to urge his eligibility as a brother-in-law, and there was absolutely nothing Prosper could do to advance the suit until Anne Marie made up her mind, for with all her amiability she had a streak of stubbornness. He would have difficulty in convincing Dale that he was helpless; and then they would have an argument, and though they would not quarrel, the atmosphere would become more and more strained, and nothing in their surroundings would serve to ease this. Prosper had always considered the setting of Sapphira gloomy, not to say weird, located as it was on that dark bayou which took its name from the moss-hung cypresses, many of them dead or dying, that shadowed it, along with a jungle growth of palmetto, swamp myrtle, red gum and a tangle of muscadine vines. The plantation house itself was a pleasant one, similar to several in the vicinity—Ivanhoe, Louisa and Sunrise among others. In each, the wide roof spread not merely over the house proper, but across the spacious gallery as well, being supported by narrow pillars and pierced by three dormers, front and back, out from the upper story. In each, the wide entrance hall was invitingly cool even on the hottest day; but at Sapphira the rooms on either side of this were more elegantly, if somewhat more austerely, furnished than in the others. The situation, despite the expanse of lawn that separated the house from the bayou, had always seemed to Prosper an eerie one, though he had been careful not to express this opinion. It would have hurt Dale's feelings needlessly, and Dale was inclined to be somewhat oversensitive anyway. . . .

Of course, he did not need to go as far as Cypremort, Prosper considered, as he idled along toward New Iberia. He could stop instead at August Scholtze's after leaving Jeanerette well behind. Plenty of people used the spacious red-painted frame building, with a grocery store downstairs and the dance hall upstairs, for a place to pass the time of day, whether or not they came with the idea of buying anything much and whether or not they intended to stay on for the evening's entertainment. August encouraged such visits and sometimes even invited his customers into his private quarters, which led from the store and which he kept tidy and cheerful, and which were shared by a dull-witted, gangling boy named Baer, whose identity August never fully explained, but who was generally supposed to be an orphaned nephew, though there were some who believed he was August's son. While August never bothered to clear up this mystery, he made no effort to disguise the fact that Baer was related to him in some way and that the two were not uncongenial. Baer helped to keep the little apartment spick and span and also helped with the cleaning and odd jobs in the grocery store and with dishwashing in the café. When visitors came to the private quarters, far from remaining out of sight, he was the one to bring forth beer and pretzels and he often joined, in so far as his limited intelligence would permit, in general conversation. None of this was displeasing to August; but he did not encourage the visitors to pass the time of day with Titine—indeed, she never appeared on the scene until the rest of the band assembled; then she arrived in a disreputable old "tin Lizzie," accompanied by the piano player, who owned this vehicle and who was immensely proud of it, as it gave him superior standing among the possessors of the battered buggies which were in far more general use. He was a very old man, but excellent at his job for all that, and was always addressed as Professor; obviously he guarded Titine very effectively from all approaches except August's.

Anyway, Prosper reflected, it would be hours yet before it was time for the dancing to begin, which meant that Titine would not be coming in from wherever she lived for some time. So far, Prosper had not discovered where she did live, though he had tried. He had narrowed down the region to a point somewhere between Bayou Patou and Bayou Warehouse, and that was the best he had been able to do. He thought he might have better luck if he were able to give her something she wanted, and evidently she was not like Anne Marie in her methods of making her wants known, any more than she was in other ways. She asked straight out for things. The last time Prosper had been at the Salle des Tuileries, she had actually argued with August, in Prosper's hearing, about some gold slippers. . . .

The band had been resting between numbers, and Titine had stayed with it, instead of taking her accordion and going out among the customers, as usual. She had just stood beside the piano, looking sulky, which was also out of character; and finally August had gone up to her and said something under his breath. Obviously he was displeased at her inaction, which was costing him trade. Usually he was very agreeable, at least in public—it was his business to be—and he was strikingly handsome in a Teutonic way. But now his rubicund face was disfigured by a scowl and he looked ugly in every sense of the word. He was a powerfully built man, and it had occurred to Prosper more than once that it would be a poor plan to pick a quarrel with him, or even to risk rousing his wrath. But Titine did not seem in the least frightened and she showed that she was displeased, too, as she answered the blond giant loudly enough for Prosper, who was lounging near by enjoying the sight of her, to hear.

"My feets is hurtin' me, them. I plain got to have new shoes."

"So why you don't get some yourself?" August had forgotten, in his annoyance, to keep his voice down.

"On account I ain't paid enough, me, to buy new shoes every time I need some, no."

"Plenty enough you are paid. I tell you get out on that floor. Only a couple of quarts I sell tonight, no more as that."

"So you think maybe I care for that, me? Not one p'ti-p'ti damn I give if you don't sell none, no. I tell you frankly, me, I got no idea to go out around them tables till I get me some gol' slippers."

"Such a *Naerrischkeit* yet, about gold slippers! Who wears them around here, maybe you tell me?"

"Nobody don't wear none. That's why I want some, me."

"So will you tell me please if there is even a place around here where you could buy them? See—it gives no such place."

"In N'yawlins, yes, you could buy plenty gol' slippers, I guarantee you."

"You maybe think I got time I should travel by Newrleens every time you get a crazy idea like that? Who will attend to the business yet, if I do?"

"Some other peoples might make it their business, them, yes, to go to N'yawlins if they know I want gol' slippers."

The prescribed interval between dances had ended. August moved away, muttering something half sullen, half menacing beneath his breath. Then, to Prosper's surprise, the bootlegger stopped in his tracks and spoke to him.

"How's Paula these days?" he inquired.

The question was even more surprising than the halt. Prosper would have said that he was very thoroughly informed about almost everything that was happening or had happened during the last ten years in the locality. But he had never known before that August and Paula were acquainted.

"Why—she's very well, thank you," he said. He spoke in a way which he feared betrayed his surprise. August did not seem to notice it.

"Keeps you company at the mill, don't she?" he inquired.

There was the hint of a leer in his voice now and this time Prosper answered more stiffly.

"She works overtime when it's necessary, just as I do," he said.

"*Ach so!* Well, all of us that sometimes must do. Remember me to her, *hein?*"

Prosper's mounting astonishment would probably have absorbed him for some time, if something else, also totally unexpected, had not happened which immediately diverted his thoughts. After August had turned away for good, Titine looked Prosper full in the face for the first time and mouthed a word that sounded like "*Dangereuse!*" At first he believed it was. Then the thought flashed through his mind that it might be "Dargereux," which was not an uncommon surname in the locality. He had never known Titine's surname, any more than he had known where she lived. If he had learned it now, it should not be too difficult to locate that point between Bayou Patou and Bayou Warehouse.

Then he knew he would not even have to waste time trying. The look had told him, plainly enough, that if he would get her a pair of gold slippers she would tell him of her own accord where she lived.

A week had gone by since then and, meanwhile, Prosper had not been able to think up any good excuse for going to New Orleans. A few years earlier it would have been simple enough—he would have just gone. That would have been all there was to it, or all there needed to be. But since the disastrous slump in the rice market, which had taken place in '21, there had so far been only a partial comeback—not enough to justify casual trips to New Orleans or, as far as that went, to justify casual purchases of gold slippers, especially as '24 and '25 had both been "salt-water years." To be sure, he had not spent anything on Anne Marie's birthday present, thanks to Captain Bob's generosity; but somehow he did not relish the idea of squandering what he had saved on his sister's present in buying one for a girl he wanted as a light-o'-love.

However, he was naturally lighthearted and, without too much trouble, he dismissed from his mind the question of how he was to find a pretext for getting to New Orleans. Turning the car around, he began to hum a song which was a perennial favorite in the locality:

> "Allons à Lafayette, c'est pour changer ton nom,
> Pour t'appeler ma femme, finir nos jours ensemble."

Halfway through the verse he stopped. Without forethought, he believed he had provided himself with an answer. He would go to Lafayette; if not actually on a romantic mission, at least in the hope and belief that he might find something there that would divert his thoughts from his problems.

Chapter Two

PROSPER HAD BEEN DRIVING ALONG ALMOST UNAWARE OF HIS SURROUNDings when a vague consciousness of some change in those familiar to him—so familiar that he did not need to watch where he was going—caused him to glance around. For the first time within his memory, the great wrought-iron gates leading to the LaBranche estate, instead of being closed and padlocked, stood wide open. Moreover, instead of being discolored by rust and weather, they were gleaming with fresh black paint. Beyond them, several men were hard at work: one was washing windows in the lodge, one was weeding the long-disused drive, and two were pruning the oleanders on either side of this carriageway. Since receiving any previous attention, the oleanders had achieved a straggling growth which had reared them to the height of trees; but in the process they had lost their air of luxuriance. Now they were being ruthlessly shorn into shape again, while withered branches and superfluous shoots were fast falling to the ground. On a sudden impulse, Prosper stopped the engine and got out of the car, leaving the dilapidated Oldsmobile parked beside the road while he went to have a look.

He now recalled that he had heard rumors to the effect that the LaBranche estate might be sold and divided into house lots to form a new subdivision; but he had not heard that such a sale had actually taken place, and it seemed unlikely that all this intensive improvement would be going forward unless there was some special reason for it. None of the workmen was close enough to the gates to make interrogations seem like casual questioning, and Prosper, whose curiosity was now piqued, had begun a mental search for some pretext to go nearer, when a black-haired girl, dressed in scarlet and leading a coach dog on a leash, appeared around the bend of the driveway. This was a figure so much more arresting than those of the diligent workmen that Prosper's momentary hesitation came to an immediate end. He watched the girl's approach, not failing to note the easy swing of her carriage, the beauty of her build, and the smartness of the suit which was short enough to reveal a generous length of slim and shapely legs. Being swift of perception and not without some experience in these matters, he recognized that the suit was costly as well as smart, and that everything worn with it was expensively appropriate: the frilled blouse, the chain bracelets, the sheer stockings, the suède pumps. Until the depression following the slump of '21, all his mother's and sister's dresses had come from Sophie's, the best dressmaker in New Orleans, and the accessories for them from equally expensive places; and Lavinia still squeezed out the money to buy one or two good outfits for Anne Marie and herself every year, and to copy, with characteristic efficiency, others which she could not afford to buy.

Somehow Prosper doubted that this girl, who was now coming down the drive, had ever needed to economize, though he could not have told why he should have so quickly decided that the suit she was wearing was not her only really good one, and that most of her other clothes were not homemade. At all events, the girl herself, rather than what she was wearing, had very quickly attracted him. She was bareheaded, and her black hair, though brushed straight back from her brow and confined by a narrow red ribbon which encircled her head, was so thick and curly that it nowhere lay flat; and when she turned slightly to one side and spoke briefly to one of the workmen, Prosper saw that her curls cascaded down to her shoulders. The dog, a magnificent Dalmatian, tugged at its leash as if impatient to be on its way, not through lack of training but through sheer vitality. The girl quickened her footsteps, adjusting her pace to the dog's and, presently, was as close to the gate on the inside as Prosper was on the outside. He hailed her.

"Hi!" he called out. "Where's the fire?"

"Right here!" the girl flashed back. "Take care, you might get burnt."

She had stopped, but she had not turned away. Prosper grinned and took a step forward.

"I'm slightly singed already," he said amiably. "And I've always heard that deep burns aren't as painful as surface ones, to begin with. So I'll take a chance."

"As far as I'm aware, nobody said anything about giving you a chance."

"Correct. That's why I said I'd take one. My name's Prosper Villac. What's yours?"

The girl made no immediate answer. She stood still, coolly looking him over, which gave him an opportunity for looking her over, too, still more appraisingly than he had before. Involuntarily, he found himself comparing her with Titine and, to his surprise, discovering many points of resemblance between the two. Both had thick, curly black hair, sparkling black eyes, noticeably red lips, abounding vitality and the gift of quick give and take. But there the likeness ended. This girl's cheeks had far more natural coloring than any Cajun he had ever seen—there was a rich glow under the tan—and she was much better built. Titine had stocky legs and thick ankles; he had told himself more than once that probably the reason she wore skirts which covered her calves was not because she was unaware that these were no longer fashionable, but because she wanted to conceal her less attractive attributes as much as she wanted to emphasize her more attractive ones. This girl had the most beautiful legs he had ever seen, slender and shapely, as he had noticed at once; and he thought she was aware of this, too, for her skirt was even shorter than fashion dictated. Titine's hands were chubby and roughened by hard work; this girl's hands were slim and smooth, and a great ring glistened on one of her tapering fingers. Prosper doubted that she had ever done anything useful in the entire course of her life. The carriage of the two girls was as different as their figures. Not that Titine was clumsy; but she lacked the complete ease, the accomplished grace of this girl. The lack was nothing to Titine's discredit, he told himself quickly. Where and how could she have learned to make mere movement a wonder and a delight to the eye? The poor kid had never had a chance. Whereas it was obvious that this girl . . .

"Has anyone ever told you that you're pretty fresh?" she now inquired, with a slight shrug of her shoulders.

"Lots of people. Is that what you're going to tell me instead of telling me your name? I hoped you'd be more original."

Suddenly she laughed, not in a silly, spasmodic way, but freely and merrily. "I don't suppose there's any reason why I shouldn't tell you," she said. "Besides, if I didn't, you'd ask one of the workmen the minute I was out of sight."

"Correct again. Only I wasn't planning to let you out of sight that quick."

The girl laughed again. "My name's Victorine," she said. "Victorine LaBranche."

"Victorine LaBranche! Moïse LaBranche's daughter?"

"'The boy guessed right the very first time.'"

Prosper looked past her toward the workmen. The man who had been washing windows at the lodge, and who was nearer the unabashed intruder and the scarlet-clad girl than any of the others, had turned to stare at them; when he caught Prosper's glance, he hastily picked up his cloth and resumed his polishing. The other workmen were apparently unconcerned or unobserving.

"Could you tell me more, as they say on the stage?" Prosper inquired. "Evidently, you were just starting for a walk and I'd like very much to join you—it doesn't particularly matter to me in what direction. Does it matter to you?"

"No, not particularly. I thought I might give my surroundings the once-over. It looks as if I might be here for some time, so I suppose I ought to know what they're like. But there's no hurry. Why don't we go up to the house? We might have a drink or something."

"If by something you mean tea or northern coffee, I'd much rather have a drink."

"You would anyway, wouldn't you?"

It was his turn to laugh. "Yes. But to be serious for a moment, just for the hell of it, it doesn't matter to me whether I have anything in the way of liquid refreshment. I'm very well satisfied with the situation just as it stands."

"You mean you're agreeably surprised because you didn't get thrown out on your ear?"

"Well, something like that. Of course, I was hopeful, all the time that you wouldn't misinterpret my innocent interest and youthful curiosity. But I confess I didn't expect to be invited into the parlor."

They had been going up the driveway as they talked, and the farther along they went, the more signs of reclamation were visible. Lawns were being mowed, flower beds weeded, and the work on the road and shrubbery intensified.

"All this feverish activity looks as if you really did mean to be here for some time," Prosper continued. "Yes, I know you said so yourself, but I thought perhaps you were just talking."

"When you know me better you'll find out I don't often just talk. I usually say something."

"I'm very much gratified at the suggestion that I'm going to know you better. It would seem to prove that there wasn't much the matter with my technique after all."

"I didn't say there was anything the matter with your technique. I just asked if you'd ever been told you were fresh and reminded you that nothing had been said about giving you a chance. But I don't see any sense in quibbling about just what I said, or just what you said, or what either of us meant by that, and then hashing it all over again. No one ever makes any progress that way."

"What do you consider the best way of making progress?"

"Why, to go ahead and say something else that does make sense! . . . Well, here we are at the house. I can't invite you into the parlor because there isn't any. But you can take your choice among the living room and the gunroom and the drawing room and the library while I see about your drink."

She disappeared, the coach dog, now unleashed, trotting along beside her. Prosper, thus unceremoniously left in the entrance hall—a somewhat somber apartment of vast proportions, encircled by life-size figures in armor—turned to the room on his right and was relieved to find it rather less overpowering. The furniture was still shrouded in its dust covers of white denim, and there were no books and flowers scattered about to give it an air of habitual occupancy; but the sun streamed in warmly through the uncurtained windows and brightened the bare floor and paneled walls. Prosper sat down in a deep chair which proved surprisingly comfortable, looked around in vain for an ash tray and decided to smoke anyhow, while trying to piece together the fragments of what he had heard about Moïse LaBranche.

He seemed to recall that the family name had originally been Zweig and that, like so many names of German origin, it had been given its French equivalent by an early settler in Louisiana, who, in this instance —again if he were not mistaken—was an Alsatian in any case, and almost as certainly a Jew, for the given names of Abel, Benjamin and Moïse had appeared and reappeared among his descendants. They had retained close ties with the homeland from the beginning and had prospered in their chosen trade as merchants almost from the beginning; eventually, they directed the thriving establishments they owned, instead of selling goods over the counter themselves. But the present Moïse was the first to design as well as direct, and to make a name for himself in New York, as well as in Louisiana and in France. He had married rather late, a beautiful woman by the name of Hortense Duandeau, much younger than himself, who was also a Louisianian, but a Christian; and he had bought this property and built this house for his bride, hoping to retire and spend his declining years there. However, she had been dissatisfied, both with the costly estate and with him, and she had found some sort of a feeble pretext for divorcing him and for keeping their little daughter in her custody. Moïse had closed the house of his dreams and had never come back there, but had gone on to greater and greater fame and fortune in New York, his creative powers increasing rather than decreasing with age. Hortense had remarried, not once but several times, each time imagining that she was mounting higher on the social ladder. As the years went by, her daughter had become less of an asset and more of a hindrance to her, a giveaway of her age, an impediment to extramarital romances. The girl had been sent abroad to school and, eventually, kept there most of the time. Now, apparently, her father had succeeded in reclaiming her; it was also apparent that, after all these years, he had come home at last—perhaps to die. He must, by now, be a very old man. At all events, it did not look as if the property were to be sold in the immediate future. Quite the contrary. The rumors to that effect, which had been the topic of local gossip, must have been false, as such rumors so often were. Possibly, in this instance, they had been instigated by old Moïse himself. Somehow Prosper felt that such a man might not care to have his plans known until they had actually been put into execution. . . .

There was a sound of footsteps in the hall and Victorine, with the coach dog still at her heels, re-entered the room where Prosper was waiting. She was carrying a vase of flowers in one hand and some ash trays in the other, and she was followed by a butler of formal and forbidding appearance, charged with a well-laden tray. When the man put this down on a near-by table, Prosper saw that the siphon of soda and the whisky bottles were flanked by a silver tea service. Up to this moment, he had not given his looks a thought. Now, at the sight of the butler, he became uncomfortably aware of his short-sleeved shirt, open at the throat, his well-worn khaki trousers and his dilapidated sneakers. He would have given a good deal for a tie, a coat and a presentable pair of shoes. The silver service added vaguely to his feeling of discomfiture.

"Thank you, Gifford," Victorine was saying. "Don't wait for the biscuits to be done—bring in the other things right away. Oh—and you might light the fire . . . I think a fire would be cheerful, don't you?" she inquired, turning to Prosper. "Not that it's really cold, but there's something sort of sepulchral about all these white coverings. I hope to get them off tomorrow. Meanwhile, a fire might help a little. At that, this room's a shade less depressing than the reception hall. I'm wondering if Father could possibly be persuaded to do away with a few of those knights in armor, or at least to keep them somewhere else. They seem so much better fitted to a baronial hall in England, which of course is where they came from, than to a suburban place in Louisiana. But they're Father's pride and joy, so I'll have to tread carefully to bring about their removal! . . . I told him we had company and he'll be down in a few minutes. He likes tea at this hour and, incidentally, so do I. But I hope that won't cramp your style any. I'm told this is very good bourbon. It's prewar stock. Not that we hold with Prohibition, anyway."

The butler re-entered the room, bringing a muffin stand, its shelves severally supplied with cucumber sandwiches, cinnamon toast and a large frosted cake. He went over to the fire, which was already burning brightly, and moved the logs about with a poker, gently and quite superfluously. Then he came back to the tea table and bowed.

"The biscuits will be ready directly, Chef says. Will there be anything else just now, miss?"

"No, Gifford, thanks very much."

The butler bowed again and disappeared. Prosper, who had risen with the appearance of the tea tray, now came closer to the table where it had been placed and looked down at Victorine, who was already seated beside it, measuring tea leaves from a silver caddy into a small earthen pot. The supercilious butler had caused him momentary discomfiture; but he had almost shaken that off, when Victorine casually announced the impending arrival of her father upon the scene. Now he felt not only ill at ease again, but more or less angry. The cockiness with which he had carried off his encounter with Victorine seemed destined to deflation and he blamed her for this.

"The tea won't cramp my style," he said shortly. "But some of the rest of this act may. You didn't say anything about a butler when you invited me to the house or tell me your father sat in on your dates. You'd better put down that spoon and mix me a good stiff drink."

"You can mix your own drink," Victorine retorted. "Then it'll be sure to suit you. I probably couldn't. And don't make any mistakes. This isn't a date. It's an introduction. You didn't have one at the gate, you know."

Chapter Three

BECAUSE, TO HIS INTENSE ANNOYANCE, PROSPER COULD NOT IMMEDI-ately think of some suitable retort to this statement, he concentrated on pouring out his highball, in which there was a very small admixture of soda to the bourbon. Victorine, meanwhile, continued to busy herself with her teamaking. Her guest had hardly taken his first long drink, however, when she rose, saying, "I think that's Father coming now," and went toward the door that led into the depressing hall.

Prosper's first impression of the old man, now slowly and painfully coming toward them, was that he cut a sorry figure. He was thin almost to the point of emaciation, and his stooped shoulders shook slightly with the effort of moving, though he leaned heavily on a cane. It was not until he had almost reached the tea table, and stretched out his free hand for support on the back of a chair, that he straightened up. The minute Prosper saw his host's face, his whole estimate of the old man changed. His skin was very dark and looked all the darker against the abundant white hair and heavy white eyebrows; his features were clear cut, regular and unmistakably Semitic; but it was his eyes that dominated everything else. They were as black as his hair must once have been and as his daughter's still was, and they were old eyes, tired and experienced and shrewd; but there was kindliness in them and there was still fire. The thought flashed through Prosper's mind that in his youth Moïse La-Branche must have been an irresistible lover, and that in the prime of life he must have been a master of women, as well as men. It was incomprehensible that such a man's wife should have left him. . . .

Moïse LaBranche extended the wrinkled hand with which he had briefly supported himself on the near-by chair. It shook slightly as Prosper took it; but almost immediately it steadied itself into a surprisingly firm handclasp. "It is very kind of you to call so promptly," the old man said pleasantly. His voice, like his eyes, was compelling; but, unlike his eyes, his voice still seemed young; it was the most surprising attribute of all. "Please sit down," he added, as Victorine helped him to lower himself into his chosen seat, "we will get acquainted while we sip our drinks, each of us with one to his own liking. That is, I trust it was bourbon you wanted, since I see that is what you have. Now I shall ask Vicky to give me my tea. If I understood her correctly, she said your name is Prosper Villac. Your father is perhaps Ursin Villac?"

"No, sir, he was my grandfather."

"Ah, yes, of course! I keep forgetting that most of the men of my own generation are—or alas! *were*—grandfathers. Many are dead now, as I assume from the way you answer my question, that yours must be. Is your other grandfather still living?"

"Yes, sir, I'm glad to say he is. My other grandfather is Brent Winslow."

"What, the great pioneer in rice breeding? You are to be congratulated on such a heritage."

"Thank you, sir. I think myself that he's the most wonderful man I ever knew—that is, I always have thought so—until now."

The words were uttered quite spontaneously. Prosper had not been unmindful of the mild rebuke at his discourtesy in starting his drink before the appearance of his host. But it had been so tactfully and so pleasantly administered that it had carried no sting with it, and it had evoked admiration rather than resentment in the visitor's breast. He had now entirely forgotten again about his short-sleeved shirt, his worn trousers and his dilapidated sneakers; the butler, being unimportant himself, had striven to make a guest feel unimportant, too; the host, who was a man among men, was restoring the guest's self-confidence. Prosper remembered having read in school Robert E. Lee's definition of a gentleman as one who never consciously or needlessly inflicted pain or even discomfort on another. He thought of this now as he looked with appreciation at Moïse LaBranche and set the crippled old man down as the greatest gentleman he had ever met, in which estimate he showed a wisdom beyond his years. His anger at Victorine had also evaporated the moment he heard her father say, "It was kind of you to call." It seemed to him apparent that she had said nothing to him about the encounter at the gate, nothing that would brand the visitor as an impudent intruder. If her father asked her just how she and Prosper Villac happened to meet, undoubtedly she would inform him—there was nothing about her to suggest the telling of shabby little lies. But for the moment he was accepted as the courteous resident of good background and good manners, who had come to pay his respects to new arrivals in the locality and give them a feeling of welcome.

"You must set me straight about the other members of your family," Moïse LaBranche continued, quietly stirring his tea. "I have made one mistake already in assuming that you were Ursin Villac's son instead of his grandson and I should not like to make another. Your father's name is—"

"He was Claude Villac. He's dead, too."

"My dear boy, I am truly most sorry—for the fact itself and for my second tactless assumption. Please forgive me."

"It's a long while since you've been here, isn't it, sir? You couldn't be expected to know everything that's happened during your absence—especially with all the other things you must have had on your mind."

"Well, it's kind of you to put it that way and, as you say, I have been away a long while. It's been difficult for me to keep in touch—or perhaps I haven't tried as hard as I should have. And I've been back only a day or two. I haven't had time yet to make amends for past sins of omission and commission. You are our first caller. We shall remember your visit with special pleasure on that account. Shan't we, Vicky?"

"Yes, Father," Victorine answered with a demureness that was somewhat startling to Prosper. Then he saw her look toward her father with laughing eyes and noticed that the old man's, too, were smiling. Obviously, not only great affection but complete understanding existed between the two, though what amused them jointly Prosper could not guess.

"Let us go back to your family," Moïse LaBranche said, handing his cup to his daughter for refilling and turning again to Prosper. "Since your maternal grandfather is Brent Winslow, your mother must be, or must have been—let me forestall another awkward mistake—his daughter, whose name was, I believe, Lorinda."

"Lavinia. She's alive and well, I'm glad to say, and very active. She manages the family rice mills—that is, I'm supposed to manage the Claudia, the new one, but she's really boss of both. My father was manager of the Monrovia and when he died she took over. Of course, that's unusual, for a woman, but she seemed very well fitted for it, and of course it pleased my grandfather that she was. Since he didn't have a male heir, the next best thing was to feel that his daughter would carry on where he left off—when he leaves off, I mean. He's still very active, too."

"But he's long since stopped making new experiments with rice breeding, hasn't he? I mean with the tremendous success he's already achieved, that hardly seems necessary."

"It isn't necessary, but I suppose he'll go on experimenting as long as he lives, because he enjoys it. However, of course his main interest is in the continued promotion of Blue Camellia."

"The impossible which he found it possible to achieve! A well-chosen name for a remarkable product. Do you know who was first reported to have said, 'If it is possible it can be done; if it is impossible it must be done'?"

"Yes, sir, Napoleon Bonaparte."

"Your grandfather told you about this slogan?"

"No, sir, I learned it in school. As a matter of fact, I told my grandfather; he'd never heard it. He just went ahead and did it."

This time, Prosper looked not at Moïse, but at Victorine as he spoke. Nevertheless, he felt sure the old man had caught the glance and, to his annoyance, he realized that he was blushing for the first time since he could remember. He had not been quite so brash as to consider that he, too, had done the impossible, that he had picked up a lady as easily as he could have a tramp—more easily, as a matter of fact, than he had been able to pick up Titine—and that he had crowned this feat by getting himself invited to her house and presented to her famous father—or at least he would not have put it all quite as crudely as that, even to himself. But, undeniably, his self-satisfied thoughts had been running in that direction. Now that he became aware of their basic falsity and incredible presumption, he had the grace to feel somewhat ashamed of himself.

"But your grandfather has a male heir now—in you," he heard Moïse LaBranche saying pleasantly. "Perhaps he has others? Or are you an only child, like your mother?"

"No, sir, I'm not an only child. I have a younger sister, Anne Marie—named for her two grandmothers. But I haven't any brothers. So I suppose I am Brent Winslow's male heir, only I hadn't thought of it that way before. I'd only thought of myself as his grandson and mighty lucky to be that."

He was feeling honest humility now and his blush, to his increasing annoyance, had deepened; he could feel it spreading from his cheeks to his neck. Moïse LaBranche, sensing his unwelcome embarrassment, quietly set about to relieve it.

"You are, indeed," he said cordially, "and I'm delighted to hear of your sister. I hope that the next time you call you will bring her with you.

Your mother will perhaps forgive me if I do not first pay my respects to her. The journey was rather tedious and wearisome, and so is the process of getting settled here again, after so many years. Of course, Vicky is doing everything she can to help me, but after all, I am an old man now— I tire more easily than I once did. And she is young, she should have companionship of her own age, and not be condemned to solitary confinement with a septuagenarian who will soon be an octogenarian. I am sure you can be helpful in seeing that she is included in your circle of friends. . . . Are you still in college?"

Prosper grinned. "I reckon I'm older than I look, sir," he said. "I finished at Louisiana State several years ago, and at that I went to college late, because I made the Cavalry Troop from Jennings that had the great luck of getting into the Rainbow Division, so I spent some time abroad. That's about all the traveling I've done. My mother meant to give me a trip around the world for a graduation present, with stops at many of the great rice-producing centers—southern Spain, Java, the Philippines, China, Japan. But shortly after that the bottom fell out of the rice market, so—"

"Ah, yes. That is another situation with which I should have kept in closer touch. But surely there has been a marked recovery already?"

"There has been some. I don't know how marked you'd call it. I suppose that depends on the point of view. We're still driving the same cars we drove five years ago. Mother used to give Anne Marie and me each a new one every year and, of course, she had a new one herself. That was about the usual scale. . . . Anne Marie finished at the Sacred Heart Academy in Grand Coteau—she didn't want to go to college, anyway, so it wasn't a hardship for her to give that up, though I know it was a disappointment to my mother. And I don't think Anne Marie has ever cared about traveling. She's very contented in Crowley."

"What does she do to keep contented?" Victorine inquired.

There was no condescension in the way she spoke; it was merely an interested and courteous inquiry. Yet Prosper found himself thinking that, when he had answered, she might find the reasons he gave for Anne Marie's contentment somewhat inadequate.

"Well—she's crazy for gardening. She has a garden at our place and she spends a lot of time at our grandmother's, too. Now she's especially gone on camellias. That's how I happened to come to Lafayette today, to see if Captain Bob—I mean Bob Mouton, the mayor, who's quite an authority —could help me locate a rare variety she wanted. He did. I've got it in my car right now. I'd drive up to the door and let you see it, but of course it doesn't look like much at this time of year."

"I'm sure your grandmother and your sister would be of the greatest help to us in restoring our long-neglected garden," Moïse LaBranche said pleasantly. "That is, if they would be so kind, and if it wouldn't be an imposition to ask for their assistance."

"They'd be very flattered," Prosper answered unhesitatingly. Then he glanced at Victorine, who had said nothing. It was just as he expected. She was waiting to have the reasons for Anne Marie's contentment explained.

"Of course, she doesn't spend all her time gardening," he continued. "The girls get together a lot for morning coffees and slumber parties and things like that. And then the whole crowd—girls and fellows both—go to dances, of course."

"You mean *thés dansants* or balls?"

"No—I think they have tea dances in New Orleans, but around here we're in our offices until nearly suppertime, which is rather early, and then go to dances afterward. At Elks' Hall and places like that."

"I see."

"Of course, we do lots of other things, too. Sunday afternoons, this time of year, we generally go out and shoot snakes."

"Shoot snakes!"

"Yes—at the levee cutoffs, you know, where we go crawfishing."

"Does Anne Marie do that?"

"Once in a while. She doesn't really enjoy it the way most of us do. But she's a good shot. Not quite as good as our mother, though. She's really a whiz! Learned when she was a kid. Paula Bennett, our secretary at the Claudia, is mighty good, too."

"I see," Victorine said again. But Prosper did not feel at all sure that she did. "I hope you'll be contented around here, too," he went on rather lamely. "We have a nice crowd of young people. I'd be very pleased to have my friends meet you and to bring my mother and Anne Marie to call. Also, to come again myself."

His self-confidence was gradually returning. Maybe Victorine did not see. But he was quite prepared to make an effort to show her and he thought he could. Moïse LaBranche, who had now finished his tea, was reaching for his cane and Prosper sprang forward to help him before Victorine, wedged in behind the tea table, could do so. The old man accepted Prosper's prompt assistance with a smile and again held out his hand, taking Prosper's in that surprisingly strong clasp.

"Do so, by all means," he said agreeably. "I have enjoyed our little chat very much, and shall look forward to others. Just now, if you will excuse me, I shall go to my room for the short rest that I usually take at this hour. But I hope you will accept another bourbon and soda from Vicky. Doubtless you and she can find something to talk about while you drink it. And then you might enjoy taking a walk together. I believe that was your plan before you came up to the house."

Chapter Four

ALTHOUGH HIS ACQUAINTANCE WITH VICTORINE LABRANCHE HAD APPARently begun so auspiciously, Prosper was very far from satisfied with the way in which it progressed. In the first place, he could not forgive her for having played a trick on him. Despite his assumption to the contrary —an assumption which all appearances seemed to support—she had immediately told her father how she and Prosper happened to meet; it was the old man's deft handling of the situation and not Prosper's own effrontery which was responsible for its smooth success. The realization of this was a considerable blow to his pride, and Moïse was hardly out of hearing when Prosper, with characteristic rashness, told Victorine that even if she had no fault to find with his technique, he did not think much of hers.

"If that's the case, perhaps we'd better not go for a walk after all," she said. "I wouldn't want to irritate you still further. Evidently, you're very easily upset. But, of course, you're welcome to another drink. Shall I pour it for you this time? I think I know now how you like it."

The last thing on earth Prosper wanted was to forego the suggested walk, and he asked himself savagely if he would ever learn to keep his big mouth shut; then he humbled himself to apologize and plead. This did no good, either. Victorine poured the suggested drink and it was very good; but it was evident that the walk was out, for that day anyhow. When he could no longer prolong his sipping, Prosper had no choice but to take his reluctant departure, though he finally wrung a half-promise from his hostess that their promenade was only postponed and, on the strength of this, made a very definite promise himself that he would return the following day.

He had some difficulty in making up his mind whether he was glad or sorry that he was prevented from doing this. When he reached home, he found his mother at her piano. She was an exceptionally fine musician and could easily have become a professional; as it was, she was generous in responding to requests for her services at charitable and civic affairs, though she never took the initiative in offering to perform; what she really enjoyed was playing in small family groups, or by herself, as she was doing now. She never seemed so relaxed or so quietly content as at such times, and Prosper stood for a few moments on the gallery, looking at her through a window before he entered the house and made his arrival known. Everyone considered Lavinia Villac a very handsome woman, and he shared this general opinion; but it was only at times like this he realized that she once had been and, indeed, still could be really beautiful. She had a faultless figure, golden hair in which the white hairs, if any, did not show, and soft smooth skin, unmarred by wrinkles; but her expression, her manner and the severely tailor-made style in which she habitually dressed at the mill combined to rob her of the exquisite femininity which Anne Marie possessed to such a supreme degree, and which made men like Captain Bob say they were afraid of her and describe her as "alarmingly efficient," instead of merely as "efficient." From the photographs taken in her extreme youth, inadequate though these were, Prosper had been able to judge that she had not always been characterized by such an expression or such a manner, nor so addicted to tailor-made clothes. He had never dared ask her what had brought about the change, but he had often wondered. As far as he knew, she had had a happy girlhood and a happy marriage; he could vaguely remember his father, who had not died until Prosper was nearly eight years old, and the great devotion of Claude Villac to his wife had been obvious even to childish eyes. But his death had not crushed his widow; though he recalled many other details of early family life, Prosper could not remember that he had ever seen his mother weep or show any of the other signs supposedly indicative of being "prostrated by grief." She had always been calm, collected and competent—too calm, too collected and too competent to meet the average male standards of beauty rather than handsomeness, except at such moments as the present one. Now, as Prosper stood looking at her, seated before her piano and dressed in one of those flowing *robes d'intérieur,* which she wore at home in the evenings, she was temporarily transformed into the type of woman he would have supposed she might normally be. . . .

As if conscious of another presence, she glanced up from the keyboard, rose immediately and, as soon as she actually caught sight of him, went out to meet him in the hall. She and Anne Marie had eaten their supper early, she told him, because Anne Marie had gone on schedule to the card party at which he had evidently forgotten he was also expected to appear. He would have to snatch a hasty bite—some gumbo had been kept warm for him—and then hurry off, explaining his tardiness as best he could. Lavinia did not say any of this disagreeably, but she did manage to convey to her son that she thought he was rather irresponsible for a man of twenty-seven; and though she listened with apparent interest to the account of his visits with Captain Bob and the LaBranches, she did not encourage him to go into much detail about either. It was obvious she thought he should be on his way to the card party, where annoyed and impatient guests were doubtless waiting for him to make up a table; and it was also obvious she had news of her own to break and that she felt she must do this without delay.

"Your grandfather Winslow has decided to go to the meeting of the Rice Millers' Association in New Orleans," she told him. "He feels it's very important for planters to get together with millers and map out some kind of a program that will convince more people in the North that rice is good for something besides inexpensive puddings—a good many of them seem to be still laboring under that delusion, instead of recognizing it as a major staple, like wheat. He's very pleased because he's been asked to make an address and head a committee for a promotional campaign. I agree that it all sounds very worth while—doubly so now that his new variety, which he's decided to call Princess Mary, is just coming on the market. He's invited you to go to New Orleans with him and I've accepted for you. I felt it was not only a kind thought on your grandfather's part, but that it represented a good opportunity for you to do some promotional work on your own account."

Prosper repressed, with difficulty, a remark to the effect that, even if he were irresponsible, he was old enough to decide for himself whether he should accept or decline invitations. Moreover, he had long since ceased to be excited by the new varieties of rice which his grandfather Winslow's successful experiments put on the market almost annually and which were generally given some family name, dressed up with a title. The previous one had been Lady Lavinia. . . .

"When does all this good work come off?" he inquired, between gulps of gumbo.

"You leave on the morning train tomorrow."

"Like hell I do! I've got a date tomorrow with Victorine LaBranche, that knockout I've been telling you about."

"Anne Marie and I will call," his mother said calmly. "That would be the proper thing to do in any case—especially as I gather your first approach to the LaBranches was rather informal, to say the least. I will explain about the importance of this conference. If she's a sensible girl, Victorine will understand."

"I'm not at all sure she is a sensible girl. But she's a damn amusing and good-looking one—about the most amusing and best looking I ever saw. Listen, Mother—"

"Yes?"

"Nothing. You go ahead and call with Anne Marie. You're right, that's the next step. You can explain I had to go to New Orleans with Grandfather. . . . Well, I'd better be getting into a clean shirt on the double, hadn't I?"

He shoved back his chair, kissed his mother casually on top of her head and bolted upstairs. Lavinia looked after him thoughtfully; she had not expected that he would take her offhand disposal of his time quite so pleasantly, especially after she heard about Victorine LaBranche. But despite her suspicions concerning the Salle des Tuileries, she naturally had not guessed about the gold slippers; and Prosper had suddenly realized that the opportunity to get these had, almost miraculously, presented itself. His mother was right; if Victorine were a sensible girl, she would understand—that is, about the importance of the Rice Millers' Association. If she were not sensible, that would be just too bad. Because, greatly attracted as he had been by Victorine LaBranche, he had no intention of giving up the chance to get the gold slippers for Titine Dargereux.

The meeting of the Rice Millers' Association lasted four days and, after it was over, a buyer from Rotterdam who had attended the conference, but who said he could not also take time for a trip to Crowley, succeeded in detaining Prosper for two days more, because the Dutchman wanted to talk at length with a representative miller. Thus an entire week was very effectually used up in ways, which however interesting they might be to his grandfather, and however important to the rice industry as a whole, were not particularly intriguing to Prosper. Moreover, he was annoyed by the questions—in his opinion, unnecessarily prying—which his grandfather kept asking about the contents of a well-wrapped box from Holmes that, on the third day of their stay in New

Orleans, made its appearance in the room which the two were sharing at the St. Charles Hotel.

"It looks like a shoe box," Brent Winslow remarked, after tipping the bellboy who had brought it to the door, for, by ill luck, he was closer to it than his grandson when the parcel was delivered.

Prosper relieved him of the box and, without making any direct answer, tried to cram it into his suitcase. The attempt was unsuccessful because the suitcase was too shallow, and he was obliged to leave the box out in full sight where, he knew, it would continue to provoke curiosity.

"But it isn't large enough to hold shoes for you. Did your mother ask you to buy some for her or Anne Marie?"

"No, not exactly."

"I wouldn't have thought so. She likes to make her own selections."

Again, Prosper gave no direct answer. He could see that his grandfather was considering other female relatives for whom a young man might conceivably have undertaken a commission and dismissing them all as improbable in such a connection.

"I suppose you young folks give prizes at your parties sometimes," Brent said at last.

"Yes, we do." Prosper spoke promptly this time. After all, the statement was quite true.

"But shoes seem to me a queer kind of a prize."

"I don't know that they're any queerer than lots of others. . . . Grandfather, I think that Dutchman must be waiting for us. He said he'd meet us in the lobby around three and it's five minutes past."

The appointment with the buyer from Rotterdam was certainly a godsend. It allayed, though it did not completely still, Brent Winslow's suspicions, and Prosper managed to continue the theme of prize-giving at parties without too much prevarication and without too much interference as far as his sense of satisfaction was concerned. He felt he had been extremely fortunate in finding a pair of gold slippers, which he was sure would appeal to Titine, in the right size. As far as that went, he had been fortunate in finding out the size. It had suddenly occurred to him, on his way to the card party, that he did not know this, and that he would have no chance to make inquiries himself before his unexpected and precipitate departure for New Orleans. But he had managed to corner Maurice Benoit who, like himself, was more or less an habitué of the Salle des Tuileries and ask a favor of him.

"Listen, 'Rice! Do me a favor, will you? Tomorrow night."

"Sure. If it won't keep me from going you know where."

"No, that's just where I figured you'd be going—especially as you had to come to this damn card party tonight to please your family. The first time Titine comes around with her accordion, say something offhand, but rather loud, to one of the others in our gang about its being a shame I got dragged off to New Orleans by my grandfather, with no notice at all."

"Okay. That's easy."

" 'Course it's easy. Then take a sort of casual look at Titine and laugh and tell her it's too bad she's got such big feet."

"Has she got big feet? I never looked at her *feet*. I've looked—"

"All right, all right. She hasn't got especially big feet, as a matter of fact—that is, they're short, but they're sort of wide. Anyhow, say just that and then send me a special delivery letter to the St. Charles, telling me what she comes back with."

Maurice grinned and winked. "I don't quite get you, my friend, but I'll do like you say. Look, we'd better get back to our tables, hadn't we? Not that there's really any hurry. Everybody's got to talking about this scheme someone's dreamed up of having a carnival next year to celebrate Crowley's fortieth anniversary. Might be a good idea at that, don't you think so?"

Prosper thought it would be a very good idea, especially as he was confident that, if there were such a festival in '27, and it was staged along the same lines as other local celebrations already in existence, Anne Marie would almost certainly be the Rice Queen—that is, if she still had not made up her mind to marry anyone in the meantime. He joined readily enough in the talk about decorations, exhibitions, contests, floats and parades as visualized for a future festival; but every now and then, throughout that evening and the next day and night, his thoughts reverted to the errand he had entrusted to Maurice; and he was greatly relieved when the special delivery arrived on schedule.

It contained only two lines. "What you mean I got big feet, me? I wear a 5-D. That ain't so big, no." Prosper, having carefully torn up this important communication, slipped away from the convention long enough to buy a pair of gold slippers, the high heels studded with rhinestones, the buckle to the ankle strap similarly ornamented, in size 5-D.

Chapter Five

ON HIS RETURN TO CROWLEY, PROSPER FOUND THAT A VERY EFFECTIVE *entente cordiale* had already been established between the Villacs and the LaBranches. The call which his mother and sister had made had been very promptly returned; Victorine and Anne Marie had taken an immediate liking to each other and were soon visiting back and forth as if they had known each other for years and it was, therefore, the most natural thing in the world that they should do so. Moreover, in spite of her guarded comments, Lavinia made it so obvious that Victorine was almost exactly the sort of girl most suitable for her son that the inevitable male reaction took place: Prosper told himself that no one was going to choose his girl for him.

He might not have told himself this so frequently or so forcefully if Titine had not entered the picture, or if Victorine had given the slightest indication that she had "fallen for him," or that she might be persuaded to do so. Prosper would have been only too glad to show her that, favorable as was the first impression she had made on him, each successive meeting had made this impression even more favorable, but Victorine was wholly unhelpful. She did not avoid him on any of the numerous occasions when they met, but neither did she create nor even encourage any when he could see her alone; and though the give and take which he had at first admired so much actually changed very little in character, he admired it less and less all the time. It required an effort to match her in repartee and he was constitutionally easygoing; besides, he was expending a good deal of energy in a different direction—namely, in trying to find the time and the place which were both propitious for giving Titine the gold slippers.

So far, he had had no luck at all in that direction. Certainly he could not present them to her at the Salle des Tuileries; and though he thought he had located, approximately, the place where she lived, he was still cautious enough to realize that it would be extremely unwise to go there without being perfectly sure that the coast was clear; an encounter with either August, or August's gumshoe man, the Professor, would not only get him nowhere; it might have very unpleasant results all around. Chafing under the delay, Prosper tried to tell himself that it did not matter, that he was a fool to hang around Titine anyhow, that Victorine was in every respect far more desirable company. But these arguments were unconvincing. Not only were the things she said hard to cope with; her whole outlook was so alien to his that he found they did not speak the same language figuratively any more than they did literally. It was not that she put on airs; it was simply that her horizons were so much broader than his, her education so much more liberal, her background of wealth and culture so much more impressive, that she constantly betrayed all this. She had been to school in both Italy and England as well as France; during her vacations she had apparently traveled to every part of Europe; and these travels embraced not only major capitals, all the way from Stockholm to Madrid, and fashionable resorts like Deauville and the Lido; they included small out-of-the-way cities and remote islands of which Prosper knew little or nothing, but to which Victorine referred so casually and with so little explanation it was evident she assumed that he did—for he was honest enough to confess that she would not have done so merely to embarrass him. She had been enraptured with the forest of palms at Elche, but disappointed in the mosaics at Ravenna; she liked quiet Ischia better than tourist-ridden Capri, but Cyprus and Rhodes better still. Her mother's plan of keeping her abroad, merely to get her out of the way, had resulted in great opportunities: her father's people—those who still lived in Alsace and who still called themselves Zweig—had cordially offered to consider her one of the family and to give her the same advantages they gave their own daughters; Hortense, nee Duandeau, LaBranche *en premières noces*, Parkhurst *en secondes*, Sturdevant *en troisièmes*, graciously accepted this invitation, even before she consented to permit Victorine to see her father except at stated intervals. The Zweigs were immensely rich, they kept open house, they went everywhere and knew everyone, not only in mercantile and banking circles, but in those allegedly more aristocratic and exclusive. Victorine thought no more of having a duke for a partner or visiting a princess than she did of going to a dance at City Hall in Crowley or spending the night with Anne Marie afterward, so that they could talk it over in the course of a slumber party.

According to the provisions of the divorce, Moïse could reclaim his daughter for half of every year after she reached her eighteenth birthday; by then Hortense was quite willing to extend the time, and Moïse and Victorine had profited by that eagerness. For the last three years before coming to Lafayette, they had spent their winters in a luxurious New York penthouse, near the great Fifth Avenue emporium emblazoned with the LaBranche name, except while they were traveling in California and the Middle West, where Moïse also owned great mercantile establishments and maintained *pieds-à-terre*. Their summers had been spent in Paris and other centers of fashion, where Moïse had supplemented his own designs by selections from the great *couturiers*. He still liked to make such selections personally and Victorine had been delighted to accompany him to the showings. It was a source of gratification to him that she had inherited his sense of style; he had never seen a girl who set off fashionable clothes better herself, or who revealed more perception and taste in the interpretation of the current vogue and the forecast of the future one. He was equally gratified because she was interested in his great establishments as a whole, and insisted on spending considerable time in them, instead of going off to college, as he had sacrificially suggested. She enjoyed their box at the Metropolitan and seldom missed the opening of an important play. Her coming-out party at Sherry's had been a spectacular success and, for that matter, so had all of her first season in society. But she wanted to know the ropes of the business, too, she said; and because Moïse LaBranche, like Brent Winslow, had no son, it was a source of pride to him that his daughter had both the desire and the ability to carry on where he must eventually leave off. Victorine's presence at the great emporiums had come to be taken more or less for granted; she made surprisingly few mistakes, and the buyers, the models, the sales force and the credit bureau all came to like her. She and her father began to make plans which would create not only a title and an office for her, but a definite responsibility of her own, when Moïse had a sudden heart attack that put an end to the project. It was absolutely essential, his physicians informed him, that he should lead a quieter existence and live in a milder climate—that is, if he expected to live at all. It was then that he had bethought him of his old home and asked Victorine if she would be willing to go there with him. Unhesitatingly, she had said she would be delighted to do so. Her father had no real reason to believe that there had been mental reservations in her ready acceptance of the complete change in their mode of life. Just the same, he had not been without his anxious moments. . . .

Prosper was not anxious so much as he was annoyed; he did not feel that Victorine fitted into the Louisiana picture and he blamed this on her rather than on Louisiana. It irritated him to hear her praises sung first by his sister, then by his mother, then by his grandfather and grandmother Winslow and, finally, by his circle of friends which, in a widening degree, soon became Victorine's circle, too. From the first she was popular, and the attributes which confused or annoyed him did not seem to confuse or annoy anyone else, which added to his confusion and annoyance. She was a beautiful dancer and, at her father's suggestion, the huge drawing room at their house became the scene of parties which either supplemented or supplanted those held elsewhere in the vicinity. The song, *Allons à Lafayette,* was heard with increasing frequency in Crowley and, when the singers caroled this, what they really meant was "Let's go to Vicky's!" Her invitations were eagerly sought and highly prized, and she herself seemed no less pleased to accept those extended to her. But quite without conscious malice, she asked questions which revealed, unmistakably, that the latter involved functions that were not up to the standards of those which she had hitherto taken as a matter of course.

The first of these happened to be a watermelon party, held at Pecan Grove, the plantation on the outskirts of Lafayette belonging to the Benoits, whose elder son Didier held a favored place among Anne Marie's many suitors. The plantation had changed hands and names several times before the Benoits acquired it; neither Anne Marie nor Prosper remembered, until their mother reminded them, that it had once been Hortense Duandeau's home—in fact, that she had grown up there, and that her wedding reception, when she married Moïse LaBranche, had been held there. By the time Lavinia had recalled this to her son and daughter, Victorine had already been invited and had accepted.

"Did you tell her where the party was going to be?" Lavinia inquired.

"Of course. At the Benoits'."

Lavinia made a gesture of impatience. "Does Victorine know where the Benoits live?"

"She hasn't been there yet, if that's what you mean."

"No, it's not what I mean. Does she know that Pecan Grove, as it's called now, used to be called Bosquet des Pins and before that Belle Hermine? Does she know that before it belonged to the Benoits it belonged to the Graviers and before that, to the Marchands and before that, to the Duandeaux?"

"I don't know. We didn't ask her all that. We only asked her if she'd like to go to a watermelon party and she said yes."

"Sometimes I think I have the stupidest children in Crowley. You'd better ask her."

"What do you want us to ask her, for the love of Mike? She can't very well live in Lafayette and never go near Pecan Grove, if she's going to see anything of us. Not with things the way they are between Didier and Anne Marie."

Prosper spoke angrily. He did not like being called stupid, and still less did he like being reminded that he had committed another *faux pas* in connection with Victorine; there had been too many already. Anne Marie, amiable and peace loving as she was, did not like being called stupid, either, but she might have let this pass; however, with unwonted vehemence, she inquired what her brother meant, talking about "the way things are"; nothing at all was decided, as far as she and Didier were concerned; she still had not made up her mind, but at the moment she halfway thought that perhaps Dale Fontenot. . . .

A tempest in a teapot occurred in the Villac household. Nevertheless, as matters turned out, there was no awkwardness about the site of the entertainment. Moïse LaBranche, in this instance, had reasoned in much the same way Prosper had: to the effect that Victorine could not live in Lafayette without ever going near Belle Hermine, alias Bosquet des Pins, alias Pecan Grove, especially in view of the fact that she seemed to be seeing a good deal of the young Villacs and that one of them was believed to have a rather special interest in the place. He had, therefore, quietly and without bitterness, enlightened Victorine as to his own previous association with it and she had taken the information in her stride. It was later that the awkwardness arose.

For Victorine had never been to a watermelon party. She was utterly unprepared for a feast which consisted solely of the featured melons and boiled corn, which was served at long crude tables scattered casually about a rather untidy yard, and which was lighted by candles in paper bags, supplemented by a large artificial moon, rigged up among the pecan trees to take the place of the real one, which was dark at that time of the month. The effects of her European upbringing were still strong enough to make her regard corn as fodder for cattle, rather than as food for gentlefolk; and the custom of gnawing it off the cob, and then licking one's fingers to rid these of surplus butter, did nothing to lessen her distaste for it. She managed to do away with one ear, eating it as everyone else did and without visible signs of shrinking, and she managed somewhat better with the watermelon, though this seemed to her almost as messy as the corn and woefully insipid to boot. When at last the satiated guests rose from the long tables and she heard murmured suggestions about going on to the Bellevue Club in Opelousas, she drew Prosper aside and whispered to him.

"Will we have supper there?"

"Supper!" Prosper exclaimed in astonishment. "Why, we've just had supper! Six ears of corn and half a watermelon ought to be enough to keep anyone from going hungry."

"Maybe you've eaten six ears of corn and half a watermelon. I haven't."

"It's your own fault then. They were there to eat."

"I don't like corn and watermelon very well. I only ate enough to be polite."

"You don't like corn and watermelon!" Prosper echoed in genuine astonishment. "What do you like?"

"Well, most things. Soup and fish and meat and vegetables—except corn—and salads and cheese and sweets and fruit—any kind of fruit except watermelon. Of course, there are some things I like better than others—artichokes as a vegetable and Pont l'Eveque as a cheese and Bar-le-Duc as a jelly and Reine Claude plums as a fruit, for instance. But I don't really care. Anything that goes into the making of a civilized meal."

"You'd better go back to France," Prosper said curtly, turning on his heel.

Of course, two minutes afterward he was sorry. He knew that Victorine was not putting on airs, that she was simply speaking candidly, that she really was hungry. But by the time he turned back to her, she was talking with Maurice, Didier's younger brother, and she danced with him most of the time they were at Farmer Veltin's, as the Bellevue Club was generally called. She permitted Prosper to take her home, but this was only on the recognized principle that a girl returned from a party with the same man who took her to it, unless, in the course of the evening, he had passed beyond the bounds of what was generally termed fresh to what was termed beyond the pale. As Prosper had not even been fresh, she could not possibly have refused to ride with him; however, when he deposited her at her front door, and said sarcastically that since she did not care for local delicacies, served local style, she probably would not want to go with him Friday night to the sea food supper at Lake Catahoula, she announced that there was nothing she liked better than sea food, but that she had already promised Maurice Benoit she would go to the party with him.

Prosper drove home with utter disregard for the state of the roads. He had no way of guessing that Moïse LaBranche, at this very same time, was admonishing his daughter in a way which was both wise and soothing. It was not his habit to stay up for her, since his strength would no longer permit him to keep such long hours without rest. But, after retiring to his room, he remained propped high on pillows in his magnificent Louis XIV bed, clad in silk pajamas made to his measure by Sulka, and reading one periodical after another, until she came knocking at his door to announce her return and tell him about the events of the evening. Then he put aside his reading material and listened intently to everything she had to say, meanwhile observing her with his shrewd and kindly eyes. On this particular occasion, he spoke with more emphasis than usual.

"We will have corn and watermelon, turn and turn about, at our table every day as long as they remain in season. You will eat just a little each time and stop when it seems to go against you. But it will not do so for long. You will learn to like it. It is very important that you should."

"I don't see why."

"Because when in Rome, you should do as Romans do. There never was a wiser proverb. And it is not based on the theory that you must be a slave to custom. It is based partly on the theory that you can get a great deal of additional pleasure out of life if you learn there is more than one good way of doing things, and that two or three or even four may be equally good, though utterly different. It is also based on the theory that gentlefolk accept hospitality in the spirit in which it is offered—that is to say, with the intent to please and not to offend and with the hope and belief that this had been done. I am sure it was the case in this instance. The Benoits are very kind people—very fine people."

"The Benoits don't know I didn't like their silly artificial moon and their horrible food and their messy service. I was very careful not to let anyone find that out, except Prosper."

"And didn't Prosper invite you to go with him to this party? Wasn't it also his hope, as your escort of the evening, that you would enjoy yourself?"

"Yes, I suppose so. But it won't hurt Prosper to be taken down a peg. He's terribly cocky over nothing—terribly provincial."

"Ah! . . . Well now, I confess he has impressed me rather favorably. I somehow had the idea that he had made the same sort of an impression on you."

"Oh, I like him! But he needs to be put in his place."

"What sort of a place, Victorine? The boy has a very good background. His parents and both his maternal and paternal grandparents have always been highly respected. His mother is extremely capable, besides being a woman of fine character; very few men have made as great a success as she has in a highly competitive field. And his sister is one of the loveliest girls I have seen in a long while; I am not at all surprised that so many young men are in love with her." Moïse paused for a moment, as if in pleasant contemplation of Anne Marie's blond beauty, and as if considering that he might well have been very much in love with her himself, if she had only been born half a century earlier. "Prosper has been brought up in a good home," the old gentleman went on. "And has had a good education; that is, I realize it has not taken him very far afield, but there is plenty of time for that still, and in going to a local school and a local college, he has followed local custom —a custom for which I believe the closeness of family ties is largely responsible. The various members of most families hereabouts do not like long separations from their kith and kin; they form a very closely knit unit. Such a unit is a valuable part of community life—more valuable, I'm inclined to think, than a contribution of outstanding scholarship or sophistication. I have always been very sorry that you were not brought up in the midst of a devoted family circle, Victorine. If I could have chosen, I would much rather have seen you reared in the way Prosper has been than the way you have been."

He paused again for a moment and Victorine knew that this time he was thinking that Hortense had left him for another man, instead of being faithful to her husband as long as he lived and to his memory after his death, like Lavinia Villac. Victorine also knew that Lavinia Villac had been a wonderful mother as well as a wonderful wife; she had not set her children an example of fickleness, frivolity and restlessness, but of loyalty, serious purpose and steadfastness. It was all too true that Prosper had had a good background and a good home and even certain advantages which she, Victorine, had lacked, for all her advanced schooling and extensive travel. Moïse, realizing that he had succeeded in making a point, continued to press it.

"Perhaps Prosper thinks you need to be put in your place," he said mildly. "After all, his mother has no doubt mentioned to him—speaking kindly and rather casually—that the Villacs and the Winslows have a good deal to overlook when it comes to an—ah—association with the LaBranches."

"Overlook!" Victorine exclaimed, flaring immediately.

"Yes, my dear. It is distasteful, even painful, for me to mention this, since your mother was once my wife—my dearly loved wife. But she has created a great deal of scandal by her conduct, not once, but over and over again, and this scandal has not been caused by idle and malicious gossip; it is, alas! founded on sad and sober truth. Families like the Villacs—and perhaps even more particularly the Winslows—do not tolerate such scandal readily and they have remained untouched by it. I would be willing to take my oath that the complete chastity of Mary Winslow, Lavinia Winslow Villac and Anne Marie Villac has never been so much as questioned; like Caesar's wife, they are above suspicion. As far as that goes, I have never heard Brent Winslow's name or Claude Villac's coupled improperly with that of any woman."

"What about Prosper Villac's?" inquired Victorine, still flaring. "I've heard lots of people say that, whenever he stays overtime at the mill, Paula Bennett, that slab-sided secretary of his, stays, too—not that I can see how she could lure him into an illicit affair."

"Neither can I," Moïse LaBranche answered mildly. "Therefore, I can't understand why you should pay any attention to such unintelligent and unjust gossip. It is not in character for you to subscribe to the unintelligent or the unjust."

"Well, there's plenty of other gossip. He goes a lot to a place called the Salle des Tuileries—a cheap dance hall over a grocery store on the road to Cypremort. Maurice Benoit goes there a lot and, once in a while, Didier goes with him—not very often though; everyone says he wouldn't have a prayer of getting anywhere with Anne Marie if he did. Dale Fontenot does some of his grocery shopping at August's—not much, because he gets most of his supplies from New Orleans or the plantation store; and he does his errands in the daytime, unless he's delayed at the sugar mill. Even then, he doesn't go into the dance hall, except maybe to say hello to his cronies and have a friendly glass with them. Anyway, he's so crazy about Anne Marie that I don't believe he knows there's another girl in the world. But lots of people think that the reason Prosper goes there is that he's stuck on a girl there named Titine, a cheap little Cajun who plays the accordion, but that he can't get very far, because August Scholtze, the bootlegger who runs this joint, is her 'protector.' "

Moïse LaBranche shifted his position slightly; he was very tired and in considerable pain and he hoped that this change might relieve him. But his speech betrayed neither suffering nor exhaustion; in fact, when he next addressed his daughter, it was with increased emphasis and something akin to severity.

"Some such talk has reached me, too," he said. "But I have not taken it as seriously as you have. Indeed, you may be very sure that if I had learned anything about Prosper Villac which I thought would make him an unsuitable companion for you, I should not have continued to welcome him to this house. He is somewhat irresponsible and impetuous, but I think he will gradually outgrow those youthful characteristics—the very fact that his mother is so outstandingly capable and his sister so imperturbably amiable may have had disadvantages, as well as advantages, as far as he is concerned. Someday he will be jolted into dependability and prudence. He is high spirited, pleasure loving and intensely virile; no doubt, he has committed a few follies along the way. But I should think they would have about run their course by now and, in any case, that is not what we were talking about, my dear. If you are looking for a Galahad, I think you may have quite a long search—and quite a dull one. Instead of doing that, if you are really attracted to this young man, and feel reasonably sure that things have not yet gone very far between him and the dance hall performer, why do you not make yourself a little more agreeable and a little more accessible—before it is too late?"

Moïse picked up the magazine he had laid aside, as if to indicate that the conversation was now at an end; but Victorine knew it was not, for he never actually dismissed her without a good night kiss and the fondly expressed hope that she would have sweet dreams. Presently, he laid down the magazine again.

"There is another thing, besides those I mentioned a few moments ago, that may be troubling those good people," he said, once more speaking mildly. "And that is the question of religion."

"Mr. and Mrs. Winslow aren't Catholics. Neither is Mrs. Villac."

"No, I understand that. Mrs. Winslow has always been a rather strict Presbyterian. Her husband, I believe, is not a communicant, but he goes to church with her more or less regularly and upholds her in all her religious activities—in fact, contributes most generously to the charitable causes in which she is interested. Moreover, they sent their only daughter to an excellent Catholic school, recognizing that it was the

only good one available in this vicinity at the time, and very properly
putting that consideration above intolerance. Mrs. Villac has remained
a Protestant herself, but she is by no means anti-Catholic, and she has
loyally fulfilled her promise to bring up her children in the Catholic
faith, though a lesser woman might have argued that her husband's early
death released her from such a promise, since she alone was responsible
for directing their upbringing. And Catholic or not, every member of
both these families is a Christian."

"You mean—they might look down on us socially because you're—
because we're Jews?"

"Yes, my dear, that is exactly what I mean. To be sure, you were baptized. I kept my promise, also—to that extent. But your mother auto-
matically deserted the Church when she divorced me and married that
poor simpleton, Parkhurst. Her desertion took a double form when she
divorced him and married the showy Sturdevant. You have never made
your First Communion or been confirmed; your mother did not take
the trouble to see that you did. The nearest place to a home you have
ever had, until recently, was given you by my Jewish relatives, the
Zweigs, and naturally they took no such steps, either. I have failed to do
so, not because I did not think of it, but because I reasoned that I had
no further responsibility in the matter, since you were a grown girl when
you came back to live with me, and never mentioned it yourself. I believe now that I was at fault. I should have taken the initiative, in order
to fulfill my prenuptial agreement that any children of my marriage
should be brought up Catholics. No age limit was set. And because of
my omission, I think I will let your statement stand as you amended it.
The Winslows and the Villacs may look down on us socially—not merely
on me—because we are Jews."

"I think it's outrageous for them even to imagine that they could!"

Moïse sighed gently. "No, my dear, it's not outrageous, it's logical—as
they understand logic. But perhaps I was wrong to raise quite such a
debatable point at this hour." His eyes strayed toward the clock, whose
hands were pointing to four. "After all, we only started out to talk about
corn and watermelon. By the way, you must learn to like court bouillon,
also, in case you do not take to it naturally. No doubt, you will be going
to court bouillon parties very soon, too. You may fare somewhat better
at those, because you will get French bread and red wine with your
fish stew and you can always make a meal of those. Still you should
take no chances. Meanwhile, I hope you raided the icebox before coming
upstairs? I'm glad, very glad. Good night, my darling, and sweet dreams."

Chapter Six

ALL THIS, OF COURSE, PROSPER DID NOT KNOW. IT WOULD HAVE CALMED and encouraged him considerably if he had, even though Victorine did not profit, as promptly as she might have, by her father's good counsel. Watching her with loving concern, Moïse admitted to himself that perhaps he had made a mistake in bringing up the question of religion; for, far from deciding that she would like to talk over her anomalous position with some sympathetic third person, as he advised, she went out of her way to proclaim herself a Jewess.

"Is there any special reason why you named that dog Levvy?" Prosper asked her one day, when they had gone to Charenton to the annual Fourth of July swimming party and she had insisted on taking the Dalmatian with her.

"Yes, two of them. First, it's an abbreviation of Four Eleven—the firehouse signal. Second, it's just a modified form of Levi. I wanted to label her as a 'dog of a Jew.'"

Prosper flushed and did not immediately answer. Victorine persisted.

"You realize I'm a Jewess, don't you, Prosper?"

"Well, I reckon I knew, somewhere in the back of my mind, that your father was a Jew. But I never thought about it much. He's such a grand person and everything."

"You mean to say you think a Jew can't be a grand person?"

"No, of course not. Look, Vicky, can't we just sit here on the beach and sun ourselves? It's such a pretty day and everything. I'm sorry I asked a stupid question about Levvy. I didn't mean to offend you."

"You didn't offend me by asking about Levvy. But you do offend me when you try to shy off from admitting you mind because I'm a Jewess."

"Good God, I haven't shied off from admitting any such thing! Besides, you were baptized, weren't you? The Duandeaux were good Catholics— at least, so I've heard; they've all moved away now. Your mother must have been one."

"Yes, she was one, but she isn't any more. You must know that, too. You must know just what she is."

Prosper flushed still more deeply.

"Vicky, I'm sorry. I keep saying the wrong thing without intending to. What I tried to say was, you're only half—"

"Half Jewish? Well, thanks for the intended compliment! But listen to me, Prosper Villac: I'd a lot rather be a Jew like my father than the kind of Catholic my mother turned out to be."

She jumped up and ran off to her dressing room. Prosper shook his head as he watched her go, and then bent over and began to pick up shells from the beach, running them through his fingers with the sand. He felt both baffled and embittered. Everything had seemed to be going so well before his unfortunate question. Vicky had fairly taken his breath away when she first emerged from her dressing room in her bathing suit. It was bright red, her favorite color, and vastly becoming; moreover, it was not only much smarter, but much scantier than any of those the other girls were wearing. She plunged into the water and swam farther and faster than any of the others, too, and then she did several fancy dives which were unfamiliar to most of them. These were not meant to be in the nature of showing off and no one took them that way; they evoked widespread admiration and—among the feminine contingent—a little awe; Prosper was puffed up with pride because it was the girl who had come with him who had created such a sensation. After they were through swimming and diving, she had flung herself down on the beach beside him, not bothering to go and take off her wet bathing suit right away, like the other girls; she said the sun would dry her off in no time and, anyway, she wanted to get a good tan. This pleased him, too. It did not strike him as daring that she should lie there in her wet bathing suit, which now clung to her lovely figure, revealing every line of it even more closely than before. By and by she sat up, shaking out her black curls, which she had not bothered to confine in a cap and which provided the only covering there was over her shoulders. All this was pleasantly provocative. No one else was very near at the moment, since almost everybody had gone off to dress, and he wondered what would happen if he reached over and put his arm around her waist, and then drew her closer and held her very near him. Only for a minute or two, of course, even if she would let him do it longer, which was doubtful; perhaps he could not get away with it at all, but somehow he thought he could and the very idea of that minute or two was intoxicating. . . .

And then that cursed dog, which had been contentedly digging for nonexistent bones at a comfortable distance, had come bounding up and Prosper had asked his unfortunate question. He did not see Victorine alone again in the course of the outing.

The next day, he called to tell her the Elks' Wives were having a dance at their Home in New Iberia and that he would like to have her go to it with him. Her answer was inexcusably mocking.

"The Elks' *Wives*? I didn't know elks had wives or a home, either. I thought they lived in forests and that they were quite promiscuous, that is, when they were—what is it called?"

"I won't tell you what it's called, if you don't know, but I think you do. And I think you know that the Elks are members of a very respectable, worthy organization, which does a lot of good, and that their wives are about the nicest ladies anywhere around. You've been here long enough to find out that much, if you hadn't found it out before. . . . All right, don't come with me. I'll ask someone else."

"Do, by all means. A nice, refined, intelligent Catholic; not a vulgar, stupid Jewess like me."

"Oh, for God's sake! I'll never ask you to another dance as long as I live!"

As the weeks went by, she began to think that he meant it. They met, frequently, of course, at the parties held in Lafayette and other places in the vicinity, for all the young people who made up "the crowd" went gaily and nonchalantly from one town to another, undeterred by indifferent roads and stifling heat. They went to fish fries at Beau Sejour and John Broussard's camp on the banks of Bayou Vermilion and to the home of Mme Plaisance in New Iberia, which was available for *sauces piquantes*. They attended the road shows and one-night stands at the Jefferson; they gathered in groups to watch the trapeze artist who performed on top of the Royal Movie Theater, to attract crowds before the show began, and listened to Frank Meyers as he sang from a box, to the accompaniment of colored slides, in the course of the show. They danced to "Papa" Celestin's band or Toot Johnson's, and to the music of the Black Swan Orchestra, which was made up of local Negroes who were waiters in the daytime. Victorine was by no means the only one who had unlimited spending money. In fact, several of the others, who had suddenly come into unexpected inheritances, threw it about much more casually than she did. The atmosphere was carefree, extravagant, pleasure loving. It was easy enough to say that one person in the crowd did not matter more than any other, as long as everybody in it had a good time. At least, it should have been. But Victorine did not succeed in saying so, even to herself, and she did not try to say so to her father because she realized he would have known better. For Prosper did not ask "a nice, refined, intelligent" girl to go to the Elks' Dance or any other dance with him. He spent more and more time at the Salle des Tuileries and, eventually, he got the long-awaited chance to give Titine the gold slippers.

Chapter Seven

AUGUST VERY SELDOM LEFT THE PREMISES DURING BUSINESS HOURS; BUT
as his patronage increased and, with it, the amount of liquor consumed,
he was occasionally obliged to go down to the Gulf to get fresh supplies
from his friends, the rumrunners. When this happened, it was his custom to put a presumably trusty lieutenant in charge of his business; but
the wooden steps leading from the grocery store to the dance hall had
been rickety for a long while and their railing was becoming more and
more insecure. He decided that it would be prudent to have mending
done and replacement made before an accident called overmuch attention to some of his activities; so he put up a large sign which read,
CLOSED FOR REPAIRS UNTIL SATURDAY, and went off, after making sure
that two carpenters were already at work.

As he gave no advance notice of his intentions, either to his customers
or to his employees, and expected to be absent himself only one night,
he did not think that much could go awry in so short a time—and, if
anything did, he would know how to mete out justice on his return. If
he had caught that one word, which might have been either *dangereuse*
or Dargereux, whispered so many weeks earlier, he would have been
less confident. But when Prosper arrived at the Salle des Tuileries
Thursday night and read the sign, he was ready for immediate action;
he had kept the slippers concealed under the back seat of his car ever
since he had bought them; and it did not take him long to locate the
shack between Bayou Warehouse and Bayou Patou in which he was
interested, because he had already thoroughly explored that terrain.

As he drove home just before dawn, however, it was with no sense
of elation. The girl who had seemed so alluring as she wove her way

among the tables at the Salle des Tuileries, playing her accordion, singing her little Cajun songs and making her little wisecracks, was almost
unbelievably less so when he had her to himself beside a bayou. Everything had been extremely easy at the end. Titine had evidently been
sure he would come, for she had been standing where the road—or what
passed for a road—ended at some distance from her parents' swamp
house. He had not even needed to risk having the lights of his car shine
on it. When she came out of the shadows and spoke to him, it had not
been with words of welcome, but with questioning greed, and disillu-
sionment had set in then and there. Did he have the gold slippers with
him? He had no trouble in guessing that, if his answer had been no, she
would have slipped away from him with a mocking laugh. When he
handed them to her, she insisted that she must put them on immediately,
that he must light a match—a succession of matches—so that she could
see. Only when she had satisfied herself that the slippers fitted, that they
were in every way what she had coveted, was she ready for love-making.
Love-making? It was an insult to apply the beautiful word of love to
anything that happened during the rest of the night.

In addition to the revulsion of feeling that had set in before he actually started home, Prosper began to be assailed by tardy anxiety regarding August's reception of the gold slippers. They would do Titine
no good if she kept them hidden at home; and since the bootlegger had
not bought them himself, he would certainly lose no time in finding out
whence they came, which should not be too hard for him; then he would
vent his wrath both on the giver and the recipient, and this might take
a very unpleasant form. Although Prosper's desire for Titine was now
as dead as if it had never existed, he shrank from the thought that she
might suffer abuse of one kind or another because of him; and though
he was no coward, he could not help remembering how often he had
thought it would be a great mistake to pick a quarrel with the powerfully
built man whom he had very certainly angered and, in a sense, wronged.
He was still preoccupied by these disquieting reflections when he arrived at the Claudia; there had been no point, after he reached Crowley,
in going to bed; he had made himself coffee, taken a quick shower and
started, in clean clothes, for the mill before the servants had arrived at
the house for the day or before his mother was stirring, though he did
not doubt she had heard him come in. Early as it was, Paula was already
at her post, and he suddenly felt impelled to ask her a question which,
previously, he had never thought worth while putting to her.

"Paula, August Scholtze asked me, a while back, to give his regards to you. I'm sorry, I forgot it at the time."

"It doesn't matter at all."

"I didn't realize you knew him."

Paula made no answer. She was apparently very busy getting her desk in order to begin work immediately.

"I never saw you at his place," Prosper persisted.

Paula stopped shuffling papers. "You never saw your sister there, either, did you?" she inquired sarcastically. "Or your new-found friend Victorine LaBranche?"

"No. But August never sends his regards to either of them," Prosper answered shortly. "He doesn't know too much, but he knows better than to do that. I'd be interested to learn where you did get acquainted with him."

"I don't particularly like the way you're talking and I don't think it's really any of your business where I got acquainted with him. But since I suppose you can fire me for alleged insubordination if I don't answer, and since I need the job, I may as well tell you it was during the war. You've probably forgotten I was with the Graves Registration Service in France. August Scholtze was orderly to one of the officers who used to come on inspection tours. I never saw much of him then and I've never seen anything of him since. I haven't the least idea why he should send his regards to me, after all this time. You needn't take mine to him the next time you go to his joint, which I suppose will be tonight. Apparently, you never heard that sage advice about its being a good thing to be off with the old love before you're on with the new."

Paula had begun to pound her typewriter before Prosper could frame an adequate reply or, indeed, any sort of a reply. He had meant to ask her, if he found she really did know August well, whether or not the bootlegger was actually violent when he was angry. But she had made Prosper forget the question. The Graves Registration Service! Well, he *had* forgotten, but that was the sort of war job for which she might have been well suited. And an orderly to an officer on an inspection tour might well have found time hanging so heavily on his hands, in 1918, that even Paula's unexhilarating company could have been welcome. But she certainly was as sour as they came now—that last crack of hers about old and new loves! Titine never had been and never would be his love, even his light-o'-love, he knew that, belatedly but with both certainty and shame. Never had he so fervently desired that something he had done could be undone as he did every time he thought about the happenings of the previous night, and this was most of the day, for he had great difficulty in dismissing them from his mind, much to the detriment of his normal occupations. And Victorine was not his love, either, his true love, for very different reasons. He thought now that she might have been, if he had not kept taking offense when no offense was meant, if he had not quarreled with her, stupidly and senselessly, over trifles. For the quarrels *had* been over trifles, nothing more. And now he did not see how he could ever try to make up with her. He did not see how he could even look her or her father in the face again. . . .

When he went home that night, his mother told him that Victorine had called him up. She had never done this, on her own initiative, before, but when he returned her call, she sounded so happy and carefree that he realized she was not thinking about offenses or quarrels. Her tone was friendly and cordial, almost affectionate. She wondered if he would care to come to dinner on Sunday—just the family.

He hesitated, but it seemed like tempting fate not to take advantage of this new propitious mood and all day Saturday he worked the more buoyantly because of the prospect that he was to see her again so soon after all. He put in a long day and worked conscientiously, trying to make up for lost time, went to bed late and slept late Sunday morning. Usually, his mother called him for Mass, but this time she did not do so and he was just about to leave the house for Lafayette when Maurice Benoit telephoned. It was evident from his voice that he was very much excited.

"Hi! Have you heard the news?"

"I've been asleep . . . what news?"

"Titine wasn't at the Tuileries last night for the grand opening."

"She wasn't!"

"No. It's the first time she's ever missed. So of course that started everyone talking. But that wasn't the half of it. She not only didn't show up at the Tuileries, but when they sent for her, she wasn't at home, either! And what's more, she hasn't been seen there or anywhere else since!"

"You mean she's disappeared?"

"Yes. August doesn't know where she is—at least, he says so and, somehow, I believe he's telling the truth. And the Professor doesn't know. Neither does her family. Now they're getting up search parties and some of our crowd are going out to help. Don't you want to come along?"

"I will, this afternoon, if she hasn't turned up by then. But I bet she will have. She probably just took off for the week end. I've been asked to the LaBranches' to dinner and I don't like to back out at the last moment. I'm not really needed, am I?"

"No. I kind of thought—well, let's skip it."

"Just as you say. See you later then."

Perhaps he *should* have joined the search at once, Prosper told himself as he drove along toward Lafayette. But he was so encouraged, indeed so elated, by the fact that Victorine, for the first time, had tried of her own accord to get in touch with him, that he thought he had a right to follow up this advantage, on the chance that it really was an advantage.

It seemed to him there could be no doubt of this when he got out of his car and found that Victorine herself was waiting for him at the door, with Levvy, as usual, at her heels, and no one else in sight. She greeted him so cordially, indeed so eagerly, that, spontaneously, he did what he had wanted to do that day at Charenton Beach and had refrained from doing—unwisely, he had thought ever since. He put his arms around her waist and drew her nearer until they were very close together; and then, almost before he had time to realize how it had happened, he was kissing her lovely upturned face and she was returning his kisses. . . .

Somewhere off in the distance, the telephone was ringing. That cursed telephone, there was no escape from it any longer, any time, Prosper said to himself, and then remembered it was to a telephone call he owed his present overwhelming happiness. Victorine did not seem to feel it necessary to pay any attention to the ringing and by and by it stopped. They heard someone answering it and afterward someone coming in their direction, so then they drew slightly apart, but they continued to look into each other's eyes, both laughing a little, from sheer irrepressible happiness because, at last, they had stopped acting like a couple of young fools and been true to themselves and to each other.

When a door opened at the end of the hall, they turned and saw that it was not a servant who was coming toward them, but Moïse LaBranche, leaning heavily on his cane. They ran forward to meet him, hand in hand, with Levvy barking joyously beside them, and Moïse looked at them with his keen kind glance and then flung his cane aside and laid a trembling hand on the arm of each.

"I am the bearer of very bad tidings," he said, speaking gently and sorrowfully. "You have probably both heard about the disappearance of the young girl who played the accordion at the Tuileries. She has just been found."

"Found! Where? Is she all right?"

The questions came simultaneously. Moïse shook his head, and the trembling hands resting on the strong young arms gripped them more firmly, seeking for support.

"She is dead. She had fallen into the rough rice bin on the top floor of the Claudia Mill. Her body was discovered by the Sunday watchman because one foot protruded from the rice—a foot encased in a gold slipper. Of course, no one knows as yet when or why she climbed to the third floor of the mill, and whether or not the fall was accidental. But it seems that the last person to leave the mill before it closed last night was—you, Prosper."

PART TWO

September, 1926

Dangereuse

Chapter Eight

THE RESPONSE TO HIS SHATTERING ANNOUNCEMENT WAS AGAIN IMMEDI-
ate and simultaneous, though, this time, his hearers did not ask the same
question.

"Who telephoned?" Prosper demanded quickly.

"What's the time that he left the mill got to do with such a horrible
accident?" Vicky asked excitedly. Moïse answered his guest first.

"The sheriff—Tobe Bennett. The Sunday watchman had called your
house and your mother answered. She said she'd notify both the sheriff
and the coroner. She told Tobe you'd gone to Lafayette to spend the rest
of the day with us . . . and he obviously thought you must be notified,
too—direct and at once. He must have telephoned here, asking you to
meet him at the mill, while your mother was calling the coroner. However, he was perfectly willing to talk to me, when I told him this wasn't
a good moment for you to come to the telephone. After all, Tobe Bennett
and I have known each other a good many years. We understand each
other."

"Father, you haven't answered *my* question. What difference does it
make whether or not Prosper was the last person to leave the mill?"

The two men exchanged glances. Then Moïse answered, speaking
even more gently and kindly than he had at first.

"It means the authorities want—in fact, they need—complete information about everything he saw and did at the Claudia last night."

"I never heard of anything so absurd! They must know perfectly well
that, if Prosper'd known where Titine was last night, he'd have told them
of his own accord the first thing this morning, when people began to
find out that her family was worrying because she hadn't come home."

"Yes, of course they realize that. At the same time, there's been a very strange—a very sad—accident. At least, we hope it was an accident—that in itself would be bad enough. It's the duty of public officials to investigate it from every possible angle. In Prosper's case, this will naturally be a mere formality. But it's a formality that's got to be observed immediately."

"That's right, honey. I've got to beat it back to Crowley as fast as I can get there."

"You mean without staying to dinner or anything?"

Again, the two men glanced at each other; despite the gravity of the situation, they could not help smiling slightly and, without stopping to consider that Moïse might regard the caress as presumptuous, Prosper put his arm around Vicky's waist again.

"Yes, honey, that's just what I mean."

"Then I'm coming with you."

"I reckon maybe you hadn't better. Not this time."

"But we've just got engaged! It isn't fair, ten minutes after we've got engaged, for some old sheriff to call you up and say you've got to tell him about every cigarette you smoked and every cup of coffee you drank and when and where last night. Of course, it's dreadful about that poor girl. Just the same, I don't see—"

"Tobe Bennett doesn't know we've just got engaged. In fact . . . in fact," he repeated, clearing his throat, "I didn't know it myself until you just said so. But I'm mighty glad you did. Remembering that will help a lot while I'm talking to Tobe Bennett." He paused and looked at Moïse LaBranche a third time. "I'd like to be sure though, before I start out, that your father wouldn't feel better if you hadn't said it and if it wasn't true."

As Prosper forced his dilapidated Oldsmobile along the road between Lafayette and Crowley, he was able, temporarily, to dismiss from his mind the grim nature of his errand, while he dwelt with almost equal exultation on the fervor of Victorine's kisses and the firmness of her father's handclasp. He had scored a great triumph, not only in winning this beautiful, self-willed girl, but in doing so with unquestioning parental approval. However, the exultation was pierced by darts of self-questioning, against which it was not proof. Victorine was, of course, the most wonderful girl in the world; but he knew, all too well, that she was not slow to anger, and he could not escape the unwelcome realization that she would be roused, quite as easily, to jealousy. Indeed, he had no doubt that part of the trouble between them, during the course of their courtship, lay in the fact that she had heard well-founded rumors about Titine's attraction for him, and that she had resented the rivalry which these implied. Her pride would have been touched by any implication that she needed to compete with a girl whom she would have considered her inferior. Vicky was not consciously or voluntarily a snob; she had quickly proved herself a good mixer and a good companion in her new environment, and Prosper felt sure that no one in their immediate circle of friends, besides himself, knew that her adjustment to it had not been altogether easy, and that she often longed for the more cosmopolitan mode of life to which she had hitherto been accustomed. But she set great store by the standards of sophistication and the code of conduct natural to one of her background and breeding; also, by the amenities which were the outward and visible sign of these standards and this code. It would never have occurred to her, until she was faced with the present situation, that she might have as a rival a common and ignorant girl, who, like her parents before her, had been born and brought up in a swamp shack, and who earned her living by playing the accordion in a speak-easy run by the uncouth creature who was her recognized paramour. Vicky would have deplored the division of attraction between herself and any of the girls whom she recognized as an equal, and she would have done her best to win the race for a man's affection, if she wanted the man herself. But she would not have felt in any way degraded by such a rivalry. The case of Titine was altogether different. The fact that the poor little tramp was dead would not help. Indeed, all sorts of sordid details, which had hitherto escaped public notice, would now be dragged into the open.

And then, what about Moïse? He must have heard gossip, too, but he could not have taken it overseriously; otherwise—as he himself had said, though Prosper did not know this—he would not have continued to welcome at his house a visitor whom he considered an undesirable suitor for his daughter. A certain number of indiscretions he would have taken for granted; a few definite lapses from grace he would have condoned. However, would he have countenanced the betrothal of his only and greatly beloved child to a man who was receiving her ardent but innocent kisses for the first time, less than a week after such a man had spent the night with a wanton, and one so easily bought that this could be done with a pair of gold slippers? Prosper did not believe that Moïse would leniently regard such conduct as a mere lapse from grace; the old gentleman would consider it, and rightly, a dual dishonor, since it involved not only Prosper himself, but Victorine as well. He would expect repentance and atonement before he would be ready to receive Prosper into his family.

However, though Prosper could not altogether dismiss such questions and the probable replies to them from his tumultuous thoughts, they were soon crowded out by others. He would have to look at the dead body of a beautiful girl which, only three nights before, had been warm against his own; as he came closer and closer to the dreadful scene, the prospect became more and more appalling. Of course, he was merely to meet Tobe at the mill, so that they could proceed together toward Toler's Furniture Store, which doubled as a mortuary establishment, where the coroner, Dr. Timoteo Davila, would be holding his inquest. But why was the sheriff so anxious to talk privately with him, and at the mill? What did Tobe really know, or think he knew? How much gossip had he heard? Did he have any inkling that the golden slippers Titine was wearing had been given her by Prosper? After all, it was one of these slippers which had led to the discovery that she was dead—dead in his mill, shod with his gift. In the warm sunshine of midafternoon, Prosper found that he was shivering, and the hands on the wheel of his car grew so unsteady in their hold that he pulled over to the side of the road and shut off the motor, while he waited for his surge of panic to pass and tried to think collectedly, blind to the beauty of the ripe field beyond the narrow stretch of still water, which was all that separated him from it.

The rice was already partly harvested and the golden shocks rose symmetrically above the stubble, which was golden, too. There were no laborers in the field, but, in view of the glorious weather, which, for weeks, had prevailed, the great red separator had been left in place over the week end, so that work could begin at daybreak on Monday. Plainly visible in adjacent fields, where the rice was still standing, binders and tractors were also in readiness. Despite the seeming stillness of the air, this standing rice waved slightly to and fro and, as it did so, it shimmered in the sunshine. Above it, the cloudless blue of the summer sky closed down benignantly. Everything in sight bespoke peace, abundance and progress.

As his spasm of nervousness passed, Prosper became increasingly aware of this, but the consciousness brought him no comfort. On the contrary, the realization that such a goodly heritage was in jeopardy added to his sense of shame and dread. Setting his teeth grimly, he started his car again and went on his way.

Except for the bulky figure of the sheriff, the Claudia's millyard was deserted when Prosper pulled into the littered enclosure and stepped out. As Bennett came forward, he extended his hand, but the usual heartiness was lacking in the firm grip of his fingers.

"This is a bad business, Prosper," he said, shaking his head.

"I'll say it is. I suppose the—the body's already been taken to Toler's?"

"Yes. Dr. Tim sent a couple of men over with a basket and asked to have her moved there. It was pretty ugly, because she'd been dead long enough to be—you know what they call it when a body gets stiff?"

"*Rigor mortis?*"

"That's the word. Well, it's plain hell to see a pretty girl in that condition. They couldn't get her into the basket without using force."

Prosper could not repress a shudder. "Good God, Tobe! I'm glad I didn't see it!"

"That's why I wanted to meet you here, Prosper. You might have to see the body. Dr. Tim said he'd make up his mind later on whether to impanel a coroner's jury. If he does call one, he feels that you, as owner of the mill, ought to be one of the five jurors."

"Man, I don't know if I could take that. Oh, I know—I was in the Army and all, but this is different."

"Well, I figured you ought to have a chance to prepare yourself— that's why I asked you to meet me here. After all, even if Tim Davila decides not to impanel a jury, he's going to be asking a lot of questions."

"Of me?"

"Of everybody, but of you especially. As I understand it, you were in and out of the mill until all hours last night, because a car that should have been held for the morning Red Ball to Beaumont was switched onto an eastbound freight and, unless something was done to route it back or load another car, the shipment would miss the boat at Port Arthur. Anyway, I was told it was something like that."

"I thought maybe I could have it loaded on another boat at New Orleans."

"All right, all right. I'm not asking you now did you see Titine Saturday night. If it turns out this was an accidental death, nobody'll ever have to ask that question. And if not . . . well, we'll cross that bridge when we come to it. But I will ask you this: Do you know anything about those gold slippers she was wearing? It was the shine from one of them, when the beam from the watchman's flashlight hit it, that led to the finding of the body. Somebody—and right now, I disremember who—seemed to feel you could tell us something about those slippers."

Prosper hesitated for a moment, kicking absently at a clod of dirt. Then he looked up.

"Yes, I can tell you something about those gold slippers, Tobe," he said. "I gave them to her. I heard her asking for them one night when she was quarreling with August Scholtze, that bootlegger Kraut who runs the Tuileries. A crowd of us were there that night and all of them must have heard exactly what I did. But I was the one that bought the slippers, when I went to New Orleans with my grandfather, a while back. The poor kid never got much pleasure out of them though; I didn't get a chance to give them to her until three nights ago."

Tobe sighed, gustily. "It'll all come out in the wash, I guess," he observed. "Well, let's get on over to Toler's. They'll be waiting for us."

It was even worse than Prosper had expected. Titine's body was laid out on a white enameled mortuary table; a sheet covered it from neck to ankles, but a bruised chin and lips were in full view—not in the ripe fullness that had made them so seductive when she was alive, but drawn and discolored. Her lower jaw had sagged, so that her stiff mouth was open, and all the chaff and grains of rice had not yet been removed from it; a number still clung stickily to her cold, bluish mouth, while others were matted in the tangled mass of her hair. Her short, wide feet, still shod in golden slippers, protruded rigidly from beneath the lower edge of the sheet, whose surface suggested the outlines of stocky legs beneath. Her dark, sightless eyes were still open, and seemed to be staring fixedly into space, though they no longer held any hint of the terror that must have filled them in her last struggle for life.

When Tobe and Prosper entered the embalming room at the rear of Toler's Furniture Store, the coroner was bending over the rigid figure on the slab and spooning rough rice out of the open mouth with a shining surgical instrument; meanwhile, he was making remarks, every now and then, to Will Duson, the publisher of the Crowley *Signal*, who was standing close by and busily jotting down notes. Joe Guerra, Tobe Bennett's chief deputy, and several other deputy sheriffs were ranged along one side of the room, talking together in low tones. On the other side were three of Prosper's strangely dissimilar relatives: his cousin, Clement Primeaux, an indigenous Cajun, sturdy and swarthy; his maternal grandfather, Brent Winslow, a transplanted midwesterner, lean and tanned, with bright blue eyes and a shock of snowy hair which seemed all the whiter in contrast to his weather-beaten skin; and Winslow's father-in-law, Jim Garland, who was still keen and spry despite his great age. It flashed through Prosper's mind that his mother must have telephoned the Primeaux and Winslow farms immediately after calling the sheriff and the coroner, and he was touched to see how promptly his kinsmen had responded by coming to his support. But he hardly stopped to speak to them now; his attention was riveted on the frozen features, waxen in the pitiless glare of an overhead light.

"That bruise on her chin!" Prosper burst out. "Somebody must have hit her! Some son of a bitch knocked her into that bin!"

"Take it easy, son," said Tobe, laying a reassuring hand on Prosper's shoulder.

"But I tell you—"

Dr. Tim, who had straightened up to greet the newcomers, interrupted. "That bruise is two-three days old, Prosper," he said dryly, "as you'd realize in a minute if you'd seen as much tissue discolored by extravasated blood as I have." The coroner was plainly aware of his superior knowledge and just as plainly gratified by his ability to use technical terms casually. "Sure somebody hit her. Maybe somebody hit her last night. But not where you see that place on her chin, or the other one at the corner of her mouth."

"Are you going to do a post-mortem, Tim?" Bennett asked. Prosper realized who had put this question, though he had not looked up. He was still gazing in horrified fascination at the grotesque form imperfectly covered by the sheet. Dr. Tim now drew the upper edge of this over the staring eyes.

"No," he replied. "And I won't be impaneling a jury, either. First place, a necropsy—" He paused briefly to let the implied correction of Tobe's "post-mortem" take effect "—won't show anything my examination hasn't disclosed already. In the second place, as far as we know, there weren't any witnesses; so a coroner's jury couldn't learn anything about the case except what I'd tell them. Hence, since the law leaves me free to decide whether or not to swear in a jury, I'll just hand down the verdict myself."

"Okay, Tim," Bennett said agreeably. "Skip the big words if you can, but make it official and for the record. What's the verdict?"

"In the first place, there is no evidence of trauma," Dr. Tim announced, "aside from those two bruises, which were definitely not inflicted last night. There are no cuts, bullet holes or broken bones, so this poor girl did not die from injuries sustained in the fall into the bin. In the second place, there is every evidence of cyanosis about the lips and eyes, which means that practically every drop of blood in her body was venous blood, which is blue, and that no oxygen had reached her lungs to turn this blood bright, arterial red." With the forefinger of his right hand, Dr. Davila was checking off each point as he came to it on the spread thumb and fingers of his left hand. He now paused thoughtfully for a moment, as though musing and, at the same time, well aware that everyone in the room, especially Clement Primeaux, Brent Winslow and Jim Garland were hanging on his words.

"In the third place," he went on, "her open mouth and her throat were full of rice grains and chaff, stuff she had breathed in during her last desperate gasps for air; so we know with certainty she was alive when she fell into the rice. The more she struggled to get out, the deeper she sank into it; it was just by chance that, in her final death throes, she convulsively thrust one foot above the surface. It was also just by chance that a gleam from that golden slipper caught the watchman's flashlight when he made his Sunday round. By the way, has anyone notified her family? For that matter, does anyone here know what her last name is and where her folks live? I never heard her called anything but Titine and I never knew where she came from."

"I can tell you," Prosper said impulsively. "The family name is Dargereux and Titine lived with her folks on one of those patches of high ground scattered through the swamps between Bayou Patou and Bayou Warehouse. You know, not far from the Salle des Tuileries, where she worked."

The coroner eyed him curiously. "That so?" he said. "Thanks for the information—it'll be helpful all around. Well, naturally, those people wouldn't have a telephone, and that area's in St. Mary Parish. Tobe, you'd better have someone from Sheriff Picou's office in Franklin notify the family and tell them to get in touch with Toler, as soon as they can, to say what they want done about the funeral, or else send one of your own deputies to bring them here."

"But your verdict—" Bennett left the sentence unfinished, on the rising inflection of a query.

"Oh, death from apnea."

"And that's supposed to mean?"

"Inability to breathe. Choking. Asphyxiation."

"So it was an accident?"

"Hell, no! She didn't go wandering around, picking daisies or something, until she stumbled into the bin, where she drowned, as you might say, in rice. She had to climb three steep and difficult flights of stairs to get onto that top floor, right under the mill roof. And she didn't do that absent-mindedly, either. She went up there with somebody, or to meet somebody, or because somebody lured her up there: somebody that knew enough about a rice mill to realize it wasn't necessary to bash her head in. Somebody who damn well realized it was only necessary to push her through one of those bin openings, or fix it so she'd fall through by herself in the dark."

"Then the official coroner's verdict is—"

"Death due to apnea, after victim had been dropped into a bin of rough rice by person or persons unknown. That means it's a case for the district attorney—Theo Landry—and he'll have to start looking into it right now. Better get in touch with him today, if he's in town, and start rounding up everyone who might know anything about this, so he can begin the interrogation tonight, or tomorrow morning at the latest. You might start right off with Villac. I don't know whether he ties in with this thing or not and, if he does, how. But he obviously knows plenty about what went on at the Claudia Mill last night."

"That's my department, isn't it, Tim?" Tobe asked quietly. "Suppose you let me handle it my own way."

"Sure, sure. I was just thinking out loud. Well, there's nothing more for me to do here. I'll be going home, Tobe; unless I get an emergency call this evening, I'll be available any time you want me. So long, everybody."

Dr. Tim closed his black satchel and walked out, closely followed by Duson and, in a more lingering way, by Clement Primeaux, Brent Winslow and Jim Garland, who shook hands with Prosper and said they would be seeing him later. Tobe turned to Joe Guerra, his chief deputy.

"Take my car, Joe," he said, "and drive on down to Bayou Warehouse. Get hold of this girl's folks and bring them with you here to Crowley, if they have no other means of quick transportation. I seem to remember that the piano player—that bird they call the Professor—lives near by and has a car of sorts. He must have, because he's the man who always drove Titine to and from the Tuileries. Very likely he'd be willing to bring them to town, and he might just as well, because I want him here for the questioning, too. Anyway, see that the Dargereux get here. And get hold of Scholtze, too. Him I'll hold if I have to. . . . It's common talk that Titine was his girl, and unless he's got a copper-riveted alibi to account for where he was last night— But never mind about that. Just see that he gets here."

"Meantime, you goin' need your car, no?" the deputy inquired.

"I'll catch a ride to Prosper's house with him and wait around. I can phone from there to the other people Theo Landry'll be wanting to question after we get hold of him. So bring the car to the Villacs' house when you get back."

"I thought maybe it'd be easier for us to talk like this than with all that gang around," Tobe said casually when they were under way. "I could see that didn't suit Duson, from the *Signal*, any too well, but it suited me and I thought it would suit you."

"It sure does. Just what did you want me to tell you, Tobe?"

"Well, just what time would you say, offhand, that you left the mill for good?"

Prosper considered a minute. "I didn't look at the clock. But it must have been late—close on to two."

"You'd been there all the evening?"

"No, just off and on. I had a lot to do. Like you were told before, we had a car loaded for Beaumont, where it was to be switched to Port Arthur for shipment to Philadelphia and, somehow, the car had just vanished. Later, I found it had been picked up by an eastbound freight for New Orleans, and I was trying to find out whether we could issue new waybills and have it shipped via New Orleans, or whether the Ess Pee could leave it at Schriever, maybe, to be picked up by the Red Ball that was supposed to pick it up here. But the Archers were having a meeting at their house, to talk over this Rice Carnival everyone's getting excited about—you know, something to celebrate the fortieth anniversary of Crowley's founding. I suppose it's more or less of an open secret that Anne Marie's almost everyone's choice for the first Rice Queen, so of course I'm pretty interested—quite aside from the fact that my grandparents, on both sides, were among the first settlers. I spent as much of the evening as I could at the Archers' house. But I went back and forth to the mill, to check on that shipment we had to get out."

"I see. I take it, if there was all that to do, Paula stayed late, too?"

"Yes. She's awfully good about things like that. I've never known her to complain about overtime. Her Aunt Amanda raises a terrible row, though. Well, after all, she's your aunt, too; you know how she is. She telephones every hour or so, to see if Paula isn't through, and then comes and sits outside, in her ramshackle old flivver and blows her horn."

"She did that last night?"

"Last night and most nights."

"She didn't come in?"

"I don't think so. If she did, I didn't see her. Sometimes Paula does ask her in, just to keep her quiet. They have a cup of coffee together and then Paula gets rid of Aunt Amanda for another hour."

"Aunt Amanda doesn't have a key?"

"No, of course not. Paula goes to the door and lets her in, when worst comes to worst."

"No one has a key except you and Paula and the watchman?"

"That's right."

"And you keep the doors carefully locked—back and front door both?"

"Yes, always, outside of regular working hours. But I don't need to tell you that, during harvesting, regular working hours are from 'can to can't'!"

"But 'can't' comes before midnight, doesn't it?"

"Yes, generally."

"After that, it wouldn't be possible for anyone to get in who didn't have a key?"

"I don't see how, except when there's a lot of work going on and lots of people around. For example, last night, I was considering calling an overtime crew to load another car, in case I couldn't arrange to get that shipment reversed. That takes a lot of preparation and moving back and forth. It would have been too much of a nuisance to lock and unlock the door to the loading dock or to the office every time one of us wanted to pass through it."

"Then let me ask you this, Prosper: would it have been possible for anyone to get in who was not normally supposed to be there?"

"Anything's possible, of course. But I'd say it was to the last degree improbable. Ordinarily, one of us—Paula, the watchman or myself— would be sure to see whoever went in or out, even if it was only while they were crossing the millyard or the switch track toward the building."

"But Titine got in."

"Unfortunately, there's no denying that," Prosper said ruefully, and paused. "But we don't know when or how and, for that matter—" He paused again "—for that matter, we don't know, do we, that she *wasn't* seen. Has anyone asked Paula or the watchman about it?"

"Not yet, of course. Things have been happening too fast. But all those questions *will* be asked."

"Someone else saw her, too. Someone who killed her."

To his dismay, Prosper found that he was trembling violently again, trembling all over. Tobe laid a steadying hand on his arm, as Moïse had done a few hours earlier.

"Take it easy, son, and if you can't do that, take it as easy as you can. I only want to ask you one or two more questions. You knew this girl pretty well, didn't you?"

"Yes."

"Does anyone know how well?"

"I reckon a good many persons suspected I had a yen for her. I don't see how anyone could have known how far it had gone, except that—"

"Go ahead and tell me. This is just between us, same as if you were talking to a priest, almost. I don't mean that sacrilegiously. I mean it— well, I guess you know what I mean. Nothing you tell me now is going any further."

"Except that I think my grandfather Winslow may suspect that I gave her a pair of slippers. The shoe box was delivered to our room and he was terribly curious about it. I didn't tell him anything, but he might guess."

"Well, good Lord, your grandfather's not going to hold a little thing like that against you—not for long anyway! He's got too much sense. I didn't mean anyone like Brent Winslow. I meant someone else who knew Titine as well as you did and might be jealous."

"I reckon that would fit August Scholtze. And he's the kind that would beat her up."

"Could he have guessed that you gave her the slippers?"

"He could have thought I might have done it. Or anyone else in our crowd that goes to the Salle des Tuileries regularly and heard her say she wanted them. Like I told you before, she did that, right out in public, one night when August was jumping on her because she hadn't gone around enough among the tables with her accordion. She said her feet hurt. She said she wanted some gold slippers. Anyone could have heard her say it."

"Who, for instance?"

"Well, both the Benoits were there with me that night and Dale Fontenot stopped by our table for a moment. Didier doesn't go there often and Dale hardly ever does. He does his grocery shopping at August's and that's all, usually. That day, he'd been delayed, so he came by our table just to pass the time of day. He never paid Titine any mind though. I'd put my hand on the block for that. He wouldn't have given her a second look, or even a first one."

"But you think there was someone, besides yourself, who might have picked her up on the statement that she wanted some gold slippers and got her some?"

"Yes. I know that's what happened. Scholtze might have given her a pair of gold slippers himself. He had her pretty well under wraps—it wasn't easy to get to her. This bird that played the piano—the one everyone calls the Professor—brought Titine to the Tuileries every night and took her home again. I think he lives somewhere in her neighborhood, and I'm pretty sure Scholtze has him keep watch over her. Anybody who wanted to give her a pair of slippers or anything else, outside of Scholtze, that is, would have to get past the Professor some way to do it."

"The answer to that is pretty obvious, isn't it, son?" Tobe replied with a hint of throaty chuckle in the words.

"You mean I managed it?"

"Sure enough."

The sheriff leaned forward, propped his thumb against one side of his chin and crooked a forefinger against the other cheek.

"What in time makes you so all-fired sure, Prosper, that more than one person gave her gold slippers?" he asked.

"I'll tell you why," Prosper said in a low voice. "I guess it never occurs to a man, right away, that any girl he goes for and who goes for him, is playing the field, even when she's—well, someone like that dead girl back there. But just at the end, when you were calling me to go, I caught sight of them and—"

"Caught sight of what?"

"Her heels. The gold slippers sticking out from under the sheet in Toler's back room had plain heels. The shoes she was wearing when she was killed—or leastways, the ones she had on when her body was found—aren't the ones I gave her."

Chapter Nine

THE SHORT DISTANCE BETWEEN THE MILL AND THE VILLACS' HOUSE HAD long since been covered. Prosper had shut off the engine and the two men had continued to sit in the motionless car, drawn up beside the curb, as they went on talking. Now the front door opened and, in the radiant rectangle thus revealed, they saw Lavinia standing, slender, erect and white clad, with the pleasant light behind her.

"Prosper, is that you?" she called. "And is Tobe Bennett with you?"

"Yes, Mother. We'll be there in just a minute."

"I thought I heard the car come up. I didn't like to disturb you though, because I thought you might be discussing something important. However, Theo Landry is on the telephone and he wants to talk with Tobe."

"Straight off, Mrs. Villac," Tobe called in response. "Thanks a lot."

Lavinia stepped back into the house, leaving the door open. Tobe turned to Prosper.

"What makes you so all-fired sure those slippers the poor girl had on aren't the ones you gave her, just from the heels?"

"Because, when I did my shopping in New Orleans, I went the whole hog. I got Titine some slippers that had heels all set with rhinestones, just the kind of flashy, imitation eye-catchers I figured she'd be crazy about."

Lavinia reappeared in the doorway. "I'm sorry to seem impatient, Tobe," she said. "Theo tells me it's very urgent."

"All right, all right," Tobe answered, with his first show of annoyance. He got out of the car, muttering something under his breath, which Prosper could not quite catch, and went quickly up the walk. There was an extension telephone in the library, at the left of the front door, and Tobe, who knew the house well and enjoyed the privileges of an old friend, strode in there without stopping and closed the door behind him. Prosper walked up to the house more slowly. Through the open windows of the living room, across the hall from the library, he could see Dale and Didier apparently both, as usual, devoting their Sunday afternoon to the effort of hurrying Anne Marie into making up her mind; it seemed evident that they had not yet been told the bad news. He would have to go in and greet his sister's guests; after all, they were not only her suitors, they were his own close friends. But he would find some sort of an excuse to make a quick getaway. However, he had just reached the entrance when Tobe opened the door of the library and beckoned to him.

"Come in here, will you?"

The prospect of further conversation with Tobe was even more unwelcome than the idea of making small talk in general company. However, Prosper recognized that he had no choice in the matter. As soon as they were inside, Tobe closed the library door behind them.

"Dr. Tim got hold of Landry all right and he's standing by, all ready to go ahead with the interrogation tomorrow or even tonight, if we can get started that soon. Of course, there hasn't been time yet to hear from Joe and August, but it won't be long now before we do. Meanwhile, I'm going to call Paula and tell her I want both her and Aunt Amanda to be available tomorrow. I won't need you at the courthouse tonight, but I may then and you'd better stay here while I'm telephoning. I'd like you to listen in, if I can get Paula. After that, you and I'll talk some more about those gold slippers. Things were just getting interesting when we were interrupted. I'd like to have a clearer idea about who you think might have given a pair to Titine, besides yourself."

"I've told you all I know," Prosper repeated doggedly. "She said, right out in public, that she wanted them and anyone who was at the Tuileries that night could have heard her say so. I also told you that I thought August might have bought the slippers for her himself. I've pointed out that he's the only man that can get by the Professor, at any time, without difficulty. Furthermore, I've told you I'd put my hand on the block that it wasn't either Dale Fontenot or Didier Benoit who gave them to her, though both of them were with me that night."

"What about Maurice Benoit? Didn't you say that he was there, too, and that he went there a lot, whereas Dale and Didier hardly ever went?"

"Yes, I did. But—"

Prosper hesitated. Without sounding self-righteous, he could not very well say that Maurice was his friend, just as much as Dale and Didier were—in fact, they were together more, because he found Maurice more congenial than the two who never strayed, or seemed to stray, from the straight and narrow path; and further that, though he did feel it was within the realm of possibility that Maurice had bought the second pair of gold slippers, he was not going to voice this opinion unless he were driven to it, much less volunteer such information. To his immense relief, Tobe guessed what was passing in his mind and respected him for it.

"All right, we'll let Maurice tell his own story—of course, he'll have to be summoned for questioning, too. So will Dale and Didier, for that matter. I take it you four had a table to yourselves?"

"Yes, we did."

"And you don't remember who was at the near-by tables?"

"Maybe I could if I thought hard. I haven't had much time yet, you know. Seems like they were mostly out-of-towners though—no one who would be interested in Titine, except that she'd liven up the evening for them."

"Well, suppose you think hard overnight and tell me in the morning. That'll be plenty of time. Scholtze will be questioned first, if we get hold of him, as I think we can, and either the Professor or my dear aunt and cousin next. They ought to be back from their usual Sunday fishing trip by this time, so—"

"Before you start telephoning, there's something I'd like to tell you, in confidence. That is, I don't suppose I'm the one to make it public first and I haven't had a chance to tell even my mother and sister yet. But I might get a call myself, any minute, and you couldn't help overhearing at least one side of the conversation, maybe both, and being puzzled, if you were still here, as you seem likely to be. I'm engaged to Victorine LaBranche."

"What do you mean, engaged?"

"What do you think I mean? I mean engaged to be married."

"*You're engaged to be married to Victorine LaBranche and still you gave a pair of gold slippers to Titine Dargereux Thursday night?*"

"Yes, and I know what else you're thinking, even if you haven't said it yet. I didn't give them to her as a Boy Scout act—I expected to get something out of it for myself. The poor girl's dead, so I don't suppose we need to go into that any further, though I don't mind telling you I'm pretty ashamed of the whole damn business. But I didn't know, Thursday night, that I was going to be engaged to Victorine LaBranche. I didn't know I was until she said so, about five minutes after you telephoned her house."

"Prosper, you've got me going around in circles. If you were engaged, how could you help knowing it?"

"I didn't think I had a prayer of getting her. I've been in love with her from the first moment I ever set eyes on her, last spring. I'd been over to Lafayette to see Captain Bob about a camellia Anne Marie wanted, and I'd actually got it. I was feeling pretty good when I started home, but I didn't have anything special to do, so when I saw that the gates of the LaBranche place were open, for the first time in years, and all sorts of activities going on, I got out of my car and wandered inside the grounds. Vicky came along, dressed all in red, with that black hair of hers blowing around her face and her coach dog tugging at its leash and—well, that was it, as far as I was concerned. But, since I've got to go into all this, I may as well tell you that we've quarreled a lot. She's kept making me feel—anyway, I have felt—that I just wasn't in her league. I've been pretty discouraged about it. That's one of the reasons —Lord, I'm not trying to make excuses, but that's one of the reasons I went for a push-over. But Vicky met me at the door herself today, and the first thing I knew, we were kissing each other. Then, as soon as you telephoned about Titine and said I'd got to come over here on the double, Victorine announced, right in front of her father, that we were engaged. He didn't raise any objections and you can bet your bottom dollar I didn't. So I guess we are, and I guess she'll be calling up to find out how things are going and how soon I can get back to Lafayette to take up where we left off, which was pretty suddenly. You wouldn't expect her to do anything different, would you?"

Tobe Bennett sat down heavily. "No, I wouldn't expect her to do anything different," he said slowly. "But I want to be sure I'm getting the straight of all this. Did Victorine LaBranche know that while you were getting to feel you weren't in her league, you went out after something easier?"

"Naturally, I've never told her so. But she must have heard gossip."

"She's going to hear a lot more than gossip now, son."

"Yes, I kept thinking of that, on my way back to Crowley. My thoughts didn't take a very happy turn, for a man who's just got engaged."

"Maybe you'd better come right out and tell her—and her father— everything that's on your mind. You heard Dr. Tim say it might be a

good plan for Theo to start the interrogation with you. I didn't think
much of that idea then, as you must have guessed, since I didn't follow
through on it, and I think still less of it now. I think you ought to have
a chance to make a clean breast to the LaBranches before you're called
on to testify at the courthouse. Maybe—"

"Maybe, after that, I won't be engaged any longer?"

"Well, that's about the long and short of it, isn't it?"

The telephone rang. Before picking up the receiver, Prosper looked
in a questioning way at Tobe, who nodded.

"Hello," Prosper said dully.

"Darling!" The one word came through so clearly and vibrantly that
Tobe could hear it as easily as Prosper. "Is everything all right?"

"I don't know just what you mean by all right, honey. As your father
and I tried to tell you, this is all pretty grim. I met Tobe Bennett at
the mill, like he asked me to. Then we went on to—to the furniture store.
I've only just got home and Tobe's here with me."

"Oh. . . . Can you tell me now what happened at the furniture store,
or would you rather call me back later?"

Again Prosper looked at Tobe for directions. "You might just as well
let her have it now," the sheriff muttered, "without too many details, of
course."

Trying his best to be both brief and lucid, Prosper gave Victorine the
gist of the happenings in the embalming room, to which they continued
to refer, as if by common consent, as the furniture store. Victorine did
not try to interrupt; in fact, she said almost nothing until he told her,
"I guess that's about all, honey." Then she spoke, more softly than before,
but still very clearly.

"I think I understand almost everything. Anyway, almost everything
that matters. But I'd like awfully to see you."

"I'd like awfully to see you, too. But I can't tell you just yet when
I can come back to Lafayette. Perhaps some time tomorrow. . . ." He
looked at Tobe a third time and a third time the sheriff nodded.

"I'll be waiting for you all day. I shan't be doing anything else. Just
waiting."

Prosper found that he had to clear his throat before trying to answer,
as he had when Victorine announced that they were engaged. Meanwhile, she spoke again.

"Perhaps you'll have a chance this evening to tell your mother and
sister about our engagement. And your grandparents. And anyone else
you think might be interested. Tobe Bennett, for instance."

"I haven't had a chance to talk with any of my relatives yet. But I will tell them, later this evening, if you're sure you want me to. I think most of them will be around—in fact, I think I heard my grandfather Winslow and my cousin Clement come in a few minutes ago, though I haven't seen them yet. Tobe and I are in the library and I've already told him, in confidence. There were reasons why I thought maybe I'd better."

"Of course there were. Especially, as Father would like to announce the engagement in tomorrow's *Advertiser* and I'd like to have him, unless there's some reason why you'd rather he didn't."

"Well—naturally, in one way, I'd like to have him tell the world. But, in another, I think perhaps he'd better not, until after I've seen you and him tomorrow."

"Why?"

"You might change your mind after I've talked to you."

"About what?"

"About wanting to be engaged."

"You haven't changed yours, have you?"

"Good Lord, of course not!"

"Then what made you think I'd change mine?"

"It's hard to explain, over the telephone. But I will tomorrow."

"All right. You can explain all you want to. But I'm never going to change my mind. Never, never, never. I love you. I don't care what people think you've done. I love you. I don't even care what you have really done. I love you. And the sooner everyone knows that, the happier I'll be. I love you."

The words came through with increasing clarity and force. Then the connection was broken. Tobe picked up his hat.

"I reckon I'll do my telephoning at home, after all," he said. And, this time, it was his voice which was husky.

Chapter Ten

AFTER TOBE LEFT HIM, PROSPER SAT VERY STILL, DWELLING, WITH THE same sense of exultation that had flooded his being when she announced that they were engaged, on the way Victorine had said, "I love you, I love you, I love you." For a few minutes, every other thought and feeling were crowded out. But, as before, the exultation was short lived and quickly impaired by other thoughts and feelings of much graver character. Tobe had shown him every reasonable consideration; it had been welcome news that he, Prosper, need not go to the courthouse that night. Now his temporary solitude, which gave him a chance to pull himself together, was welcome, too. But Prosper knew this solitude would not last long. He had been right in believing that he had heard his grandfather Winslow and his cousin Clement coming in; since then he had heard various other footsteps and many other voices. His mother was an only child and he had moments of being thankful that this was so; he was fond of his relatives, in a dispassionate way, but he was rather glad there were no more of them. His father, Claude Villac, had been one of seven, four boys and three girls, and all except Claude were living; moreover, with the exception of his uncle Onezime, who was a priest, all had married and all had produced children. Prosper had to stop and count the number of his first cousins. Nor was this the end. His Cajun grandfather's cousin, Phares Primeaux, had early been left a widower, and Ursin Villac had joined forces with him, first in homesteading and then in rice farming; they had lived in the same house, utilized the same cattle shelters, worked in the same fields; their children had grown up like brothers and sisters. Phares' elder daughter Mezalee had become a nun and was a teacher at the Academy of the Sacred Heart in Grand

Coteau; his elder son Fleex had committed suicide, under strange and tragic circumstances; they were both far removed from Prosper's orbit. But Marcelite, the younger daughter, was married to a very prosperous farmer named Alcée Bazinet, and Clement, the younger son, now ran and owned the place which had belonged jointly to his father and uncle, and which he had greatly and profitably enlarged. In addition, he helped in the supervision of Brent Winslow's adjacent and highly valuable property. Marcelite and Clement were not only Prosper's cousins and close friends who, as such, would rush to his side in any emergency; they were among his most important patrons. He could not afford to offend them, especially at a time like this, when he would need every ally he could get. Yet he dreaded unspeakably to see them. In fact, he did not want to see anyone except Victorine, not even his mother, not even Anne Marie. . . .

He looked around him, finding his very surroundings suddenly distasteful. When the house, which was one of Brent Winslow's wedding presents to his daughter Lavinia, had been built, there had been two rooms on either side of the long central entrance hall: a parlor and sitting room on the right, a library and dining room on the left. Lavinia had been dissatisfied with this arrangement from the beginning; she had not wanted a small stiff parlor and a small nondescript sitting room, connected with each other only through one narrow door, but one big comfortable and tasteful living room, in the same space. Her bridegroom had not agreed with her and she had bowed to his wishes—then; however, before he died, she had won him over to her way of thinking, and the pleasant, homelike room, where all the different members of the family were now assembling, was the only one that Prosper could remember, on that side of the hall. But the library and dining room had remained unchanged, largely, he suspected—though Lavinia had never said so—because she had agreed they should, in return for the concession about the other arrangement, and because, with excessive scrupulosity, she had continued to feel this agreement was binding. The library ceiling, which was ornamented by a design of golden garlands surrounding crimson squares on a background of buff, and the plate of wrought iron, which concealed the coal grate when it was not in use and which depicted a domestic scene at a well, had always been very generally admired; they were even more so, now that they could be pointed out as features of household adornment more than thirty years old, which was venerable for Crowley. The fact that the dark paneling which formed the dado below the wallpaper did not leave much room for books, and the further fact that only a mahogany fretwork, surmounting velvet portieres, separated the library from the dining room and precluded any long period of quiet for reading, had never loomed large in anyone's consciousness. Lavinia had always been more interested in music than in books, and her grand piano, the best that money could buy, dominated one end of the living room, where the low shelves underneath the windows accommodated the works of reference on camellias, which occupied Anne Marie's leisure hours. Prosper, like most of his friends, read westerns, whodunits and popular magazines to the exclusion of almost everything else, except circulars dealing with the breeding and milling of rice, and, at that, the amount of time he devoted to reading was negligible, now that he was no longer required to do any in connection with his studies. It was not until he had seen the vast book-lined room at the LaBranches', with its galleries, its sliding ladders designed to reach the upper shelves with ease, and its treasure trove of first editions and rare prints, that Prosper realized what a library in a private house could look like; it was not until he heard Vicky and her father casually discussing current biographies and histories, written in three or four different languages, which kept pouring into the house with almost the same regularity as groceries, and listened to the father and daughter as they quoted, with equal ease and lack of self-consciousness, from classical works of which he had never even heard, that he had begun to appreciate the part which books played in some people's lives.

Well, it was a mercy that Vicky did love books, and that reading came to her almost as naturally as breathing. That was what she would be doing now, except when she was taking Levvy out for a run through the grounds—reading, while she waited to hear from him again. Prosper wished he could select some volume at random from one of the sectional bookcases set along the paneled walls under the scrolled ceiling and bury himself in its contents. He rose and searched restlessly, but could find nothing that seemed likely to divert his troubled thoughts. Besides, the light was bad, both because of the dark paneling and the inadequate fixtures, and Lavinia and Anne Marie would have to start setting the table for a buffet supper any moment now, to provide for all those well-meaning relatives whom Prosper could hear, constantly arriving, and whom he ought to go in and see. Verna, who had come to the Villacs as cook when Lavinia was married, and Callie, who had been first Prosper's nurse and then Anne Marie's and had stayed on afterward as house girl, were still in Lavinia's employ; but they had Sunday afternoons off, as well as at least one afternoon during the week, and when they were out, Lavinia and Anne Marie got supper themselves and made light of it, no matter how many guests there were. In this respect also, the Villac house was entirely unlike that of the LaBranches', where there was not only the formidable English butler Gifford, who had so upset Prosper the first time he had gone there, but half a dozen other servants of various nationalities: a chef, a second cook, a valet for Moïse, a personal maid for Victorine, a chambermaid, a parlor maid, a kitchen maid, even someone who was called a stillroom maid, whose duties had never been made clear to Prosper, any more than the purpose of a stillroom had been. He had failed to straighten out the functions of all these servants and the reasons why it was necessary or desirable to have so many. But he had discovered that several were always in attendance. He doubted if Victorine had ever made a cup of tea for herself, much less got supper on the table for ten or twenty persons. Not that she couldn't—of course that girl could do anything; and maybe, when they were first married, she would like to, so that they could be by themselves. That was what he would like. But perhaps, since Moïse was so old and feeble, she would feel she should continue to live in his house. Prosper would understand, if she did. He wouldn't like it half so well as a little house of their own, but he would understand. At least, she wouldn't have 'steen uncles and aunts and cousins butting in all the time. . . . *When* they were married! He'd better make that *if* they were married! He sat down and again became the prey to manifold anxieties, to the exclusion of all joyful thoughts.

The door of the library opened quietly and his mother came in and put her arm around his shoulders. He was grateful because she did not at once snap on one of the lights which, though inadequate for reading, would have been strong enough to make him blink uncomfortably, just at that moment. He was also grateful because she did not seem to resent the fact that he had not sprung up, as soon as she entered, and greeted her with courtesy, if not actually with cordiality. She spoke with unwonted gentleness.

"I know you don't feel like talking with anyone, Prosper, or even seeing anyone. I had a chance, just after you and Tobe got here, to tell Dale and Didier and Anne Marie about what had happened. I mean the barest facts—of course, I didn't know more myself then. But now, my father and mother and grandfather are here and all your Primeaux and Villac relatives."

"Just as if it were a wake, you mean," he said bitterly.

"No, dear, I didn't mean that—you know I didn't and you don't mean it, either. You know they've come from the kindest motives."

"I'd much rather they left me alone. I should think Grandmother and Grandfather Winslow and Grandpa Jim would realize that, even if the others don't."

"I think perhaps they do, but they know the rest don't. I've never forgotten what my mother-in-law said to me about Cajun families when I was very young and inexperienced. In fact, I think I can repeat it almost word for word, after all these years: 'With us, *chère*, it ain't just one man, him, an' one girl, her, w'at's married with each other, no. It's the whole family w'at counts, all two of the families, an' the families looks out for everybody that's in the families, them. That's the way we do, us, an' it's a good way, I guarantee you, me.' All the Primeaux and Villacs felt that way, and they still do; they're rallying around because they know you're in trouble and they want to help. They'd misunderstand if your grandfather and grandmother and Grandpa Jim didn't come at a time like this. And it would be too bad if there were a misunderstanding, wouldn't it?"

"I couldn't care less, on that score."

"Prosper, you're not acting like yourself at all. That isn't strange. I know this has been a terrible shock to you. But you can't stay in here, all alone, the whole evening. You'll have to come into the living room and show your appreciation of your family's kindness—even if it is mistaken kindness. Besides, the whole situation's under discussion now. You'll have to throw any light on it that you can."

"I can't throw any light on it at all. You've already told Dale and Didier and Anne Marie what Tobe told you to begin with, and Grandfather and Grandpa Jim and Clement must have told them and all the rest of you what happened at Toler's. There won't be anything more to say until we know whether Joe Guerra got hold of August and the Professor and the Dargereux family."

"We ought to be hearing that any moment now, and you ought to be in the living room to take the message. Besides—"

"Yes?"

"Well, I think perhaps I'd better tell you this before you go in. Dale may not be staying much longer. He says he thinks he ought to go over to Toler's."

"What for?"

"To be there when the Dargereux family arrives. He says they'll need help, that they're terribly poor, that they wouldn't have enough money to pay for—well, you know, the necessary things."

"I shouldn't think they'd be as poor as all that. Titine must have earned some money."

"Yes, but she didn't share it with her family. She had the Professor keep it for her. At least, that's what Dale says."

"How on earth would he know?"

"Of course, I didn't ask. I'm only telling you what he says about it. And he says the Professor wouldn't turn over any of it to the family, unless he were forced to. So Dale thinks someone ought to help out and that he's the one to offer. He says there's bound to be enough trouble about the funeral, trouble that'll make the family unhappy, without having the worry about money besides, when he's got plenty."

"What kind of trouble?"

"Why don't you let him tell you himself? After all, I'm not a Catholic, I'm not sure I understand everything he's saying. But I do understand this—Anne Marie's terribly upset."

Prosper winced. That was what hurt more than anything else. His mother could stand up to trouble, even bad trouble; he knew she had done it, over and over again. The same was true of the staunch Winslows, the indestructible Garland and all the sturdy, earthy tribe of Villacs and Primeaux, as well as their in-laws and their progeny. So, he was increasingly aware, could the LaBranches and, after all, that was not astonishing: as a child, Moïse had seen his family triumph over poverty and obscurity and he had fought his way up, not only to actual wealth, but to distinction and power; he had accepted the wreck of his marriage without bitterness, and had returned to his homeland to face disability and death with serenity. Victorine was a fighter, too, and Prosper was tardily certain that this was all to the good, as far as he was concerned; she had in her all the elements of strength and endurance which would make her a conqueror over fate, like her father. But Anne Marie was different; she had never wanted or needed to fight; she had always been sheltered, cherished and beloved. No one had ever said so much as a harsh word to her. And now he, her brother, who worshiped the ground she walked on, was responsible for her misery. Lavinia, divining part of what was passing in his mind, spoke quickly.

"Don't take it so hard, Prosper. Of course, Anne Marie's just as sure as I am that you're not responsible for this terrible accident."

"It's a little early to be sure of that, isn't it?"

"Of course not. Of course we know it's as amazing and appalling to you as it is to us. When I said Anne Marie was upset, I wasn't referring to anything you'd done or that anyone might be stupid enough to think you'd done. I was referring to what Dale is doing."

"Why he'd rather cut off his right hand than upset her!"

"That's what I thought, too. And I believe she really had come to a decision. I believe she was going to tell him tonight that she'd marry him. She was counting on you to get Didier away first. Of course, she didn't know, when she planned all this out, that there was going to be a terrible tragedy, or that we'd have a crowd of other people in the house, or anything like that. And now, if Dale insists on going off to Toler's before anyone else leaves—"

Prosper got to his feet; if he had sent Tobe going around in circles an hour or so earlier, his mother was certainly having that effect on him now. He did not even try to delay her long enough to tell her his own good news, the only good news of the day. He opened the door and crossed the hall with her at his side.

As he expected, the living room was full. The Winslows and Jim Garland were sitting at one end of it, the various Primeaux and Villacs, with their husbands and wives, filled the center and, at the farther end, near the piano, Anne Marie was sitting between Dale and Didier. Her eyes were lowered, her cheeks were flushed and she was twisting her handkerchief nervously around her pretty pink fingers. Didier's face was completely expressionless, but, as Prosper advanced toward this group, after the briefest of greetings to the others, Didier averted his eyes. Dale, on the other hand, looked straight at Prosper and rose to meet him. His fine, sensitive face, always serious of expression, was more than usually grave. He spoke slowly and with great earnestness.

"I feel I ought to apologize to everyone for saying and doing the wrong thing," he said. "I didn't mean to—I don't want to. When I told Anne Marie I felt I ought to go to Toler's, I thought she'd understand. I thought I'd just slip out quietly and come back by and by, if I could, and that, with so many others here, no one would notice I'd gone, or whether I came back—except Anne Marie and Didier, of course. Now it seems she didn't understand and that, somehow, everyone's in on this and that everyone's puzzled and wants an explanation. It's very simple really. I know something about the Dargereux through kinsfolk of theirs that have worked at my sugar mill. Titine's mother and father have always both been terribly shiftless. I don't think Michel Dargereux ever had a steady job or even tried to do what he could with the little land he owns. He mostly just sits and fishes in the bayou and lets the world go by and his wife's just as no-account as he is. They had two or three other children before Titine, who've all died. One was drowned, and one had typhoid, and one got kicked by a horse. They never had much care, I'm afraid. But somehow, Titine survived and managed to get to school for a few terms. I'm told she was always good at wise-cracking from the time she was just a little kid and that she could always carry a tune. Then she had a chance to learn how to play the accordion and she had enough initiative to go out and get herself a job. I think we ought to give her credit for that—also, for having enough sense to save what little she earned and to have it kept where no one could get at it to waste it. Her folks were sort of proud of her—they wouldn't work them-selves, but they had a dim realization that their daughter wasn't as lazy as they were and then, she was all they had left. They're going to grieve over her death, just the way any of you would if you lost a daughter—more, in a way, because they know she didn't have a good name, that she probably can't be 'passed through the church'—that is, she can't be buried in consecrated ground. She wasn't given the last rites and it must be years since she's been to confession or Communion and—well, I don't need to talk about the rest. The most her folks can hope for is that the priest will come to their shack after the wake, wearing ordinary clothes, and say a few prayers there, and maybe another short one at the grave, which would have to be somewhere on their land, not in a regular cemetery—and Lord knows most of their land is swamp. They'll take this harder than anything that's ever happened to them. Lots of you here know that."

There was a murmur of assent among some of his hearers. Others shook their heads, not in denial of his words, but in shock or sadness. All waited for him to go on.

"I didn't mean to make such a speech," Dale said apologetically and with still greater earnestness than before. "As I told you in the begin-ning, I thought I'd just slip out quietly. I'm sorry I couldn't do it quietly; however, I still mean to go. And I'm sorry I've had to take up your time by explaining all this, when you've got lots of other things that need talking about. It seemed to be necessary though. So I'll just say again that I want to be at Toler's when the Dargereux get there, to tell them that I'll meet all the bills for the coffin and the embalming and that the first thing tomorrow morning I'll go and talk to our priest and see if there's anything that can be done about the funeral. I think August would offer to pay the expenses of that, but he can't get to Toler's before the Dargereux do—he'll have to go straight to the courthouse. And he's a

Lutheran, if he's anything, which I doubt, so he wouldn't have any influence with the priest."

Dale paused for breath, but everyone sat very still, waiting for him to go on, even expecting, without quite knowing why, that he would do so. They were not mistaken.

"There's another reason why I want to go," he said. "Of course, it has nothing to do, directly, with the girl's death; but it does have something to do with the way she was found. The watchman's flashlight picked up the gleam of a gold slipper. I heard her say, a few weeks back, that she wanted some gold slippers. She didn't have many pretty things, the kind girls want—every girl, I guess, and I thought it would give her a sort of lift if she knew someone really paid enough attention to what she said to do something about it. Ten days or so ago, I met the Professor on the road between Cypremort and the Tuileries. He was driving alone and so was I; I asked him to pass back by my house and have a drink, as it wouldn't be far out of his way. He said he'd be glad to and we had a pleasant little visit together. I gave him a drink and he sat down and played on my piano. It seemed mighty good to hear music in that room again—there hasn't been any there in a long while. Of course, you all know I've been hoping there would be more pretty soon, but . . . well, anyway, I asked the Professor if he thought it would be all right for someone like me to buy Titine gold slippers. . . . I didn't want her to think I was trying to put her under obligations to me and—well, God knows I didn't want that bruiser Scholtze to think I was doing anything . . . well, I guess we needn't go into that, either. Somehow I felt as if the Professor, who might have been considered that poor girl's guardian, in a way, would give me a straight answer. But he stopped playing with kind of a musical crash and looked at me in a queer way. I realized I'd got off side somehow. So I handed him a twenty-dollar bill and said, 'Here. This ought to give you a guarantee I'm not trying to put anything over. Take this money and the first chance you get, buy Titine the best gold slippers this will pay for. And don't even tell her who they're from.' After that, his whole attitude changed, and he played again for a while—the man really has astonishing talent—and we had another drink or so and he left.

"I've sort of been waiting to hear from him, but he hasn't said a word, so I never really knew whether or not he bought her those slippers. That is, I suppose he did, since she was wearing gold slippers when her body was found. I've told you all about it first, because sooner or later it's bound to come out anyway, and I'd rather you heard it from me and, second, to make you see—if anything can—why I feel as if I ought to—"

He paused and looked about him, first at Anne Marie, who had averted her face, and then at the others, noting that Prosper, too, was looking at his sister. Dale sighed and went on.

"Well, it can't be long now before the Dargereux get to Crowley, so I'll ask you to excuse me and be on my way. There are one or two things I want to talk over with Toler before the family gets there."

Chapter Eleven

HE LEANED OVER ANNE MARIE, AS IF HE WERE ABOUT TO PUT HIS ARM around her shoulders and rest his head against her shining hair; from the other end of the room, it looked as if the act had been as real as the obvious yearning, but actually, he had not touched her. After a moment's hesitation, Dale straightened up and faced the assembled company in the same direct way that he had looked first at Prosper and, afterward, at everyone else. Then, in the quiet, controlled voice that had marked his speech all the time, he said again, "I'm sorry," and added, "Good-by," before turning away and starting through the rear door of the living room toward the back entrance of the house.

"Hol' on one li'l minute, my frien'! I got it in my mind, me, I'm comin' with you. Yes!"

Save for the occasional subdued murmurs, everyone had remained exceptionally silent and motionless all the time Dale was talking. Now Clement Primeaux had risen and, with surprising speed and verve for so stocky and stolid a man, wedged his way among the closely placed chairs, where he and his Cajun relatives had been sitting, to the more open space by the piano. Then he, too, turned and faced the assembled company.

"I take shame, yes," he said harshly, "that it had to be somebody outside the fam'ly to show us what's right for people to do. We been sittin' yuh, us, like we small children in school, that can't do nothin', no, till the teacher tells them. I say I take shame. . . ."

"Hey, wait a minute, Clem," Bazinet protested angrily. "I don't see how you got any call to talk like so!"

"How much you think I care, me?" retorted Clement, brushing the issue aside with a sweep of the hand, its blunt fingers spread wide. "Those Dargereux peoples goin' have to find some place to stay, no? That Landry, him, ain't goin' let them take their young dead girl back tonight and, even if he did, how they goin' get back by their bayou? So I'm goin' over to Toler's, me, with Mist' Fontenot, and I'm tellin' those po' peoples they can stay by my house on my farm long as they need to."

"That's mighty kind of you, Mr. Primeaux, and it provides for an emergency that hadn't even occurred to me," said Dale. "I'll be proud to have you come with me."

"Those folks is peoples, same as you just said," agreed Clement. "And it's us, yes, the fam'ly that's got bad trouble, too, should of thought about that biffo' you did." He swept his thick arm in an accusatory indictment of the whole gathering. "If you could wait fo' one li'l minute, Mist' Fontenot, I got one other piece that's got to get said yuh and now. I'm goin' tell those peoples, me, that if anybody says they can't bury that po' li'l dead girl, her, in this cemetery or that cemetery, they can bury her in my cemetery lot, back of the orange grove, on the prairie. I guarantee you, me, I ain't forgot how my *maman* had to baptize three of her childrens her own self, or how she and my daddy, him, buried them without no help, in the ol' days, biffo' Father Vialleton, him, could get around to do all like he wanted to for everybody."

"Oh, I'm sure that won't be necessary," Lavinia began. "These aren't the old days any more. That poor girl's body will find a decent resting place somewhere."

"Sho' will it," Clement continued doggedly. "That's what I'm sayin'. And, w'ile I'm sayin' it, I got it on my mind, me, to say what some of you know and some of you don't. After those three li'l children that was my brothers and sisters got buried out in the prairie, and after the groun' got consecrate' by Father Vialleton, it came a hurr'cane storm one October. Trees got blown down, chimbleys also, and also the little crosses on them three graves, yes. So what my daddy did? After the storm done passed, he put back the crosses where he figured out they belonged, them, and always he said they was put back on the consecrate' groun'."

"Clement, why have you got to talk about all those family things from long back, I ask you?" Marcelite Bazinet interrupted shrilly. "Besides, what has our family, a respectable family, got to do with anyone like the Dargereux girl?"

"She ain't no worse of a sinner, no, I tell you frankly, than some I could name; and one of them is buried in my cemetery lot already," Clement flung at her, his brows drawn down in a bristling scowl.

"What's more, there's always flowers on his grave. Don't forget we got a suicide in our fam'ly, what the priest said couldn't be buried in no consecrate' groun'. But our daddy, him, stood up and said part of that cemetery lot back of the orange grove never did get consecrate', he remembered it real good from that hurr'cane storm, and he would make it man to man with anybody what had it on his mind to say Daddy got to throw my po' brother's body in some swamp." He shot a brief glance, almost of apology, toward Lavinia. "I ain't tryin' to hurt nobody, me, not now, no. But Daddy and me, we done bury Fleex our own selves, and his body's sleepin' peaceful where his po' li'l brothers and sisters got buried biffo' the groun' ever did get consecrate' at all. So if no priest won't come to help bury that girl for the Dargereux, and they want to have her put in our lot where my dead brothers and sisters is at, them, I not only give them lief, me, but I'll help them do it. That is what I got on my mind, and not nobody, no, goin' change it or either stop me from doin' it, not no more than they could stop my daddy, him!"

He turned to Dale. "I got to thank you, yes," he said quietly, "biccoz you polite enough to wait while I said what I got to say, me. I'm ready, now."

The silence which had already been so profound, now took on a quality of horror. It was true that all Clement's hearers did not know everything he had laid bare in his rebuke to Marcelite, though it was easy enough to guess that, in the latter case, he was referring to some youthful indiscretion of hers, which she would not have cared to see brought to light. But most of the persons in the room knew that his father and mother had buried some of their children themselves, because there was no one else to do it; also, that later, when there had been an argument as to how much of the ground was consecrated, Phares Primeaux had won out about the burial of his eldest son, Felix. What was more, everyone knew that Felix had accidentally shot his cousin, Claude Villac, and that his suicide was the result of his desperation. The impassioned reference to Felix, by the younger brother who had adored him, the coupling of past with present tragedy in the home of persons intimately connected with both was the more overwhelming, because the outburst was so definitely not in character: for years, Clement had passed as a being devoid of any violent emotion; not even his nearest relatives guessed he had nurtured the greatest grief of his boyhood to such a degree that it was as poignant as if the wound had just been inflicted. Now it had found vehement expression under circumstances which made its effect doubly tumultuous.

The slamming of the back door, as Clement closed it behind himself and Dale, startled everyone anew. Nevertheless, the sudden noise lessened the tension in the overcharged room, and brought the unnatural silence to an abrupt end. Jim Garland began talking to his daughter and son-in-law, in a lower voice than usual, but otherwise in his normal way. The Villacs and Primeaux, obviously still not united in their feeling about Clement's attitude and action, began to argue among themselves. Lavinia, the color completely drained from her face, but her manner as calm as if one shattering blow had not followed another, leaned over Anne Marie.

"Come, dear," she said. "We mustn't let anything that Dale and Clement have said and done upset us. They both had their reasons. Suppose we try to start getting supper?"

"How could anyone want any supper after that? I'm sure I don't. I want to go to my room."

"I know just how you feel, honey," Prosper said, as soothingly as he could, considering that he was badly shaken himself. "I'll go up with you and stay for a few minutes. You don't mind, do you, Didier?"

Didier moved uneasily in his chair, but he looked Prosper in the face, for the first time since Dale had begun talking. "No, I guess not," he muttered.

"I'm sure Annette and Marcelite will help Mother get started with supper, and I'll help finish, when I come back," Prosper went on, speaking with an effort. "But before we go, I've got something to say, too. It won't be quite such a long speech as Dale's, but I hope it'll make more sense to most of you."

Anne Marie looked up at her brother. He forced a smile as he glanced down at her.

"What's that old cliché about every cloud having a silver lining? Well, we seem to be surrounded with pretty heavy clouds, whichever way we look. But one of my own special clouds has got a lining that isn't just silver—it's pure gold. I'm engaged to be married."

"Good," shouted Jim Garland from the other end of the room. "Hurry up, tell us about it!"

"That's what I'm trying to do. The most wonderful girl in the world has told me that—well, I'm going to say it right out. She's told me that she loves me. She's told me so not once, but over and over again. What's more, she told me not before we'd heard about this—this awful thing at the mill, but afterward."

"Good for her!" Jim Garland was shouting again and, this time, there were echoes to his shout. "Go on, Prosper."

"We were more or less on our way to an understanding of sorts, but not so far along that she couldn't have backed out, mighty easily, if she'd wanted to. And she didn't. She said, right in front of her father, that we were engaged, and then she called me up here, an hour or so ago, to say a lot more."

"You're not talking about Vicky, are you?" Anne Marie asked incredulously.

"Of course I am. Did you ever hear of anyone else I wanted to marry? Of course, you haven't! Come on, honey, I'll go up to your room with you. Excuse us, will you, folks?"

Anne Marie rose, somewhat reluctantly. The atmosphere was indeed gloomy, but Prosper's revelation of a golden lining had done a good deal to brighten it. She was afraid that, if she were shut off upstairs, she might miss some other even more exciting development. But she could not very well admit a complete about-face; she suffered herself to be led from the room by the same rear door that Dale and Clement had taken. After she and Prosper reached her pink and white bedroom, he helped her settle herself on the cretonne-covered chaise longue, patterned in roses, and arranged its lacy pillows behind her.

"There!" he said. "Now have a good cry and then go wash your face and get out of your clothes and climb into bed. I'll bring you a tray after a while. I know there's some shrimp gumbo and some peach ice cream and a lady cake; they ought to taste good to you. But before I barge in with food, I'll come and make sure you're not asleep. You might feel like taking a little nap after a while."

"Oh, Prosper, you really are a dear! You don't think I was unreasonable just now, do you?"

He hesitated, torn between complete candor and unswerving devotion. Then he chose his words carefully.

"Well, you see, honey, I think it was pretty hard for Dale to say what he did—to do what he did. Of course, he wanted to stay with you and, of course, he didn't want to stand up in front of all those people and give a long explanation of his actions. It would have been a lot easier for him if you could just have said, 'All right, come back as soon as you can,' when he told you he thought he'd better slip out for a few minutes and, if he could have, then Cousin Clement wouldn't have done what he did."

"That was the worst of all! How could he talk that way about Fleex, right in front of you and me—in our home? Fleex killed our father!"

"Accidentally. He loved our father. He wouldn't have done anything to hurt him for the world. It was his horror over what he'd done that made him kill himself."

"You sound as if you were trying to excuse him. And someone else must be doing that, too, if there are always flowers on his grave."

"Yes, that did come as a surprise, as—as a shock. But let's not talk about that now. Let's go on talking about you and Dale. I can see that it would have been hard for you to let him go, without asking any questions, when you'd just made up your mind to marry him."

"It was *terribly* hard. How could I understand having him act like that? You said yourself, just a few minutes ago, that it didn't make sense."

"No, honey, I didn't say exactly that. I said I hoped what I was saying would make more sense to most of the people who were listening than what he'd said. Because I got the feeling you weren't the only one who didn't understand he was doing the hard thing because he thought it was the right thing. However, *I* understood all right. Dale Fontenot was telling a perfectly straight story, not hiding anything, not adding anything. Also, he was saying a kind word for a girl who's dead and to whom no one else is going to grant any good points at all, because she had got herself a bad name. And he was going to help some people who are so no-account he thought no one else would lift a hand for them, even if they had lost their only child and didn't even know how they could give her a decent funeral. Of course, Cousin Clement's taking care of all that now, but Dale had no idea anything like that would happen. He did all this explaining and then went away—which must have been mighty hard for him. He had reason to think you were going to tell him, at last, that you'd marry him, and that was what he wanted more than anything in the world, just as I want to marry Vicky more than anything in the world. He's waited years to have you say a certain thing and then he had to go off without hearing it. I've always thought Dale was the finest fellow I knew, but I never in my life had as much respect for him as I did this evening."

"Prosper, you're standing up for him just because he's your friend."

It was on the tip of his tongue to say, "That's not the only reason, and you might stand up for him because you're his sweetheart." But he had never spoken that way to Anne Marie and he could not quite bring himself to do so now. She shifted her pillows and went on.

"You know perfectly well he had a guilty conscience! All that talk about paying for the slippers as if it were merely a generous gesture!"

"But that's exactly what it was! Do you suppose, if he had had a guilty conscience, he would have looked twenty people straight in the face, the way he did, and made up a story like that as he went along? Dale's naturally very sensitive, actually rather shy; he's lived all by himself for years, in one of the gloomiest places I ever saw in my life, and that's had its effect on him, too. He's become more and more withdrawn, less and less self-confident. You must know that. If he hadn't, he wouldn't have let you keep him in suspense all this time. He'd have found some means of bringing his suit to a head. And, when it comes to a guilty conscience, I wish I had one as clear as his."

Anne Marie sat up among the tumbled pillows. "What on earth do you mean?" she asked excitedly.

"I mean just what I say. Dale asked the Professor to buy a pair of gold slippers for Titine because he knew she wanted them a lot. He didn't even give them to her himself and he didn't want anything from her in return."

"Do you really believe that?"

"Of course I really believe it."

"Well, I don't. And I don't know why you say you wish your conscience was as clear as his."

"I can't give you all the details now. But try to bear this in mind: I'm supposed to be the last person that could have seen this girl alive. Everybody around here knows I used to hang around the Tuileries. And a lot of things could be brought out at the interrogation or inquiry or whatever they'll call this investigation to show why Titine Dargereux came to my mill Saturday night—and died there."

"You mean anyone might think that you—you—had reason to—that maybe you killed her?"

"Yes, a lot of gossipers and tongue waggers are going to couple my name with that of a dead girl. I can't stop them from talking. Nobody can."

"Oh, Prosper, this is awful! It's simply awful!"

"I didn't want to point out all this to you, but you practically asked for it, with your suspicions about a fine man like Dale Fontenot. There are going to be just as many suspicions about me—a lot more, in fact—and harbored by a great many more people. Before you condemn Dale Fontenot, try to understand that when it comes to being suspected and regarded as guilty, your brother's in there forty to the acre!"

Anne Marie was weeping openly now, and Prosper, feeling the swift stab of pity for the sister he had idolized so long, bent to put his arms about her. But she pushed him away.

"Have you even stopped to think for a moment what a terrible scandal this will create?"

"I haven't been thinking about much else all the afternoon."

"Do you realize that the whole family will be involved in it? Do you realize that I won't have a chance in the world of being the first Rice Queen, when I'd set my heart on it—you who always said you'd do anything in the world for me!"

Prosper had been sitting on the edge of the chaise longue, close to his sister. Now he rose abruptly and looked down at her with an expression she had never seen on his face before. A girl, a girl about her own age, had just died a horrible death, and the effect of this death on Anne Marie had not been one of sympathy and shock. It had caused her first to doubt the good faith of a man who had been her devoted suitor for years and who, in all that time, had never given her the slightest reason to question his singleheartedness; and then it had caused her to grieve, not because the fair name of her family would, with reason, be sullied, but because such a stain would deprive her of an honor she coveted. Ever since Prosper could remember, Anne Marie had been his idol; and now, on top of all the other tragic events of the day, he was discovering that his idol's slim, arched, delicate feet were made of clay. For a moment, he gazed at her, almost unbelievingly; then he turned and started out of the room.

"Prosper, what made you look at me like that? Why are you going off and leaving me all alone when you know I'm so unhappy?"

He paused on the threshold, but only for a moment. "If you don't know, without being told, I'm afraid it wouldn't do any good for me to try to tell you," he said. "It didn't do any good when Dale tried, and he's a lot better at explaining than I am. Anyway, I've got to go downstairs. The message must have come in from Joe Guerra by this time."

It had. Joe telephoned, Prosper's mother told him, almost as soon as he had gone upstairs with Anne Marie; she stopped to speak with him in the act of slicing a long loaf of French bread. Joe had been fortunate in finding everyone he had been sent after. The Dargereux seemed dazed, rather than grief stricken; they had said very little and asked almost no questions; but they had made no objections when Joe told them they must come to Crowley with the Professor, who, though naturally very much shocked, was articulate, co-operative and comparatively calm. Joe had seen him start off in his Ford, with the Dargereux on the back seat, and they should be at Toler's almost any time now. August had, at first, seemed inclined to be ugly, but Joe had succeeded in convincing him that it was to his own best interest not to resist the summons he had received, and he had consented to go along in Joe's car. They, too, must be well on their way to Crowley by this time. The grocery store and dance hall had been closed and Baer had been left in charge of the building. Of course, he was not very intelligent, but, after all, there was not much that could happen there that night. . . .

"And you don't have to go to the courthouse while August is being questioned, as Tobe told you," Lavinia concluded, as she started slicing bread again. "I wouldn't be surprised if he didn't require you to go to-morrow, either—after all, he knows you've got a mill to run, and that there'll be even more than usual for you to do, with Paula out—I understand she's going to be questioned next after August. Anyway, we've got a reprieve for this evening, so let's make the most of it. We'll all feel better if we eat a hearty supper and talk about that good news, which has helped a lot, my dear, coming in the midst of so much bad news. I'm happy to tell you that I'd rather have Vicky for a daughter-in-law than any other girl I've ever seen."

"And I'm happy to hear you say that. Especially as I assume you'd rather have had Dale Fontenot for a son-in-law than any other man you've ever seen. Perhaps one gain will make up for another loss."

"Another loss?" Lavinia echoed, lowering her voice. "There won't be another loss. Anne Marie's upset now, but that doesn't mean she'll change her mind in the end, after she's taken so long to make it up."

"Perhaps she won't, but you can be mighty sure Dale will—in fact, that he already has. Anne Marie may think she isn't through with him, but if he isn't through with her, he isn't half the man I believe he is. And that may hurt Anne Marie's pride, but I don't believe it'll hurt her much otherwise. I think Didier will do just as well for her purposes." To his mother's amazement, Prosper was speaking scornfully, and his eyes strayed in the direction of a daintily laid tray, covered with a fine cloth of embroidered organdy and set with Dresden china. "Why don't you let Didier take Anne Marie's supper up to her?" he inquired. "It might be an opportune moment."

Chapter Twelve

WHILE THE VILLACS AND THEIR STRANGELY ASSORTED GUESTS WERE STILL trying to pretend they had good appetites, and resolutely talking about Vicky, though Titine was uppermost in their thoughts, August Scholtze was ushered by Guerra from a dimly lit hallway of the courthouse into a narrow, high-ceilinged room. The bootlegger blinked his eyes against the sudden flood of bright illumination from a central electrolier, surprisingly ornate in the bare chamber's other lack of *décor*, and slouched in the direction of a long table, toward one end of which Guerra directed him. The deputy immediately joined a group already gathered at the opposite end: Landry, Bennett, Davila and Malvina Walton, the capable and impassive court stenographer; then, taking a chair from the other side of the table, he scraped it along the floor to bring it a little behind Bennett, and leaned forward, whispering to the sheriff, who tilted his head back and listened attentively, though without taking his eyes off Scholtze. When Guerra finished speaking, Bennett nodded in obvious agreement and told August to sit down. The tone was noncommittal, but it was clear he had voiced a command rather than a hospitable invitation.

"All right, I do it," retorted Scholtze, resting his pawlike hands on the top of a chair back. "But first, somebody better tell me what gives. I got rights, you know. And even if you don't know, I do."

For a moment, no one spoke. The only sound in the room was the morose buzz of a mud dauber, futilely trying to fly through a long windowpane where the blaze of light from the electrolier was flashingly reflected. The high walls, bare in their coating of calcimine from chair rail to ceiling, showed that other wasps had built mud nurseries there from time to time; but all the original white pigment had faded to an indeterminate hue, which might eventually turn either gray or yellow with age. From the chair rail to the floor, the walls had been painted a scrofulous brindle, marred and streaked by generations of match scratchers.

Landry, a short, round-bodied, round-faced man, whose habitual expression, resembling that of a Kewpie doll, deceived those unfamiliar with his terrier eagerness as a prosecutor, was the one to break the silence. "This is an investigation into the circumstances surrounding the death of one of your employees, Scholtze," he began, "a girl named Titine Dargereux. And don't try to look surprised. The whole damn countryside knows by now that she was found dead in one of the Claudia Mill's rice bins early this afternoon."

"I do not feel for looking surprised," Scholtze conceded, pulling a chair violently toward him and flinging his big frame into it. "But if I did feel for looking surprised, I would do it. I would look surprised as hell. You understand that?"

"What's biting you, Gus?" snapped Davila. "There's no call for you to have a chip on your shoulder. Nobody's done you anything outside of bringing you here for questioning, the same as lots of others."

"Oh, so nobody has done me nothing? That's what you think? Well, I feel for thinking different, see? Maybe when comes a deputy to arrest you, *mir nichts dir nichts*, you got a right to act like it was nice. Not me!"

"You're not arrested . . . yet," Landry interrupted. "But if you want to be, you can get prompt service. As Dr. Davila told you, a number of persons have been called in for questioning, you among them. In other words, you're here simply as a witness; a material witness. I'm not even putting you under oath. But if you're going to be hardheaded, if you want to obstruct an investigation into what Dr. Tim thinks might be a murder—"

"Yah, I don't obstruct nothing. It's you, acting like everybody's guilty already. I hear plenty people say you would even charge yourself with murder if you think you could get a jury to say you got to hang."

Tobe Bennett rose slowly and leaned forward across the table. "You keep a civil tongue in your head, Scholtze, or I'll work you over myself, for resisting arrest or something," he said warningly.

"But I ain't arrested. Dr. Tim just says so."

"You will be, if necessary. I'll think of a charge later. For wearing blue silk sleeve garters, maybe. So you be good, and you'll keep out of trouble—for a while, anyhow."

Scholtze glowered at the sheriff, but relaxed in his chair as Theo Landry began fumbling among the papers on the table before him.

"That typewritten transcript of Dr. Davila's findings at the inquest is here somewhere," he murmured. "And some of the reports on what several of those waiting to be examined have told us informally, though we haven't called them in for official questioning as yet." He leafed through a file of papers Mrs. Walton handed him, and then addressed Scholtze directly. "Now here's the story as we have it so far, Gus. The Dargereux girl was alive Saturday night when she left her house about two hours earlier than usual, but not, as usual, with that piano player called the Professor. With someone else, and in a flivver; a tin Lizzie like all other tin Lizzies, so it may be difficult to identify it unless—" He paused significantly and eyed the listening bootlegger with an air of thoughtful appraisal "—unless someone comes forward and tells us it was his car and where he was driving the girl, and so forth and so on."

"You mean me, maybe?"

"Hear me out first. After that, if you want to alter what we have pieced together, no matter how trivial or how important the change might be, you can do so. . . . We know, for example, that when she left the house she was wearing her old black shoes, but carrying a paper parcel, which could have held another pair of shoes—a pair of gold slippers, for example. Her accordion, as usual, was in the Professor's keeping, so it is natural to conclude she intended to go to your night club, the Tuileries; but she never got there. She may have come direct to Crowley, or she may have come here much later; all we know is that her body was found in the Claudia Mill. We don't know who brought her here, or who met her here, but we'll find that out, sooner or later, and when we do, we'll learn why she came to Crowley, instead of to the Tuileries where she—"

"I could tell you that right now, already," Scholtze interrupted. "She comes to Crowley because I told her plain she got to give back those gold slippers before she shows her lying face in the Tuileries again. I never asked her who she got them off of, because I didn't feel for knowing him. So the feller must be somebody which lives in Crowley yet."

"When did you tell her that?"

"Friday. Friday night."

"Your club was closed Friday night, wasn't it?"

"I give you right about that. The carpenters and painters and *Gott weiss wer noch* was all over the place to get it finished already for the grand opening last night."

"So where were you when you talked with her?"

"In my living quarters. The carpenters and painters didn't go in there. She didn't come to play her accordion. She come just for a private visit."

"I see. And you simply asked her to give back the slippers on which she had apparently set her heart, and she simply said yes, she would. Is that your version of it?"

Scholtze gave the district attorney a sullen glance.

"No, I never asked her," he growled. "I *told* her what she got to do."

"And she said she would . . . just like that?"

"She says she will do it, *ja* you bet she says it, after—after—"

"After you beat her?" suggested the district attorney.

"Beat nothing. That wasn't no beating. I slapped her two-timing little face for her, that is all. Did I say two-timing? I should say three-timing, or maybe four-timing yet. *Gott weiss* how many timing me she is!"

"But you did strike her?"

"*Jawohl*, but not beat. You got to let women know who is boss, and that is all I do. I slap her on the mouth where she been lying to me."

"And after that?"

"After that, she promises me she will give back the slippers already. I say she better not forget, if she does she will be sorry like she never been sorry in her life yet, and I gave her one more little *Patsch* so she should remember. . . . And after a while, she goes home. At least, she says she goes home; and the Professor, who brought her to my place, says that is where he took her, after he finished cleaning up last-minute stuff in the dance hall, so we could be ready for the grand opening."

"When did the Professor tell you that?"

"Saturday night he tells me yet, when he shows up early with no Titine. I say where is this two-timing little piece at? And he says all he knows is that when he gets by her house to bring her to work like always yet, she is gone. She leaves word by her folks to say she first got to do something about some gold slippers before she comes to work or the boss will be mad with her. She leaves early in this car, and nobody seen who was driving it."

"Could it by any chance have been your car?"

"How could it be my car when I am at the Tuileries a good two-three hours already and never left there until afterward, like *Gott weiss* how many people who seen me could tell you?"

"Doesn't your nephew sometimes drive your car?"

"Baer, you mean? He don't drive it without I am there, too. He is a good boy, but *nicht ganz beisammen,* like we say. It means he ain't crazy like they put people in the *Verrucktenhaus* for, but he don't think so fast. So he got orders to never drive the car lessen I am with him."

"He never disobeyed those orders?"

"Sure, once in a while, maybe. Boys ain't supposed to be no angels yet, with wings on. But when I catch him, I give it to him good, with a switch, where it hurts. I don't spoil no *Junge.* So he knows better as to take the car now."

"In other words, if it was your car, somebody besides you or Baer was driving it?"

"Somebody besides me. I got to give you that much. But I don't use the car early that evening, and since Baer works downstairs, opening package goods and keeping watch on the store, I naturally don't see him. But I know what I do see; when I tell the Professor I'm going by Crowley and see what is what with this girl maybe with some feller—somebody that gives her gold slippers *noch*—I find my car right where I always leave it, and it's got plenty gas in the tank, too."

"Then you did go to Crowley last night?"

"What did you expect from me to do? Here I am, on the grand opening night yet, and I got no girl singer! You think maybe I don't feel for wanting to know what gives? How many Saturday night grand openings do I got to lose?"

"Please answer the question. Did you or did you not go to Crowley last night?"

"All right, all right, all right. So I *did* went to Crowley. I say to myself this funny business got to stop and now it is time to stop it. To the Professor, I say he should watch things until I get back, so nobody starts nothing and the waiters or either the customers don't steal me blind yet, and I go to Crowley."

"In *your* car?"

"That's right. My car."

"Did you go alone?"

"Sure! All alone. Nobody comes with me. I want that Baer he should come, too, and I call him, but with all the *Geschrei* and the worry, I don't wait when he don't come. Maybe he is out making a delivery, and I am going crazy with no singer. So I tell the Professor he should watch everything until I come back, and I go in my car to Crowley."

"Why Crowley? Why not New Iberia, Lafayette, Abbeville, or some other place?"

"Because I think it could be only about two-three persons that would give her those gold slippers, and out of those the most likely one got his home and his mill in Crowley. So if she really goes to give him back the slippers, Crowley would be where she goes. That is how I feel for it. And where she goes when she gets here would be to the Claudia Mill."

"Why? Spell it out for us, now."

"Because that *Esel* Prosper Villac would let any girl if she is even halfway pretty talk him out of anything, and I feel for it that he is the one what gives them to her."

"And so you drove to Crowley? What time would that have been?"

"I never looked at no clock, but it must be about nine o'clock. The Professor could tell you better as me, if you'd let him in here, by he ain't so excited like I was."

"Did you go back to the club any time after that?"

"Sure I go back. I go back in time to close up, put away the cash in the iron box, pay the waiters and musicians."

"And what time did you get back?"

"This time I did look on the clock. People was still sitting around and drinking, but no music. I get back ten minutes behind three."

"In other words, you were gone about six hours, roughly from nine to three. How long a trip is it from the Tuileries to Crowley?"

"How long it takes, you mean?"

"Yes. Let's see, from the Tuileries to New Iberia is about a dozen miles, from New Iberia to Lafayette is eighteen, and from Lafayette here is about twenty-three. Call it right at fifty-five miles. How long would that take you?"

"Not much more as two and a quarter hours; two and a half, maybe."

"Well, call it two and a quarter hours each way. That would mean you were in Crowley from a little after eleven to one o'clock in the morning. Right?"

"No, it ain't right. A little after eleven, yet, is what *you* say when already you got to know it takes me two and a quarter hours, you say it yourself. So, if I jump in my car out the second floor of the Tuileries and start *punkt* nine o'clock, it is still anyway *doch* fifteen minutes after eleven when I get to Crowley; not by the mill, yet, but by the time I start, after I look to see have I got gasoline enough, *und so weiter, und* by the time I drive by the mill, where I go on the wrong street yet and got to come back, it is anyways half-past eleven, not no little after eleven like you say."

"All right, Scholtze, have it your own way. At least you didn't leave till one, by your own say-so. Now—where were you and what were you doing during that hour and a half?"

"I go by the mill and I don't find nobody there, only the watchman. He says Miss Bennett's *Tante* comes for her twice, and the first time she raises a *Geschrei* about it ain't right a girl got to work all hours in the night. The second time was after Villac comes back already, *und* Miss Bennett goes home with her *Tante*, and right after that Villac says he got to go someplace, and after Miss Bennett is gone away, he goes, too."

"But you did not hear all this yourself?"

"No."

"And you did not see Miss Bennett when she went out?"

"No."

"I take it you know her by sight? You'd recognize her if you did see her?"

"Sure, I'd recognize her. I knew Paula Bennett and a lot better than just by sight, a long time before she was ever Villac's secretary."

"And you did not see Miss Bennett at all last night?"

For the first time since he entered the room, Scholtze appeared obviously ill at ease. "I never talked to her like I did to Ten High, if that's what you mean, and she never didn't see me," he said defensively.

"But you did see her?"

"Well, I tell you how it was, Mr. Theo. Ten High tells me Villac's been there off and on ever since so soon after supper, before Miss Bennett left and after she has gone yet. He says Villac acts like a crazy man, running in and out, first by the front, then by the back where the loading dock is, then by the office, then back to town, hollering about some carload that is lost, and running up to look in the bins has he got enough to load another car right away. . . ."

"Never mind about what the watchman said," the district attorney broke in. "We'll find that out from him. What we want from you is what you did when you found the mill deserted, except for Ten High."

"I had it on my mind already to get the whole thing settled, so I says to Ten High will he let me in to see if nobody is there, and he says he couldn't do that. Then he changes his mind and says well, go ahead and look around, but don't tell nobody and for God's sake don't strike no matches nowheres at all. So he lends me a flashlight, and—"

"I wonder what made him change his mind?" mused Tobe Bennett aloud. "It wouldn't be that you crossed his palm with silver, maybe?"

"I never did!"

"Okay, with paper then? Green paper? And don't go getting too virtuous on me or I'll have to take steps. Besides, we've got Ten High outside waiting to be called in for questioning."

"*Nu*, and since when is a law against giving somebody a tip? That Titine could have got rich on tips if she wasn't a tart in her two-timing little heart. I suppose you never give no waiter a tip or nothing like that?"

"Nobody said it was against the law," Landry suddenly snapped. "All we want to know is whether it happened, and you've already told us it did. So you searched the mill, and what did you find?"

"I never found nothings at all. Not one single *verdammt* thing! I look good, too, because I got to think even if she went off with Villac, maybe they leave something behind, like a paper package with shoes in or something else. But I see nothings, I tell you."

"When you looked all over, did you by any chance look into the rice bins?"

"So crazy I ain't. Rice I am not looking for, but a *Dirne* with maybe a feller already."

A loud knock drew all eyes in the direction of the door. It opened, and a fat, perspiring man, in belted khaki trousers, shirt sleeves and ten-gallon hat entered and then—absurdly, in view of his nearly three hundred pounds of weight—tiptoed toward the group of officials, his shoes squeaking loudly. They clotted around him attentively as he whispered in a rumbling monotone; then Bennett nodded vigorously to his chief deputy, and the fat man followed Guerra squeakily from the room.

"Mind if I ask a few questions about what Barousse just told us?" asked Davila.

"Help yourself," agreed Landry.

"How long do you suppose that search of the mill took you, Gus?"

"I don't know. I never looked at no clocks."

"Oh, come on, Gus. I'm not asking for a stop watch report. Were you there long enough to have made a thorough search? Or did you just give a quick look around?"

"I looked good, like already I told you. It don't take so long. Outside the machinery, it gives nothing except the wood chutes that the rice goes through, and the bin floor on top got nothing at all, only the bare, slick floor with holes in so somebody can look down and see how much rice is in each one."

"Well, how long did it take you, as near as you can judge?"

"Ten minutes, maybe. Only long enough to climb the stairs up and come the stairs down."

"All right. Let's say it took twenty minutes, and ten minutes more for your conference with Ten High. That's a total of half an hour. Do you follow me so far?"

"Sure, Doc, but you got it wrong when—"

"Let me finish. It was about nine o'clock when the Professor told you Titine had disappeared, and you decided the thing had to be settled, once and for all. At least, that's what you just said. So it took you a little more than two hours to get there, half an hour at the mill and a little more than two hours to get back, which would have brought you back shortly after one-thirty. Yet you said you didn't get back until a little after three."

Scholtze shifted his muscular bulk about on the wooden chair, moistened his lips and brushed his palm over the bristly crop-cut of his blond hair.

"I got back just in time to close up," he said at last.

"In other words, you got back an hour—give or take a few minutes either way—after you should have been there, had you gone right back after looking through the mill. Can you account for that time, Gus?"

Again the big man fidgeted.

"I can tell you where I was at and what I was doing, *ja,*" he said moodily. "But if you mean do I got witnesses to prove what I say, no, I got not one single *verdammt* witness. You just got to believe me."

"I'll take it from here, Dr. Tim," interrupted Theo. "Be careful to get every word of this down correctly, Mrs. Walton, please." He turned to Scholtze. "All right, Gus. Give us your account of that hour. Maybe we can dig up some witnesses you wouldn't be knowing about. If this case ever comes to trial, Dr. Davila, Sheriff Bennett and Mrs. Walton will all be in a position to testify to what you tell us now. You have a right, therefore, not to answer."

"Come to trial!" echoed Scholtze. "You mean you got the idea *I* killed that young girl?"

"She's certainly dead," observed Davila.

"But I would never kill her. *Um Gottes willen,* I am crazy about her! That is why I can't stand it she goes out with other men, two-timing on me. Villac maybe I could have killed if I find him with her Saturday night. But not Titine. This you must got to believe!"

"That's as it may be, Gus," agreed the district attorney. "On the basis of all this, do you want to tell us what happened at about the time Titine was killed? By the way, one thing I haven't mentioned, and you're entitled to know it now, before you make up your mind to talk or not to talk, is that on the basis of his medical examination as coroner, Dr. Tim here gives it as his opinion that the girl died sometime around midnight, Saturday, give or take a couple of hours either way. In other words, she died sometime between ten o'clock Saturday night and two o'clock Sunday morning, an interval which includes the very time when you say you were in Crowley, and more particularly the hour or so you haven't accounted for. So it's up to you to decide whether or not you want to tell us more."

"*Aber gewiss,* certainly, sure I talk. I got nothing to hide. Plenty men already yet made a damn fool out of themself over a woman, and plenty more men going to do it, too, just so long as it gives men and gives women. . . . What I did before I go back by the Tuileries to close up for the night? I let the watchman see me drive off, but I park in the next lane and walk back to where I can see, but nobody sees me. Then I wait, because I know like I am sitting here—and I still know it, too—that if she meets Villac by the rice mill either she is *noch immer* there until yet, or they go away some place together. I ask myself, *also,* where will that *Schweinhund* Villac take the young girl? He is not in the mill, because I just looked there, *nicht wahr*? He can't take her home by his mother's house and it's too-too plenty early to take her home by Cypremort. Anyway, she is sure to work the late shift by the Tuileries, because that is her biggest money night in the week. So maybe he will bring her to the club. But whatever they do, they got to come back to the mill first."

"Why?"

"The Professor tells me before I leave the club yet how she got to have the accordion with her, because he looked already in his car and it ain't no accordion there, like it has been since Wednesday. Also, she got that paper bundle with her *noch dazu,* like her folks said, and I don't see no accordion and no paper bundle with shoes wrapped up in when I looked around the place, but I got sense enough to know there must be a *Haufen* of places where they could be hid. And I know they got to come back to pick up them things when—"

"What makes you so sure they were left there?" Bennett suddenly shot the question at him, with the effect of a lunge. So vivid was this impression, that Scholtze drew back involuntarily as though from a threatened blow. But he recovered his composure almost at once.

"I don't like to say things like that in front of no lady," he parried.

"Go right ahead," snapped Bennett. "I'm sure Mrs. Walton will make allowances, in view of the fact that your life might depend on the answer."

"All right, then, if Mrs. Walton will excuse the way I say it," he replied. "You are a grown man, Tobe, also Mister Theo and Dr. Tim. I ain't saying you ever done nothing like that, but if you ever in your life was to take out a *Schatzi* to make love, like it was late at night and—well, I guess you know how I mean—would you let her carry a big accordion under one arm and a paper bundle with shoes under the other? Remember, you start out from a mill where they got a *Haufen* places to hide things. I ask you like any man asks another man. Don't you got to give me right about it?"

Theo Landry rose and started toward the door.

"Before I tell you, or let these gentlemen tell you, whether we might agree with you, let me show you something." He opened the door, beckoned to someone beyond it and returned, followed by Chief Deputy Guerra, who carried with gingerly care an object fouled and begrimed with all manner of refuse, through which, nonetheless, flashed an occasional gleam of ivory and mother of pearl.

"Recognize it?" asked Theo, holding it up for Scholtze's better inspection.

"*Na, endlich!*" he exclaimed after one brief moment of hesitation. "It is her accordion. Where it comes from at last?"

"It was found under a pile of trash in the back yard of your home, Scholtze. That was what Barousse came in to tell us a few minutes ago. And in the light of this find, and your own statement of what you did between eleven Saturday night and three Sunday morning, I'm holding you for the grand jury—as a material witness, for the present, and until such time as they decide whether you're to be indicted on a charge of murder!"

Chapter Thirteen

LANDRY'S ANNOUNCEMENT WAS FOLLOWED BY A BRIEF CONFUSED INTERVAL in which Scholtze so volubly protested his innocence of any complicity in Titine's death that the tumbled mixture of accented English and guttural German was almost incomprehensible. "This here is a *gottverdammt Schandhaft*, a *verfluchte Schweinerei*," he raged. "This here is a free country, like they were always saying when I buy Liberty bonds, we got to save the world for democrats, and not do things like does the Kaiser. Is it this here you make the world safe for, to put a man what ain't done nothing on the jailhouse yet? How I know the *verdammte* accordion got in my yard? Better you should find out who put it there, maybe, as take a man to the—"

"Pipe down, you!" Guerra admonished him roughly.

"You don't understand, Gus," explained Landry. "Being held as a witness doesn't necessarily mean being put in jail. All we got to do is go see Judge Campbell and have him fix an appearance bond for you. Then you put up the money, and agree to come back when you're called before the grand jury. Either that or you get some property owner to sign your bond."

"I put it up mineself, yet," sputtered Scholtze. "How much you want for to let me go?"

"I don't want anything. The judge will decide your bond. I suppose it will be about three hundred dollars. Do you carry that much around with you in your pocket?"

Scholtze grinned. "That is feed for chickens, *noch*." He dug into his trousers' pocket and brought out a thick roll of greenbacks, tightly encircled by a heavy rubber band, which he stripped off. "Money you want?" he continued, "*und* money you get already. *So geht's in dieser Welt!*" He moistened the ball of his right thumb with his tongue, peeled off three hundred-dollar bills and tossed them onto the table. "*Drei hundert* is a big nothings, I bet you. It gives plenty more right here. Now can I go?"

"First we have to see the judge. I can't fix your bail, you know."

The various technical details were finally achieved and the other waiting witnesses were released, though notified to return at nine in the morning, at which time Paula Bennett would probably be the first one Mr. Landry would question. On his way home, Tobe dropped by the Villacs' house and, beckoning Prosper into the library again, told him he would not be called for interrogation before Tuesday at the earliest, most likely not even then.

"I still think there's a chance it won't be necessary to call you at all, son," he said. "What I'm hoping is that this case will break wide open and the real killer be spotted before you need to speak your piece. Maybe I'm too optimistic, but at least I've got this much settled with Theo Landry: if there's any reasonable way to do it, you're to be the last person questioned."

"Tobe, I'll never be able to thank you enough," Prosper assured him feelingly. "I know now, better than ever, why my dad set such store by you. And you can be sure that when you want me, I'll be ready to talk."

Upon returning to the living room, Prosper found that a number of those who had done more or less justice to Lavinia's bountiful supper, and then fidgeted through the restless hours that followed, were still seated in stilted groups. This was not only because custom decreed they must not "eat and run," but because they hoped for some reassuring word about a tragedy whose omen cast a long shadow over the whole family. Prosper's report of what Bennett had just told him provided this reassurance and, despite Dale Fontenot's failure to return, the visitors dispersed in an atmosphere of general cheerfulness, tempered with decorous recognition of the sober dignity accorded any death in the community. As soon as the last good nights had been said, Lavinia, still very pale and still completely composed, began to straighten out the disordered living room, emptying ash trays, putting chairs back into place and generally restoring order.

"Can't you let all that go until morning, Mother?" Prosper inquired. "Callie and Verna can do it for you then. The dishes, too."

"I know. But I hate to leave a place cluttered up overnight. I always have. Somehow it seems even worse the next day, and it would set Callie and Verna a bad example to find the house looking like this—they'd think they could go off, leaving things in this state, when it *wasn't* their night out. Besides, I imagine we'll be having a good deal of company off and on, right along, and beginning early in the morning. I wouldn't want any of our relatives to come into the living room when it wasn't in order. I'll have to leave for the Monrovia early, as usual, and there'll be extra cooking to do, without adding extra cleaning to that."

"All right then, I'll help you. . . . By the way, I haven't seen anything of Didier since he went upstairs. Have you?"

"No. I think you were probably right—this was an opportune moment for a visit with Anne Marie."

Prosper glanced at his wrist watch. "The opportune moment seems to be somewhat extended," he said rather dryly. "I believe I'll go up and get the tray. After all, the dishes on that have to be washed, too."

"Let's leave them for the time being and see if he doesn't come down of his own accord. He may do so before we have the rest of the work done, and the moment you burst in might not be so opportune."

The repressed quality which marked the change in her voice from natural to unnatural control, and which Prosper had learned to associate with the further tightening of her normally firm lips, was very marked. He felt it wiser not to attempt an immediate answer, and silently began to wash the stacked dishes. He had been trained, from childhood, to make himself useful about the house and he worked with deftness and dispatch. When the last of the tableware had been dried and put back into place, his mother returned to the living room and motioned him toward a chair beside the one in which she seated herself.

"I want to talk to you some more about Vicky," she said.

"Aren't you pretty tired? Wouldn't you rather go to bed?"

"I shan't go anyway until Didier leaves. You know I'm rather old-fashioned about things like that, Prosper. We'll give him a few minutes more and then, if he hasn't come down, I'll take some sort of action. Meanwhile, I hope you won't mind if I offer you a bit of advice."

"I don't mind your offering it. That doesn't mean I'm promising to take it."

"Of course not. It's only this: if I understood right, you said, when all the others were here, that Vicky had told you she loved you, over and over again, not just before you got the bad news from the mill, but afterward."

"Correct."

"In other words, when she knew you were the subject of scandal and perhaps worse?"

"Correct again."

"All right. This is my advice: don't tell her you know you're not good enough for her. Don't tell her she ought to put you out of her mind, at least until your name is cleared. Tell her instead that you hope to be more worthy of her confidence someday, but that, meanwhile, it means every-thing in the world to you to have it now—that and her love. Tell her you know, with her help, you can fight through somehow."

Prosper looked at his mother in amazement. He could not remember when he had heard her speak so urgently and, with sudden clarity, he realized she had known some man who had failed to do what she was recommending in such deadly earnest, and that the consequences of this failure had been tragic. Obviously, he could not ask her to reveal, di-rectly, any more than she had indirectly. But the hopeful thought that she might do so someday and that, if she did, they would be closer to-gether than they had ever previously been, flashed through his mind.

"Thanks, Mother," he said quietly. "Like I said before, I'm not prom-ising to take your advice. But I appreciate it and I'll think it over care-fully. I'll go further than that: I'll promise not to do anything that's exactly opposite of what you've suggested until I *have* thought it over and talked with Vicky again—I don't mean on the telephone, I mean face to face. However, I don't seem to feel capable of any more very coherent thoughts tonight and, of course, I can't see Vicky until tomor-row evening at the earliest. I believe I'll call her up, but just to tell her the latest news and say good night, because I imagine she's waiting to hear from me. Then, if it's all right by you, I'm going to bed. I'll look in at Anne Marie and Didier on my way to my room, and drop a hint as to the hour. Under the circumstances, it's a little late for visiting and I'm sure he'll want to be at the courthouse early tomorrow morning, because that's where Maurice has got to be, even if he isn't the one called on to testify first."

The hour fixed for attendance did, indeed, seem unreasonably early to Didier, especially as the schedule previously outlined by Landry as probable proved to be the one that was carried through. The witnesses waited in the hallway—the Benoits stormily, Dale patiently, the Profes-sor nervously and Amanda stonily, while Paula—to whom the chair oc-cupied by Scholtze the previous night had been indicated as the one she should now take—underwent questioning in an adjoining room. The

general seating arrangement was much the same as before, except that
Guerra was now stationed outside to summon the witnesses. The buzz of
the mud dauber no longer sounded through the room; the window had
been opened and it had escaped, unless it had died of exhaustion or been
captured by a spider. The pleasant early morning breeze had dispelled
some of the room's mustiness; otherwise, it was even less attractive than
before, as the overflowing ash trays were still unemptied and the un-
swept floor still littered with paper. Paula, whose appearance was always
extremely trim during working hours, looked almost painfully neat in
contrast to all this clutter. She had never bobbed her hair; it was brushed
smoothly back from her forehead and gathered into a small round bun
at the back; as an added precaution against untidiness, it was closely
confined by a net. Her spotless shirtwaist dress of gray voile was buttoned closely at both neck and wrists, and she wore no rings on the
capable-looking hands which she kept quietly clasped; at no point did
she seem disposed to fidget with a pencil or a piece of paper. Her feet,
shod in sensible shoes, were placed primly side by side, and the length
of lisle stockings which showed above them was considerably shorter
even than Mrs. Walton's, who dressed in somewhat the same general
way, though less pronouncedly so; Malvina had been known to wear
skirts which came only a few inches below her knees; Paula had never
made any such concession to current fashion, which both she and her
aunt Amanda termed "disgusting."

"Just for the record, Paula, will you give Mrs. Walton your full name
and tell her where you live?" asked the district attorney; and when this
information had been supplied, he continued: "Also for the record, you
were born here and have lived here in Crowley all your life. Isn't that
correct?"

"Except for the time when I was overseas with the Graves Registration Service of the A.E.F.; and of course while I was going to business
college in Lafayette."

"And how long have you worked at the Claudia Mill?"

"It will be six years in December."

"What are your duties there?"

"I keep the books, type all the letters. . . ."

"From dictation, of course?"

"Not always," Paula replied, bridling a little. "Any more than I say
'Claudia Mill' when the telephone rings and then hand the receiver
straight to Mr. Villac. Much of the correspondence I handle myself.
Many inquiries I take care of without bothering him."

"Would you say, then, that you are a sort of assistant manager at the Claudia?"

"In a way; I am assistant *to* the manager, I suppose."

"At any rate, you are thoroughly familiar with the mill, both in its structure as a building and in its functioning and operation?"

"I certainly am."

"Now on last Saturday night . . . by the way, do you often work late at the mill? By late, I mean at night, of course."

"Everybody in Crowley knows that, Mr. Theo. You know it as well as I do. During the harvest, everybody in every rice mill works early and late and in between times, too."

"I'm merely trying to establish whether you worked late last Saturday night and, if so, whether this was customary or merely an unusual situation on this particular night."

"Certainly, I worked late on Saturday night. We're right at the beginning of our rush season."

"How late would you say, Miss Bennett?"

"I couldn't say for sure. It would be just a guess."

"That will be good enough. Maybe we can get at it this way. You went home for supper?"

"Yes, but sometimes my aunt brings supper to the mill for me when we really get caught in a squeeze."

"But this particular night—I'm talking about Saturday night now—you went home. About what time?"

"About six o'clock. My aunt called for me in the car."

"But you *do* live in what would ordinarily be called walking distance of the mill?"

"Yes, but my aunt says it isn't best for a young girl to be out on the street alone by herself, especially after dark."

"I'm afraid I didn't think of it as being 'after dark' quite as early as six in September." He might have added that he did not think of thirty-three, which he knew to be approximately Paula's age, as representing such youthfulness as to be in need of careful vigilance. Wisely, however, he let this pass, and merely inquired, "So Miss Eaton usually calls for you?"

"Usually. Sometimes Mr. Villac says that he'll drop me off at my aunt's house, if he happens to be leaving about that time; and sometimes Cousin Tobe takes me home. Those days, I telephone my aunt not to come. But even then, she sometimes asks me to wait anyhow, so she can come and get me herself. And she always sees to it that there's a gun in the door pocket of the car, just for extra precaution."

"Extra precaution against what?"

"Why, anyone with evil designs!"

Again, Landry decided it was better not to argue a point and merely said, "So, apparently, Saturday night was one of the times she decided to come for you herself?"

"Well, Saturday night, Mr. Villac never said a word about dropping me off at home, because he was too upset and busy."

"Upset? Was there any reason for him to be upset?"

"A whole car of sacked rice would be reason enough, I should think. It was supposed to be picked up about three in the morning by the west-bound Red Ball, to go to Beaumont and Port Arthur for the steamer *Texas Belle* to Philadelphia. It was all loaded and sealed, and on the siding by the depot, where the engineer of the mixed local train spotted it."

"It wasn't on the mill spur then?"

"No. The engine of the mixed local pulled it off our spur and spotted it on the depot siding. The big locomotive on the Red Ball would pick it up on that switch, but naturally, it wouldn't hunt around for cars on the mill spurs."

"And what happened to it?"

"One of the eastbound freight trains coupled it on by mistake, and was taking it on to New Orleans."

"How did you find this out?"

"Well, all we knew at first was when the depot agent asked how come the car was gone. He thought maybe Mr. Villac had changed the routing for some reason."

"And then?"

"Well, then everybody was rushing around. That was about six o'clock, when my aunt came to take me to supper. I told Mr. Villac I would be ever so glad to stay until things were straightened out, and usually he would have asked me to do it, because he depends on me a lot, and knows how glad I am to help him. But he seemed terribly upset and said 'no, no, you go with your aunt, I can handle whatever's coming up here, you run along now.' So I went home with Aunt Amanda."

"That was about six o'clock. How long before you went back to the mill?"

"Less than an hour."

"Let me ask you this: as long as Prosper Villac told you he could handle anything that might come up in connection with this situation, and would not need your help, why did you come back?"

"Mr. Villac telephoned later and said he would have to leave the mill for a while, and would I please come back to catch the phone calls. Sometime after I got back to the mill, which was before seven, a telephone call came from the railroad freight office in Lafayette, to say the missing car had been located. This must have been a little after eight, but I'm not sure of the exact time. Anyway, the railroad people said they would spot it at Morgan City, where the Red Ball stops anyway, so it would be picked up by the same train that was supposed to take it in the first place; but a lot of new waybills would have to be made out, dead-heading the car to Crowley, and then putting the original papers back into the file, and—"

"Yes, yes, we can understand that." Theo was getting rather tired of hearing about the missing car and all the trouble it had caused. "What I would like to know—in fact, what all of us would like to know very much—is whether Mr. Villac told you why he had to leave the mill at a time of such emergency?"

Paula hesitated.

"I—don't—I mean, I can't really remember."

"Are you sure you can't? If I said, for instance, that he might have wanted to meet someone, would that refresh your memory. . . . Yes, Joe, what is it?"

Guerra had entered rather hurriedly and, approaching the end of the table where the group of officials had been listening to Paula's story, was whispering to Bennett. Tobe turned to Landry and then to Davila.

"Sorry to interrupt, Theo, but Toler wants to know whether Dr. Tim would be willing to release Titine Dargereux's body for burial? Seems there's a special reason—"

"Oh, hell, yes!" Dr. Tim replied. "Any time. We know she was alive when she fell or was pushed into that bin, otherwise there wouldn't have been any rice in the respiratory tract. . . ."

"Meaning . . . ?" asked the district attorney.

"If she hadn't been breathing, her throat and trachea would have been clear. But she had breathed in a lot of rice, like a person drowning in grain."

"And the beating?"

"Nothing to that; I mean nothing she wouldn't have got over as soon as the black and blue marks faded. Sure, let them bury her, if it's going to be any consolation to them."

Guerra hurried from the room. Landry, who had obviously been displeased at the interruption, repeated, with increasing emphasis, the question he had asked Paula just before it occurred and which she had not yet answered.

"As I was saying, are you sure you can't remember whether Mr. Villac told you why he had to leave the mill at a time of such emergency? If I said, for example, that he might have wanted to meet someone, would that refresh your memory?"

"I couldn't swear that it would, Mr. Theo."

"I'm not asking you to. You're not under oath. I mean, this isn't as if you were testifying in a court, where you could only say what you actually saw or knew of your own knowledge. Here, you can tell us what you think, what someone has told you, what you heard, anything at all. This is an investigation, you know, not a trial. What we're seeking is information, not evidence. So try to remember if Mr. Villac said anything about having to meet somebody."

"He might have. I know there was a party at the Archers' to discuss plans for a rice carnival and he seemed to think he ought to sit in on the discussion. I believe he expected to see the Benoits there or maybe somewhere else. It seems to me he did say something about meeting one of the Benoit boys, but whether it was Didier or his brother Maurice, or whether it was at the Archers' or not, I couldn't swear, Mr. Theo. Honestly, I couldn't."

"But you're sure that if he did say he had to meet someone, it was one of the Benoits? It couldn't have been anyone else? It couldn't have been the Dargereux girl, for example?"

"Mr. Villac wouldn't lower himself to meet trash like that!" flashed Paula. "A strumpet from some shack in the swamps, a—a—common little something that sings in night clubs. . . ."

"Easy, there. You're talking about a dead girl."

"I'm sorry, Mr. Theo. I know we're not supposed to speak ill of the dead, but that doesn't make her any decent kind of person that a self-respecting man would associate with while she was alive. So I *know* Mr. Villac wouldn't have had anything to do with her. Even if he *did*, he would never admit it to people, would he? He would never tell *me* about it, anyway."

"Well, let it go at that, for the time being. He telephoned you, said he had to leave the mill for a while—it might have been to meet one of the Benoit boys, either at the Archers' or somewhere else. That is, you think so, but you can't be positive. So you went back to the mill around seven?"

"That's right, a little before. Aunt Amanda and I hadn't finished washing the supper dishes when Mr. Villac phoned. She was rather put out and, while she was driving me back to the mill, she kept saying, it was a shame the way men treated women, here was Mr. Villac not even giving me time to swallow a bite of supper, no consideration, but that was always the way men treated girls, she remembered when she was young how—"

"You say you returned to the mill a little before seven. Was Prosper Villac there when you arrived?"

"Yes, but he left almost right away. He acted as if he were glad to see me, saying how now he could get away, and he wouldn't have bothered me if it hadn't been so dreadfully important."

"So you were there alone for a time. Let me ask you this: during that time could anyone who wanted to slip in unnoticed and could such a person perhaps have hidden in some out-of-the-way corner?"

"Oh, no! Besides, I wasn't alone. The watchman was there."

"But the front door, and the back door—the one that leads to the loading dock and the spur track—these were open, weren't they?"

"I didn't notice about the back door, but I suppose it was open. It naturally would have been. If it wasn't that some hoodlum could get in and damage the machinery or steal milled rice, it wouldn't really be necessary to lock anything but the office."

"You had a key to the office, of course?"

"And to the other doors, likewise."

"Did your aunt go in with you?"

"No. She was still talking about how terrible it was for me to have to come back to the mill, and how it was just like a man to make me do it, so she had better go back and finish the dishes by herself, but she didn't propose to have me stay at the mill until all hours, while other people were off gallivanting with God only knows who, and such as that. So she went back home."

"Did anyone come to the mill while you were there?"

"Mr. Benoit did. Mr. Maurice Benoit, I mean."

"Was he looking for any particular person? Did he say?"

"Only that he wanted to talk to Mr. Villac, and that it was important. I said Mr. Villac might be looking for him, too, at the Archers'. I was going to ask him if he knew whether Mr. Villac wouldn't go there to find him, but the telephone started to ring, just then, and I turned back to answer it. It was the railroad freight office at Lafayette, and when I finished making notes on everything they said, Mr. Benoit was gone."

"Could he have been somewhere in the mill where you would not ordinarily see him?"

"There are hundreds of places, at night especially, where persons would not be seen unless you were making a search for them."

"Let me amplify that question. While your back was turned, answering the phone, and if the watchman at that time was inspecting the millyard, would it have been possible for one or two persons, no matter whether the name was Benoit or Joe Blow, to have slipped into the mill and up to the top floor, just under the roof where those bin openings are?"

"Certainly it would be possible. I had my back turned to the office door, and all I was paying attention to, anyway, was what I was writing, so I could leave a memorandum for Mr. Villac."

"So much for that. Now who was the next person you saw, if anyone? You didn't by any chance see August Scholtze, did you?"

"August Scholtze!" flashed Paula, almost as angrily as she had replied when Landry referred to Titine. "Indeed, I didn't!"

"You know August Scholtze, don't you—I mean, you know him by sight?"

"I met him years ago, in France, when I was with the Graves Registration Service, and he came to our headquarters at Romagne, as the orderly of an officer who was making a tour of inspection through American cemeteries, Argonne among others. It was a very brief and casual meeting. I'm not sure I'd recognize him now."

Landry glanced at Bennett, who lifted his eyebrows slightly. Neither had forgotten the contradictory statement which Scholtze had made the night before, and the discrepancy in the two replies interested them both. However, there was nothing in Landry's speech or manner to indicate that he was conscious of prevarication somewhere.

"But if you had seen anyone, unconnected with the mill, prowling about at this time, you would remember that, wouldn't you, whether you recognized such a person or not?"

"Of course I would. And I didn't see any such person."

"Well, I'll repeat myself, as I did once before: who was the next person you saw, if anyone?"

"'Zebe Peyronne, the watchman."

"The one everyone calls Ten High?"

"That's right. The only way I happen to know his real name is that I keep the pay roll records."

"Anything special in his seeing you at that time?"

"No, he was just making his rounds. I remember asking him why he didn't go upstairs, but just looked around the first floor. He said he wouldn't make the whole round until after everybody had left, that it didn't mean anything right now, unless I wanted him to look up there for some reason. So I said no, just to do his work like always. About that time, or a little later, maybe—anyway, the watchman was still there, or he had come back by the office for a small cup of coffee—I heard my aunt out in the millyard blowing the horn on our car the way she does when she's out of patience, and Mr. Ten High was running around to the front of the millyard to see what was the matter."

Tobe Bennett interrupted the recital with a chuckle.

"I sh'd have thought Ten High was used to Aunt Amanda's carryings on by now. She's been acting like that since Hector was a dock-tailed pup."

"Oh, he's used to her all right, Cousin Tobe," Paula explained, "and he knows the squawk of that horn better than I do. But he can't take chances at night, and has to go see if anything is wrong. Anyway, by the time he got to the car, I was already out there, and telling my aunt I couldn't possibly leave yet, so if she would come into the office, I would fix coffee for us. I had put the water on to boil already, and was making fresh drippings, because I figured Mr. Villac would want some by the time he got back. Anyway, he likes to have fresh coffee on hand all the time."

"Let's go back over that some more, Miss Paula," suggested the district attorney. "To begin with, did Miss Eaton come back to the office with you?"

"Yes, she did. So did Mr. Ten High."

"Would that have been right away, as soon as you and Ten High got to the car where she was sounding the horn?"

"No, not right away. At first, she always makes like she won't come in, but in the end she mostly does. She doesn't have much fun, and one of the things she likes is to be coaxed. So for maybe five minutes—just a little while, anyway—she made Mr. Ten High and me tease her to come in and have some coffee, and maybe wait in the office until I was ready to go."

"Five minutes or so, eh? And was anyone watching the mill during that time?"

"Why, we were all right out front in the millyard!"

"But would it not have been possible while you were there in front for someone to have slipped in through the back door from the loading dock without you knowing it?"

"Maybe they *could* have done it, but—"

"And what is even more to the point, would it not have been possible for someone, who was already in the mill, to have slipped out through that back door and to have disappeared without being seen by anyone?"

"We-e-ell, I suppose so. But nobody did."

"Nobody that you know of, you or the watchman, either, for that matter. However, we'll come back to that later. As I understand it, Miss Eaton finally did come into the mill with you, into the office, that is, where you were making or preparing to make coffee. I suppose you all had coffee then?"

"When it was finished, Aunt Amanda and Mr. Ten High and I each had a cup of coffee."

"Then the watchman left on his usual rounds?"

"That's correct, Mr. Theo."

"And your aunt—did she stay until you were ready to leave?"

"Oh, no! Right after she finished her coffee she wanted me to go home with her, but I told her I could not go yet, that Mr. Villac had left everything in my hands, and she sniffed and said I was a fool to be doing his work while he was gallivanting around the countryside wining and wenching. . . ."

Again Sheriff Bennett chuckled.

"That's Amanda for you, every time," he grinned. "Can you imagine folks actually talking like that? If I'd heard that business about wining and wenching in darkest Africa, I'd look around the corner of the nearest elephant to see where my aunt Amanda Eaton was."

"Anyway," Paula continued, "she went away, and I tended to my work until Mr. Villac came back."

"How long after your aunt Amanda left was that?"

"Right about half-past ten, maybe ten forty-five. He had telephoned once before then, and I had given him the memoranda. He already knew about finding the car, but said he'd alerted a loading crew, and arranged for another car to be spotted on our spur, just in case the Red Ball failed to pick up the first car at Morgan City, but he had checked, and the car was now on the Red Ball."

"You said earlier in the evening that, when you first got back to the mill after supper, Prosper looked upset. Did he still impress you as looking upset when he came back about ten-thirty?"

"Not upset, no, but tired like somebody that is just used up until nothing's left."

"Did he say anything special?"

"No, only how tuckered out he felt, and how old Dupre at the depot had said the car had been located and left at Morgan City, and how I had been notified and could tell him all about it. He thanked me for helping out, and then said for me to call up Aunt Amanda and go home, that he would wait there until the Red Ball came through, when he would double check to make sure our missing car was really on it. I started to say he was too tired to wait there until three or four o'clock in the morning, but he said it would be all right, the next day would be Sunday and he could rest. So I called Aunt Amanda to see if she was still up, and she said she would come right over and get me. I expect I was gone shortly after eleven."

"You went straight to your aunt's home?"

"That is what I did."

"You saw no one, stopped to see no one, talked to no one on the way?"

"Not a soul. But, as our car left the millyard, an automobile passed us going toward the Claudia siding, then turned and followed us a piece."

"Anyone you knew or recognized?"

"No. We were quite frightened at first, and hurried to get out in front of our house. As we did so, the other car turned again and left. I thought that perhaps—"

"Yes? You thought that perhaps—?"

"Perhaps it might have been someone to see Mr. Villac, someone who thought he might just be leaving the mill, and when he saw he was mistaken—"

"You're sure it was 'he'?"

"Well, I must say! I didn't see who was driving, certainly. But I shouldn't think . . . I mean, I don't know any women who would be driving around by themselves that time of night."

"You and your aunt were."

"But that's different. We were just driving from the mill home, not following cars."

"All right, then. Until the contrary is proved, we'll assume it was a 'he' that followed your aunt's car Saturday night. What did she say to it?"

"She just kept telling me, 'See, Paula? That's why I'm always saying a girl can't be too careful. If you had been by yourself, that creature would not have turned back, I'll venture to say! But when he saw there were two of us, he gave up his evil designs.'"

"Wining and wenching!" murmured Tobe Bennett.

"And then?" asked the district attorney.

"We went into the house as fast as we could, and locked the door.

Aunt Amanda wanted to phone Cousin Tobe to have the 'creature,' as she called him, locked up. But I asked her how she would tell Cousin Tobe what the car or the man in it looked like, so she decided to let it go at that."

Paula's narrative was once more interrupted by a knock, which again heralded the entry of Joe Guerra. He remained just within the door, carefully closing it behind him.

"This Professor . . ." he began, and then paused as if uncertain what to say next.

"What about him, Joe?" asked the sheriff.

"He says he can't wait no more. He says he's got to go."

"You tell him he'll wait until we get good and ready to give him leave to go. Who's he think he is?"

The door behind Guerra opened suddenly and the Professor's lean figure squeezed past Guerra's bulk.

"I'm nobody," he said, his wrinkled countenance without emotion. "Just nobody. But you try to keep me here, Mr. Bennett, and I'll put a bad mouth on you from Mermentau to Lafourche."

"You'll do *what?*" asked Tobe, rising.

"I'll fix it so folks'll cross the road to keep from passing the time of day with you. Lookee here! I don't live in this parish and I don't vote here. But you'd be surprised how many folks know me. And if you try to keep me from that funeral—"

Bennett slapped his forehead.

"By God, I'd plumb forgot. That Dargereux girl . . . so she is being buried today!"

"She is, and right in your parish, Mr. Bennett."

"What do you mean, in my parish?"

"I mean on the Primeaux farm. Clement Primeaux told the folks they could bury her in his family graveyard out yonder, and that if anybody didn't like to come by, he'd help dig the grave and lower the coffin his own self, as he and his father did for that brother of his. And, Mr. Bennett, you might be the high sheriff, and you and this goon here are big enough to hold me, but if you keep me from going to that poor little girl's funeral and showing a lot of poison-tongue gossips that some persons have respect for the dead—"

"Ah, hush your talking, man," said Bennett, flapping his large hand in dismissal. "Of course, you can go to the funeral. You don't mind adjourning this inquiry for the rest of the day, do you, Theo?" Then, in a whisper inaudible to the other, he added, "I don't need to tell you how many Primeaux and Villacs there are in that part of the prairie, or what would happen once they all got on the warpath—as I think they may have already!"

Chapter Fourteen

THOUGH HE HAD NOW HAD ENOUGH EXPERIENCE AT THE MILL TO KNOW better, it did not seem possible to Prosper that Monday could present as many problems as Saturday, all requiring immediate solution. Moreover, Paula's absence inevitably made a great difference in the speed with which routine work could proceed. Finally, when this difficulty was surmounted and most emergencies had, apparently, been met, Ervin Stacy, the expert grader who was receiving rice coming in from the fields, called Prosper to say that an immediate conference was needed with Howard Lokes, one of the largest rice-producing farmers in the area, who was a steady patron and who was threshing that day. It was extremely important that Lokes should be kept satisfied, since he was good for approximately fifteen thousand barrels of rice and, normally, no better grade was received at the Claudia. This season, however, the crop was not up to scratch, much to the surprise of everyone at the mill; and because of the various important aspects of the case, Stacy naturally felt that the proprietor should be the one to decide what action must be taken. Prosper, inwardly cursing the delay this would entail, nevertheless agreed and called in Wayland Foster, his cautious buyer. After consultation, a call was put through to Lokes, and both grader and buyer waited with Prosper in his office until the farmer could join them there. A sample of each load was then brought in for examination, and it was obvious to all, though Lokes would not admit this, that the rice was very poor grade. As courteously and as patiently as he could, Prosper explained—though actually Lokes needed no such explanation—that the Claudia would lose a large sum of money if five dollars a barrel—the market price for grade one—were paid for such an inferior product.

Lokes argued hotly that his tenants could not and would not stand for a reduction, since their expenses were as high as ever; if the Claudia would not meet the maximum price, the rice would be taken elsewhere. He did not actually say there was any other reason why he would not have been sorry to seize a pretext for doing this; but, from his manner, it was not difficult for Prosper to guess what was in the farmer's mind, and he hastened to agree that, since this was the first time that their product had not come up to standard, Lokes and his tenants deserved some consideration; perhaps a compromise could be found, satisfactory to both sides. In principle, Lokes replied, he might consider some such arrangement; but the afternoon wore on and still no definite figures had been fixed. Foster finally rose, glancing at the clock, and said perhaps he had better see about some more coffee. As soon as the prudent buyer was out of the room, Prosper offered Lokes four dollars and a half per barrel; it was better, in his opinion, for the Claudia to take a loss than to forfeit the support of Lokes and his tenant farmers, especially in view of what might be taking place at the courthouse. Lokes continued to raise objections, but when Foster reappeared, accompanied by a colored boy carrying a coffee tray, he grudgingly said that, perhaps, they had better settle on something like that, rather than to stay there all night. Prosper could not have agreed more wholeheartedly.

Earlier he had checked with his mother, who had already left the Monrovia, and spoke to him from home, where his uncle Onezime and his uncle Odey had now arrived; the former had found another priest to look after his parish in the Delta for a few days, the latter a teacher who was willing to take over his classes at the university. She was then on the point of going out to the family farm with them. She had waited to give Prosper an account of the day's happenings, but now she thought that she would be on her way. Did she want him to come with her, Prosper asked. No, that was not necessary. He had better be on his way to Lafayette. He did not wait for the suggestion to be made a second time.

Vicky was watching for him at the front door and opened it for him herself, just as she had the day before. But this time she did not wait for him to put his arms around her waist and draw her toward him. She instantly placed her hands on his shoulders and kissed him, not as if this were just the natural way in which to greet him, but as if it were the only way; and, so swiftly that it seemed miraculous, the tension of his troubled thoughts was eased, the confusion clarified, the tumult stilled. He could not have told why the thought had flashed through his mind that this was the kind of kiss a devoted wife would give an equally devoted husband, when he came home, tired and worried, at the end of a day's work: not the casual kiss of indifferent habit, depleted of ardor because it had been too often and too carelessly given, in the course of a long humdrum married life; not the kiss, either, of avid hunger for passionate experience, devoid of any sensation beyond unfulfilled physical craving; but a kiss of tenderness, of faith, of lovingkindness and of confidence that all these feelings were returned in full measure. The conviction of this was so strong that he yearned, unutterably, to put it into words, and deplored his inability to do so; then he realized this was not necessary, that Vicky knew it anyway, that she had intended her kiss to be like that. An almost overwhelming sense of undeserved privilege, together with one of boundless gratitude, swept over him; he raised his hands and, taking hers from his shoulders, turned the palms upward and kissed them, lingeringly, almost reverently, before he embraced her.

"Wouldn't you like to come and see my sitting room?" she asked when he released her. "You've never been off this floor, and I think it's really pleasanter on the second story, and we'll be all by ourselves there. Not that I think anyone would burst in on us, if we went to the library. But somehow the other seems—well, a little more intimate. At least it does to me. Does it to you?"

"It sure does. And I'd like very much to see your sitting room anyway. That is, unless your father might feel I was—well, presuming a little, if I let you take me up there."

"Father suggested it himself. He wants to see you later on, too, of course. But he knew we'd want to be alone for a while first."

She led the way up a massive staircase, elaborately carved, which gave Prosper the impression it had been imported from some medieval castle, like the armorial figures in the great entrance hall. However, there was nothing oppressive about the atmosphere of the room into which Vicky ushered him, though the radiant sunshine which must have flooded it earlier in the day had now faded to the quiet light of "first evening." A gentle breeze stirred the curtains of fine Indian muslin that hung, in straight simplicity, at the open windows—in fact, there was a conspicuous absence of frills and furbelows everywhere. The walls were unpapered, but their cream-tinted surface served as an effective background for some fine flower prints and water colors of picturesque faraway places. And there was no lack of color in the room. The comfortable chairs were upholstered in quaintly figured *toile de Jouy*, and the one large rug, which covered most of the hardwood floor, repeated the glowing shades of the chintz. Well-filled, open bookcases flanked the fireplace and on the upper shelves of these were numerous signed photographs, not enough to give a cluttered look, but sufficient to indicate that Vicky had friends in many parts of the world and that some of these had illustrious names. A flat-topped desk, spacious enough to be serviceable, but neither so large nor so severe of outline as to suggest the needs of a man's office, rather than those of a young girl's private sanctum, stood at one end of the room; on this desk was only one silver framed photograph—that of Moïse LaBranche, taken when he was in the prime of life. At the other end of the room, beside a half-opened door which gave a glimpse of a bedchamber beyond, was a gate-legged table, on which current magazines had been set to one side, in order to allow room for a well-laden tray. Vicky walked over to this and began pouring out bourbon.

"I know how you like your drink now," she said smiling. "And I'm sure you need one, coming straight from the mill. I've got sandwiches here, too—caviar, smoked turkey, ham. I wanted to give you a special treat, but I'm not so certain about your taste when it comes to things like that."

"The drink will sure go to the right spot. But I really don't need anything to eat, Vicky."

"You may, before you get your dinner—we're planning it rather late. And I was brought up on the theory that drink, like ink, needs a blotter."

"All right then—caviar. I'm not sure what a caviar sandwich is like, but I'll be glad to find out. Are you eating and drinking with me? And can't I help you get things ready?"

"I'll eat and drink with you, if it will make you feel any better. But it would make *me* feel better if you'd go and sit down over there and light a cigarette while you wait for me to join you."

Ordinarily, he would have protested; but he was at one and the same time too tired for argument, and too grateful for the rest and the refreshment which were offered him as if they were now his right, in this house. Vicky mixed his highball quickly and expertly, set it on a small round tray with a couple of caviar sandwiches, and brought it halfway across the room to him, setting it down on a small side table where he could conveniently serve himself. Then she returned to her source of supplies, mixed her own highball, and came back.

"What makes you try to talk until you've had your first drink?" she inquired. "You can start telling me things with your second. You'll feel better by then. Meanwhile, I think it's pleasant to sit here together, don't you?"

He could not tell her how pleasant, and again he realized he did not need to explain the way he felt, that somehow she knew it already. They had managed to establish a companionship so complete that it required no words to give it meaning at a time like this, no caresses to give it warmth. He quickly drained his glass of half its contents and gulped down one sandwich in short order. Then, already more relaxed, he began to drink slowly and to nibble at his second sandwich instead of devouring it. Vicky had thrown a cushion down in front of his chair, and had seated herself on it, leaning her head against his knees. She did not say anything at all, and she took only an occasional sip from the small glass she had provided for herself. When she saw that Prosper was almost ready for a refill, she rose, smiling but still without saying a word, and took his glass from him. On her return, she saw that he was smiling, too.

"This chair has nice broad arms," he said. "Couldn't you come and sit beside me now, and let me put one of *my* arms around you? I don't need both to handle this highball, and you don't seem to be doing much with yours anyway."

"I think that's a very sound suggestion."

She moved the cushion out of the way, dispensed with her drink altogether, and seated herself as he had indicated. The companionable silence continued until he had emptied his second glass. Then he set that down on the little table and stubbed out his cigarette.

"Are you comfortable where you are?" he inquired.

"Very."

"Would you be more comfortable or less, do you think, if you were sitting on my lap?"

"More."

He laughed. For twenty-four hours it had not seemed to him possible that he would ever laugh again. He drew Vicky onto his knees and she nestled against him as if she had always known this was the way and the place that she wanted to come to rest.

"I think I can talk quite rationally now," he said. "Perhaps a little less rationally and with more frequent interruption than if you were on the other side of the room. But I wouldn't have you go there on that account—or any other. Do you want to hear what's happened since I telephoned last night?"

"Yes, in substance. Then I'd like to talk about us."

"All right, I'll keep the news flashes brief."

Nevertheless, once started, he found the same sense of relief in speech that he had previously found in silence. The only items he omitted from his recital concerned Anne Marie; he could not bring himself to say anything about his sister which would be a reflection on her, even to Vicky. But he did tell her of Dale's help to the Dargereux, and of the former's departure from the Villacs' house, when it would have been to his advantage to stay. Then Prosper interrupted his narrative to make an observation.

"You ought to have fallen for Dale, instead of me."

"Much good it would have done! To all practical purposes, Dale doesn't know I exist! Anyhow, why?"

"Well, he's got everything you ought to have."

"You mean his father was an ambassador and his mother was an F.F.V. and he went to La Rosée and Princeton and has a huge gloomy house filled with antiques and ghosts—at least, I suppose his mother, being a Virginian, wouldn't have thought Cypremort was complete without just the right kind of a ghost. And I never saw a place where a whole flock of them ought to feel more at home!"

Prosper laughed again. "Those are some of the reasons—not the ghosts, but the rest of what you said."

"But, Prosper, I've known any number of ambassadors and F.F.V.'s and Princeton graduates! If that was all I was looking for, I'd have been married ages ago."

"No, I didn't think that was *all* you were looking for. But Dale has a lot more than that to offer."

"Maybe. To Anne Marie. And I might have given her a run for her money, if I'd been interested. But I was looking for someone like you. Go on with your story. What happened next?"

Feeling wonderfully encouraged and a little lightheaded, Prosper continued. He did not stop to make any more observations and Vicky did not interrupt him, either. At last he heaved a sigh.

"That's the gist of everything. Now what did you want to say about us?"

"You didn't make me any direct answer, last night, when I said I'd like to have our engagement announced publicly right away and that Father agreed it should be."

"Well. . . ." Prosper hesitated for a moment, but despite the fact that he had not committed himself to a promise about his course of action, neither had he neglected to think over his mother's advice, with increasingly favorable results. "I'd rather it weren't, until all this mess is cleared up," he said slowly, "but I suppose there's no real reason why it shouldn't be. I took you at your word and told the assembled family last night. So the news will be all over both Acadia and Lafayette parishes by this time anyway. I don't suppose it matters if it spreads farther, that being the case."

"All right. Then Father'll send the announcement to the *Advertiser* tomorrow. . . . And, of course, I'd like a ring. I don't mean because I want you to spend a lot of money on jewelry for me. I mean—well, you know that famous line in the Book of Common Prayer, don't you?— the one about 'an outward and visible sign of an inward and spiritual grace.'"

"I'm afraid I didn't know the line, but it's a good-sounding one and I'm very much touched that you think it applies in this case. Also, I'd like very much to give you a ring, and my credit must still be sufficiently good so that I can get you almost any kind, in reason, that you want, even if there isn't much money in the cash drawer. Have you thought what stone or stones you'd prefer?"

"Only that I'd like a circlet of some sort, what some people call a gypsy ring, not a solitaire. And colored stones, some anyway, rather than just diamonds."

"That shouldn't be too hard to manage. I might even get you one right here in Lafayette, if you want it straight off. I could get you another, handsomer, later on."

"I shan't want anything handsomer. I just want a present from you—a present that will show everyone what it means."

"All right, honey. I'll measure your finger and get you a ring tomorrow. I'll bring it with me the next time I come to see you. What else?"

"I'm afraid you're going to make more difficulties about the next thing. I'd like to get married right away."

He straightened up so suddenly that he dislodged her from her comfortable position. "In the midst of this mess!" he exclaimed, repeating the unpleasant word he had used before. "Why, honey, you must be crazy!"

"I'm in love. I suppose all people in love are more or less crazy. But I think I'm as sane as most."

"I don't, if you'd marry a man who's involved in a murder case! It's bad enough to admit you're engaged to a man like that. It's unthinkable that you should marry him."

"I don't see why. I should think it should go a long way to proving I know you're innocent."

"But you don't know anything of the sort!"

"Of course I do! Of course, I know what Father said yesterday is true—that you'll be called as a mere formality."

"Vicky, you're an angel, and all that, to have so much confidence in me, but—"

"It isn't so long ago you thought I was a perfect devil, just because I didn't like corn and watermelon and didn't know about Elks' wives and things like that."

"I never thought you were a devil. I'll admit that sometimes—"

"I made you so mad you couldn't see straight?"

"I've been a bad-tempered fool, I know that, honey, but I'm not so much of a fool that I'd let you—"

"I wish you'd lean back in your chair again, the way you did before—there, that's much better. But you needn't argue with me. You even got so mad about Levvy you couldn't see straight."

"By the way, where is Levvy? I've just realized I haven't seen her today."

"It's about time. Levvy has gone visiting at the fire department. I'm hoping the visit will be productive. I thought that this winter would be a fine time for her to have puppies. It hasn't been easy to plan for that, while we were wandering around from one place to another, but I never meant to have her a thwarted old maid, any more than I mean to be one myself."

"Vicky, you are the limit. You're not going to be a thwarted old maid simply because I won't let you marry a man who may be tried for murder."

"Oh, we've got as far as a trial now, have we? A few moments ago, we were just talking about being involved. I see I'll have to work fast. Well, I'm working as fast as I can. When I found you couldn't get here until late afternoon, I went to see the Bishop and—"

"Vicky, you didn't!"

"Yes, I did. Father went with me—he and the Bishop are old friends. He was just as nice as he could be—the Bishop, I mean, of course—Father's always just as nice as he can be. Father explained that I'd been baptized in the Church and he blamed himself because I'd never made my First Communion or been confirmed—he shouldn't, really, because it was all my mother's fault. Anyway, the Bishop said that as long as I'd been baptized and you were a practicing Catholic there wouldn't be any real difficulty. I could be married at home or in the Rectory any time. Of course, if I wanted to be married in the Cathedral, I'd have to wait until after I'd made my First Communion, and it would take about six weeks to arrange for that—I wouldn't have to wait to be confirmed, because the intention would be evident. So, if you're bound and determined to put me off, we'll wait six weeks and then we'll have a great big elaborate wedding and invite everybody. I'd enjoy that in a way. Most girls do. But I want so much to marry you that I'd be willing to give up all those extra trimmings. What do they amount to anyhow? What counts is being married! Darling, you don't know how much I wish you didn't have to go away, that you could stay here all night, so that before morning every bit of me would belong to you. Then no matter what happened afterward, they couldn't take that away from me. I'd be your wife. I might even have your child!"

Suddenly she buried her face on his shoulder. He was not sure, but he thought she was crying, not senselessly or hysterically, but as quietly as possible, from the very depths of pent-up and profound emotion. He was too shaken himself to answer her, just as earlier he had been too much touched to do so; but again, he realized she did not need or expect an answer, that she had poured out her heart to him in the belief that he would understand and that, having done so, she would presently be relieved from stress and strain. As soon as that happened, she would face him again with a confident smile. Meantime, he sat very still, holding her close and, presently, he began to murmur words of endearment that he had never uttered or wanted to utter before. He could not even be sure that she heard him, but that did not matter, either. What mattered was that his moving lips were against her soft dark hair and that she was in his arms.

Chapter Fifteen

HOW LONG AFTERWARD LEVVY CAME BOUNDING INTO THE ROOM, NEITHER
Prosper nor Vicky knew. Except for the light that came streaming
through the open door, leading into the upper hallway, the sitting room
had long been in darkness. The great dog rushed straight toward the armchair where her mistress was ensconced and, leaping up, tried to lick the
hidden face, meanwhile making sounds of mingled uneasiness and affection. Vicky sat up and shook back her tumbled curls.

"It's all right, Levvy," she said soothingly. "Lie down!" And, as the dog
did not immediately obey, she repeated the order, more emphatically.
"You see!" she went on, turning to Prosper, "Levvy's in such high spirits,
she won't listen to me. And, as you know, she's generally docile as a
lamb. . . . If you want to see me in high spirits, instead of having me sob
on your shoulder—"

"Oh, for God's sake, Vicky! Don't start joking about this again. It's—
it's a serious situation. And as for having you sob on my shoulder—well,
that was the grandest thing that ever happened to me, coming on top of
what you'd just said. I'll never forget it as long as I live. But it won't
make me change my mind."

"Something will," Vicky retorted, still speaking lightly. "Something
will make you forget those damn scruples of yours." She slid from
Prosper's knees and stood in front of him, straightening out her dress.
"Meanwhile, it must be long past dinnertime. I suppose we ought to go
down and see Father. We've left him alone for hours."

"I beg pardon, Miss Vicky. Mr. LaBranche isn't alone and he said I
wasn't to disturb you, but that if you did send for me to say that you
were not to feel hurried on his account, because he had congenial com-

pany. You didn't send for me, to be sure, and I'm sorry Levvy got away from me. But you know how it is—when she's separated from you for any length of time, it's hard holding her back."

The speaker was standing on the threshold and, as Vicky snapped on the nearest light, Prosper saw a solidly built, elderly woman, whose large, steel-rimmed spectacles overshadowed, but could not obscure, the ruddiness of her face or its cheerful and affectionate expression. Her gray hair, parted in the middle, had the crisp look of natural waves that had been arbitrarily smoothed down, and the same attempt at severity had obviously been made in respect to her clothes. The high collar of her white blouse parted to disclose a small neat black bow, and a starched white apron almost concealed the plain black skirt which came nearly to her ankles. As Prosper rose, a little stiff from sitting so long in the same position, Vicky took his hand and led him in the direction of the doorway.

"It's high time you two knew each other," she said happily, "in fact, it's long past time. Nannie, this is Mr. Prosper Villac—my fiancé. I'm sure you've heard Gifford and other members of the staff talking about him. Prosper, this is Mrs. Sarah Donovan, mostly called Donovan. She was my nurse when I was little, so she's still Nannie to me, and I think that's what she'd like to have you call her. She was the best nurse any naughty child ever had. Now she runs the house for me and still tries to run me. You know from personal experience that no one has had very good luck trying to do that. I know she's been vainly wishing, for ages, that she could come through here so that she could draw my bath and then get me into clothes that she considers suitable for dinner. I think she's been very forbearing, don't you? Suppose we give her a break! She'll turn you over to Gifford and I'll join you downstairs in a few minutes— well, maybe not a few, but twenty anyway."

Donovan came forward, hugged Vicky hard and kissed her resoundingly, first on one cheek and then on the other. "You know I'm wishing you every happiness in the world, lovey," she said heartily. Then she turned toward Prosper and bobbed. "You've got yourself a prize, I don't need to tell you that, sir," she said, with equal heartiness. "It's a long time I've been hoping to have a chance to say so to your face. But my duties don't take me much in the part of the house where you've been up to now. That is, of course I go through all the downstairs rooms the first thing after breakfast, to make sure the maids didn't overlook anything they ought to have done—they're well-meaning girls, you understand, sir, but they're all young and some haven't had much experience before. After I'm sure everything's tidy, I go over menus with Chef, while I wait around until Miss Vicky rings for her breakfast tray. Levvy's right there with me, listening for that bell, too. Do you know, sir, I've never known this dog to make a mistake? There's half a dozen bells in the house and some of the maids can't tell them apart to this day. But Levvy knows which is Miss Vicky's and she doesn't stir from my side till she hears it, and goes off with a bound, though it might be almost ten o'clock before—"

"Go on, Nannie, don't give me a bad name with Mr. Villac! If he thinks I'm such a sleepyhead as all that, he might get the idea I wouldn't make a good wife for a man who's at his rice mill by seven every morning. And we mustn't brag too much about Levvy. Of course, we know she's the most wonderful dog in the world, but he doesn't appreciate her."

"I'll warrant there's nothing I could say, or anyone else, would make him feel you wouldn't be the best wife in the world for him, Miss Vicky. And if he doesn't know yet that Levvy's the most wonderful dog in the world, the day'll come yet when he will, you mark my words. So stop your chatter for now. . . . If you'll come with me, Mr. Prosper, I'll have you shown where you can get yourself a good wash and then I'll be back to this bad baby of mine."

Ten minutes later, Prosper, having been duly turned over to Gifford, who still regarded him with almost as much condescension as on the occasion of the former's first visit, entered the library to find Moïse—immaculate in dinner jacket and gleaming shirt front—deep in conversation with "Bedon" Martin, whose tall hat, from which he derived his nickname, lay on the table beside him and who was clad in formal dress. This costume, unlike his host's, had nothing to do with any compulsion toward changing for the evening, and neither was it immaculate; it was his habitual garb, worn morning, noon and night, and, as the same outfit had served him for many years, it had inevitably long since begun to show signs not only of wear and tear, but of soil. It was not perhaps the original, which he had sold all his other clothes to buy, long before, in order to appear clad like his classmates at Johns Hopkins for their graduation; even so, it bore so close a resemblance to the one which he regarded as responsible for much of his subsequent success that he had never worn anything different. While he was on his way home from Baltimore, there had been an attempt at robbery in the train, and Georges Armand Martin had been the "hero" who prevented the holdup. Several newspapers had printed an account of this daring deed, together with

Martin's picture complete in Prince Albert and high hat. When he reached his native Breaux Bridge, after his long absence, he was primarily recognized as "the doctor who had caught the robber"; and since, as a young physician just out of college, he needed all the recognition he could get, he decided to remain faithful to his representation in the paper. In some communities, this might have caused him to be unfavorably labeled as an eccentric; where he lived and practiced, it added to his prestige and his popularity; and when he ceased to devote much time to medicine, in order to devote more to politics, he maintained that politicians, like doctors, needed to be easily identified. If there were ever any dispute on this score, he had stilled it; he had long been a successful officeholder, serving several times in the state legislature, and was now city judge in Lafayette.

Like everyone else in the vicinity, Prosper knew the judge, Dr. Bedon Martin, as well as he knew the mayor, Captain Bob Mouton, and held him in the same affectionate, if somewhat amused, regard. Ordinarily, he would have been as delighted to see the one as the other. Just now, he would have much preferred to see Captain Bob. True, the mayor, not infrequently, made lighthearted references to *"la chair, la chair"* in referring to those peccadilloes of his own which he confessed with unfailing regularity and, under different circumstances, might well have made some reference to the fleshly attributes which had given *la pauvre* Titine such irresistible allure; but Prosper knew he would not have done so now. Captain Bob was kind and tactful and essentially religious; he would have been sensitive to the fact that any kind of a jest on this subject would be ill timed, and would have confined his comments largely to civic improvements and to camellias. Prosper was less easy in his mind about the topics Bedon might have chosen. Of course, as city judge, he had no association with and no power in the district court; but he and Moïse might very well have been discussing Titine's death from legal angles, and the thought of this made Prosper uncomfortable. He was immensely relieved when Martin rose with alacrity and shook him warmly by the hand.

"My old friend Moïse here has been telling me some very good news about you, Prosper," he said cordially. "You're greatly to be congratulated. Of course, I'm aware there's some bad news which concerns you closely, too. But the good news affects you much *more* closely. Don't forget that."

"I'll try not to, Judge."

"Try not to? What do you mean, *try?* Look here, I know what kind of stock you come from. You mustn't be the maverick of the herd, as one of our distinguished statesmen said about an equally distinguished cousin of his with whom he happened to disagree politically. I want your assurance that you won't forget."

"All right, Judge. You've got it."

Martin picked up his tall hat and Moïse stirred in his chair, reaching for his cane. "You're sure you won't change your mind and stay for dinner with us, Bedon?"

"For *dinner*? At this hour? I had mine long ago! But thanks for the invitation, Moïse, just the same, and for the good visit we've had. Don't you forget, either."

The two older men exchanged meaning glances, but there was no explanation of what Moïse ought not to forget. "Couldn't I take you home, Judge?" Prosper asked. "Or have you your car?"

"No, you can't take me home and I don't have my car. I have my horse and buggy. From the clouds, I thought a storm might be blowing up, and you know I don't ever use an automobile in bad weather. What's more, I have my own way of using a hitching post. No offense, my boy. I'm obliged to you, just as I am to Moïse for his dinner invitation, and decline it in the same spirit."

"At least let me go to the door with you."

"Why yes, I'll let you do that. I'd rather have you than Gifford and I see Moïse is just getting ready to ring for that Admirable Crichton."

The visit closed on a note that was friendly all around. Prosper stood in the open doorway, watching the judge as the latter plodded down the drive toward the old hitching post, his coattails swaying slightly behind his tall slim figure, the long locks of his white hair visible beneath his high hat. The grandfather's clock in the corner of the library was chiming as Prosper re-entered, and Moïse waited until after it had struck nine before saying anything. Then he spoke more forcefully than was his habit.

"Dinner won't be announced until I ring, and I think we can be sure of a quarter hour to ourselves before Vicky comes down. In fact, I've given orders to Donovan about delaying her a little, which I believe will be understood by them both. I've given you a chance for an undisturbed talk with my daughter. Now I want my chance."

Again, Prosper felt uncomfortable, as he had when he first caught sight of Judge Martin; but though this time his anxiety was not assuaged, neither did it take the turn he expected.

"My old friend the judge doesn't meddle much with medicine any more," Moïse said. "He's too busy with his affairs of state . . . you know about the only time he was ever beaten when he ran for office, don't you?"

"I think so, sir. He advanced two hundred dollars toward campaign expenses to a 'coming young fellow,' didn't he, because he was tired of not having any opposition? Then this coming young fellow up and got elected mayor! That's the story, isn't it?"

"Yes, and I guess it's true, for Martin told it to me himself again to-day. 'I'll never pay another man's expenses to have him beat me,' he said, roaring with laughter and slapping his knee, as if it were the greatest joke in the world. . . . Well, that isn't what I started out to tell you, and I must be getting garrulous in my old age, or I'd have come to the point faster—especially when I know I've got to talk against time. As I said, and as you doubtless knew anyway, Bedon doesn't meddle much with medical matters any more. Everyone thinks of him as Judge Martin instead of Dr. Martin, and if he hadn't gone broke in Baltimore and figured in a train robbery when he didn't have a thing in his pockets but his ticket home, he wouldn't have attracted much attention either way. But he's a mighty sound physician just the same and, every now and then, for old time's sake, he'll visit a former patient or a good friend. He was here today because I'm both. I asked him to come and have a look at me. I wanted to find out whether he'd say the same thing that all these specialists, with their newfangled methods and notions, have been telling me. Well, he did."

"I knew you weren't well, sir, but I didn't realize the trouble was serious. I hope—"

"It is serious. Vicky doesn't know that, either—she must think Bedon's visit was purely social. But I've had several slight heart attacks and one that wasn't so slight. It was that one which decided me I'd better come home. Because Lafayette *is* my home. All the other places have been just way stations. But this is the place where I was born and the place where I want to die."

"Some time! Not for a long while!"

"Some time, yes. And that some time might be almost any time now, my boy."

Prosper tried to find an adequate answer, and discovered that he was only muttering incoherent sentences, compounded almost equally of genuine concern and genuine affection. Moïse held up his hand.

"That's all right. I know how you feel without your saying so. At least,

I know how you feel about *me* under the conditions I've just outlined. I don't believe you've considered how they'd affect Vicky."

"No, I haven't. I'm not quite sure—"

"You're not quite sure what I mean? Well, that doesn't surprise me. There's no reason why you should have tried to figure it out. But I'll explain. If I should die—that is to say, when I die—she'll be very much alone. She won't go back to her mother—there's a breach that'll never be closed again. If she were still fancy free, she might return to the nearest relatives we have—the Zweigs in Alsace-Lorraine. They've been very good to her, they're very fond of her and she's very fond of them. But Vicky's head over heels in love with you and you're in trouble; nothing on earth would persuade her to leave Lafayette."

"Yes, I reckon that's so," Prosper murmured, vividly recalling the recent scene in Vicky's sitting room.

"I think you met her old nurse today for the first time—Sarah Donovan. A very respectable, very trustworthy, very efficient woman and devoted to Vicky. She can hardly be classed as a servant, in the usual sense of the word. But, after all, that's what she is. She'll have enormous responsibility when I die—and practically no authority. Legally, Vicky's of age. She hasn't any guardian but me. Her fortune isn't tied up in any trust fund. What's a good deal more to the point, she hasn't a watchdog. Oh, yes, in the literal sense, and Levvy's a good one. But this is a case for a watchdog in the figurative sense, which happens to be much more important, under the circumstances. She needs a man in the house—a man who has authority as well as responsibility—a man who loves her as much as she loves him. In other words, she needs you, Prosper."

"But—" he began and stopped.

"I'll be completely candid. Perhaps you'll think I'm being brutally frank, though I don't mean to be. However, this is a time for plain speaking. I wouldn't have chosen you for a son-in-law, even before the present scandal arose. I won't go into all the reasons. Some of them you'd probably guess anyway and some of them don't matter greatly. But I knew Vicky had chosen you and, whether you believe it or not, she's a one-man girl. There are such girls. In fact—" He stopped short and Prosper had the impression that Moïse had caught himself just in time to prevent saying something he would have regretted. "I preferred to abide by her choice, rather than to have her marry the wrong man—I mean, the wrong man *for her*," Moïse went on. "She believes with all her heart and soul that you are the right man for her. Hence you are. Since this is so, I cannot too strongly second what I know Vicky has said to you herself:

don't delay your marriage to her. The engagement will be announced tomorrow. Marry her here in this house, quietly, as soon thereafter as you can arrange to do so. Let me have the privilege of giving my only daughter in marriage."

Not allowing Prosper time to frame an answer, Moïse struggled to his feet and touched a bell. With an immediacy which suggested that Vicky, as well as Gifford, had been listening for it, she came into the room. There was a freshness and a fragrance about her which suggested that she had, indeed, stepped from a scented bath only a few minutes before; her dark hair was still damp around her temples and, this time, she had tied it back with a white ribbon. She had discarded her tumbled dress for another, and the one she had on now was made of white lace; it floated softly around her in cloudlike folds. She came over and stood between the two men, looking attentively first at one and then the other. But it was to Prosper that she spoke.

"I believe something has happened already to make you change your mind," she said joyfully.

Moïse did not permit Dr. Martin's verdict, of which Vicky was still unaware, to cast a gloom over the rest of the evening. Plans had already been made to have a festive little dinner, at which the finest porcelain and crystal should be used and vintage champagne served; although there were only three at table, it had the gala effect of a party given to celebrate *fiançailles*. Later that week, Moïse said, they must have a real party—Prosper's mother and sister, his grandmother and grandfather and great-grandfather and as many of his Villac and Primeaux cousins as he'd like to invite.

"You don't know what you're saying, sir," Prosper replied, grinning in spite of himself.

"I have an idea, and they'd all be very welcome. But if you like, we'll wait and ask them to the wedding and confine this next dinner to the immediate family. Perhaps that would be better. What do you think, Vicky?"

Vicky thought perhaps it would. They discussed these and other plans, but not for long. Moïse confessed to fatigue and, though he did not admit it, Prosper found that he was practically dead on his feet. There was no lack of ardor in the way he said good night, but, for all that, his farewells were not prolonged; and it was with a sense of relief that he found, when he reached home that, except for the lights at the rear entrance, in the hallway and on his bedside table, the house was in complete darkness. That meant that his mother and Anne Marie and the various visiting relatives must already have gone to their rooms. There would be no more explanations, no more arguments, no more disclosures, no more emotional upheavals that night.

A note from Anne Marie was pinned to his pillow. She had gone to a slumber party and would not be back until breakfast time, if then. Mother was not coming back from the farm and neither were Uncle Onezime and Uncle Odey. Titine Dargereux had been buried at Cousin Clement's that afternoon and there had been a terrible scene at the funeral. Everyone there was still very much upset, and all sorts of new wild rumors were flying around. It was just as well Prosper had been in Lafayette and had known nothing about this.

Chapter Sixteen

CLEMENT PRIMEAUX, STANDING WELL BELOW GROUND LEVEL IN THE excavation he was working to deepen still further, looked up from his labors, seeking to read the portent of the low scud of clouds fleeing northward. Sometimes the breezes, blowing steadily from the south across the prairie, where there was no windbreak, not only marshaled legions of such small clouds, but presaged hurricanes. This possibility was by no means to be discounted at the end of a long hot summer, like the one just drawing to a close. When it happened, it brought destruction to everything in its path, as it had when it ripped into splinters the crosses which marked the graves of his little brothers and sisters, and scattered the fragments far and wide. However, Clement felt confident there would be no such devastating storm today; every now and then the fleeing clouds revealed ragged patches of clear blue, through which areas of sunlight streamed to the ground. Probably there would not even be rain—just wind, rippling the crops which were still standing, but not shattering the bearded heads of the rice in the golden fields as yet unharvested. Reassured, he bent again to his task, the blade of his ditching shovel, bright from use, flashing as he stopped every now and then to smooth the rectangular sides of the low wall with which he was surrounded. When he resumed his digging, he deepened, with each powerful downward thrust of the blade, the grave he was preparing for Titine Dargereux.

Once he paused to refresh himself from a vacuum bottle of strong, highly sugared black coffee, pouring it into the metal top which served as a cup, and sipping it gratefully. While he stood resting after this draft, he noticed the hurtling approach of an automobile on the road from

Crowley—a road whose straight course along the meridian was broken only by sharp right and left jogs at township lines, as these narrowed to allow for an eventual meeting of all meridians at the poles. The speeding speck grew and took recognizable form as one of the Benoits' blue Reo Flying Clouds. With a wrench that made the tires scream as they scraped over the graveled roadbed, the car careened in at the Primeaux cattle gap and came to a halt in the lane where the driver, dismounting, became recognizable as Maurice Benoit. Clement regarded the visitor with dispassionate gravity, neither welcoming nor forbidding.

"I think, me," he observed, "this could be the very firs' time I see you drivin' like hell without you be racing, yes, with you' brother Didier, him. Nothin' ain't wrong, maybe?"

"No. I just found out how you'd offered to have Titine buried in your family plot here. You ask me, it's a lot of jibber-jabber, this business of saying she hasn't been to confession and didn't have the last rites and so on. How could she have the last rites when she was murdered? Anyway, the poor kid's dead, and God help the son of a bitch that killed her. But in the meantime, I came out to help, if there's anything you want me to do, or anything I can do."

"Tha's surely good of you, yes," Clement replied quietly, "but there ain't nothin' to do outside of dig, an' I guarantee you, me, I can do it faster as you, an' two people in a place like this just gets in each other's way. You wouldn't know, maybe, when they comin' out yuh with the—the—coffin, them, *hein?*"

"No, but it won't be too long," Maurice said. "They still have to polish a lot of brass, with Dr. Davila filling out papers sixty to the acre, and making those two Dargereux—neither one of them with sense enough to figure out how much twice two is, unless somebody gives them the answer—sign statements that the body can be exhumed if it has to be for the trial, and all that."

"You got maybe an ide-yuh, no, how many's comin' out?"

"No way of telling. Of course there'll be the hearse; Toler said they could use that and he'd even furnish the driver without charging Dale Fontenot for it. Dale paid for the coffin and the embalming, you know. Scholtze went to Toler's as soon as he had been released on bond and offered to do that; but Dale had got ahead of him, and that made Scholtze madder than he was already, if such a thing's possible. Today's hearing was adjourned after nobody but Paula Bennett had been questioned, so I'm reasonably sure the Professor's coming out. In fact, I understand he as good as dared Theo Landry to keep him at the court-house."

"I expec', me, I better make plenny-plenny hurry then," said Clement, putting up his vacuum bottle. "I got no other cup out yuh, Mist' Benoit, no, or you could have some of this coffee; but you go by the kitchen, my wife Laurelle got coffee ready. At leas', I tol' her to keep on drippin' it till she got plenny-plenny more'n enough, her, by I didn't know how many was comin' out. She got *cush-cush et caillé* an' biscuits an' syrup, too, so if you' hungry, just help you'self while I keep goin', me. Maybe by this time, Laurelle got extra gumbo made, too, but she got nobody, no, for to help, not outside our li'l girl, Ad'line; an' that stuck-up sister of mine, Marcelite, ain't been near us, her, no, so I can tell you someone w'at ain't comin'—tha's Marcelite an' her husband. Her an' me don't see this yuh funeral with the same eyes, no. But I'll get along all right without no Marcelite, nor neither her husband. An' anyway, you' plenny welcome to w'at we got for to eat an' drink."

"Thanks a lot. Some coffee and a biscuit will taste mighty good. After I've had them, I'll duck over to the Winslow place and see if we can't rustle up some flowers there. I know they always have loads—I'm sure of coral vine and roses and zinnias anyway, and Mrs. Winslow might even have a few early camellias. She's a wizard when it comes to raising those. I'll be back with blossoms of some kind in no time."

Maurice took himself off, leaving Clement deep in thought as he continued to dig, placing the dirt taken from the excavation in neat mounds at the head and foot of the steadily deepening rectangle; in this way, he was assured that those who lowered the coffin, standing at the sides, would have level, dry footing and he took pride in the consciousness that he was providing this. At the same time, he could not help wondering why Maurice Benoit seemed so eager to make a public display of sympathy for a girl to whom he had never shown any consideration in her lifetime. This was especially astonishing to Clement, since Maurice's brother Didier was taking no part, public or private, in seeing that some decent show of dignity attended the burial. The night before, he had let Dale Fontenot leave the Villacs' house without making any offer of assistance; indeed, Clement had been given the impression that Didier took an unseemly advantage of Dale's departure and Anne Marie's apparent resentment, to press his own suit. To be sure, Maurice had not been among those present at the time, and though he had once been among Anne Marie's many suitors, Victorine LaBranche had attracted his attention almost immediately after her arrival in Lafayette and, since then, Maurice had not interfered materially with Didier's courtship. Yet the Benoit brothers were keen rivals in practically everything else and always had been. Their father had been obliged to give each of them identical automobiles; disputes over whose turn it was to drive, or to use a single extra car on a given night, would otherwise have led to blows. Ordinarily, they drove from point to point, at breakneck speed, racing one another. Throughout the autumn, each pitted his bird dog against the other's in a sort of two-man field trial. It was even said that, during the war years, their commanding officer had been forced to ground them, and finally to assign them to separate air service commands, since otherwise each would try to outdo the other in aerobatics. And now, abruptly, one was making a show of readiness to be of assistance to the afflicted, while the other was holding himself just as ostentatiously aloof. Why?

Clement was still asking himself this question, when he became aware that another car had turned from the highway into the lane and was approaching the house. It was moving at a moderate rate of speed, but without halting, which suggested that its driver knew the lay of the land. Though he was temporarily lost to sight as he passed on the farther side of the orange grove, even the first brief glimpse had given Clement the feeling that there was something familiar about him. The feeling was intensified when he heard the newcomer's voice, responding to cries of welcome from Laurelle, Adeline and Happy, the youngest member of the family, who had been named for his dead uncle, Felix; and, a few minutes later, Clement recognized his cousin Onezime Villac, as the priest from the Delta came through the trees and opened the gate of the little cemetery. Clement threw down his shovel and hastened forward.

"How I am glad to see you, me, yes!" he exclaimed, gripping his cousin's hand hard. "I never had no ide-yuh you could be comin'!"

"I never thought of anything else from the moment Lavinia telephoned, yesterday. I got hold of Father Gubler at Barataria and started asking him to take over for me; before I'd finished the first sentence, he interrupted to say that of course he would. Then I drove straight to Baton Rouge, and when I got to Odey's, I found he'd already got someone to substitute for him in his classes. I spent the night at his house, and then he and I hit the road for Crowley together, as soon as I'd said Mass this morning. I haven't seen Prosper or talked with him yet—Lavinia seemed to think it might be just as well if I didn't, until tomorrow; he's having all kinds of trouble at the Claudia and there were pressing reasons why he needed to get off for Lafayette. But Lavinia came straight over to the house from the Monrovia, as soon as I telephoned, and she had rooms all readied up for company and a good hot meal just waiting to be dished out. You can count on her every time."

"You got it in you' min', then, how she is pretty sho', her, to come out yuh today?"

"Of course. She and Annette will be along a little later, with Odey. As far as my other sisters and my other brother are concerned, Odile and Pauline haven't had time to get here, but they both telephoned, and we've even heard from Olin, for the first time in years. Annette's husband is away at some bankers' convention, so he can't come, but Annette said to tell Laurelle she'd be on hand to help, as soon as she'd made sure there was someone to stay with the children when they got home from school. Mrs. Winslow's coming to help, too—she's been baking pies all the morning, and she sent some over by me—I stopped at the Winslows' first, because I thought maybe I could do some such errand along the way. Young Benoit had just got there, asking for flowers. How does he come in on this, anyway?"

"Tha's the extactlies' thing I been askin' my own self, me. I got to admit, yes, how him an' Prosper been good-good frien's for the longes', an' maybe he got it in his min' how this yuh is the right time to show it, so everybody, them, can see plain. Just the same, I tell you frankly, me, it ain't like he's in the fam'ly, him, an' standin' by his blood relations the way you an' me an' Odey is doin'."

"Well, I suppose it doesn't matter what his motives are, does it? Anyway, he needn't have bothered about the Winslows' flowers. They were already being loaded into a truck, enough to decorate the *salle* and cover the coffin, and Mr. Winslow and Mr. Garland are bringing them over. I suggested they go to the house first. I wanted to have a chance to talk to you alone if I could."

"You go right ahead, Onezime, and say w'at you want."

"Well, it's this way, Clement. Of course, I wanted to stand by Prosper, just as any member of the family would, when he's in trouble. But that isn't the only reason I almost broke my neck to get here quickly." Onezime paused and looked across the open grave which Clement had not quite finished digging, toward the tombstone on the grave beyond it. "You know that when Fleex died, I didn't come," he said in a low voice. "And I've always been sorry—sorry because I didn't help you and *Nonc,* when you were grief stricken, and sorry I didn't stand up for Fleex, whatever he'd done. After all, we were raised together, and he was a lot more like my brother than my cousin. But then Claude was *really* my brother and Fleex had killed him before he killed himself . . . oh, I know—" he went on hastily, aware of an attempt at angry interruption, "it was an accident, a terrible accident. But just the same, it had happened. And I was a young priest then—young and intolerant. Even if it hadn't been for the rule of the Church about suicide, I'd have felt—"

"Titine Dargereux wasn't no suicide, her," Clement said harshly, "an' just the same, the Church—"

"I know, I know. The rulings of the Church must seem unduly severe sometimes to laymen, but I must ask you to believe that there's a reason for every one of them, though we can't take time to go into those now. What I started to say was, I've learned to have a good deal more tolerance toward sinners, whatever their sin was, than I had when I was younger. And when I found I'd be permitted to say a few short prayers at the services here, I wanted to do it more than I've wanted to do anything since I can remember. I felt in a way it would make up for what I didn't do—what I couldn't do—for Fleex."

"Not nobody ain't never goin' make up to me, no, for all w'at happen' when Fleex died," Clement said, still harshly. Then he added, with less brusqueness, "But at leas' I got to admit it was real-real kin' for you to come yuh, an' I put my hand on the book, me, Lavinia feels the same, an' Prosper, too, when he hears how you done come. I'm too-too glad, me, yes, you with us, Onezime; that I would swear to, on my dead papa and mama's grave, I would swear to it. Yes, an' I'm plenny glad Mi'z Winslow comin', an' also Annette, her, not just for to help Laurelle with all she got to do, but to help that po' Mi'z Dargereux, too. . . . *Bien!* Now you done had you' say, an' I done had mine, yes? So you better go up by my house. The women mus' be needin' a man to at leas' watch, I bet you. Me—I'll be comin', too, so soon like I get this yuh finished right."

He watched his cousin out of sight and went to work again. Fifteen minutes later, placing his hands on the turf at the grave's side—the broad, calloused hands with short blunt fingers—Clement muscled himself out of the excavation. It was finished. There should be time before the cortege arrived for him to clean up and don his best suit and uncomfortable shiny shoes, much as he and his father had done before they lowered the coffin that held Fleex's body into the newly made grave close by the one he had just dug for Titine.

When Clement reached the house, there were two more cars in the yard besides the truck which had brought the flowers that Mrs. Winslow was now arranging in the *salle*. Lavinia and Annette had brought flowers, too, she told him, although—and there was a touch of pardonable pride in her pleasant voice as she said it—neither of them had quite as many to bring as she did. Onezime and Odey had both offered to go to the cemetery with her to finish the arrangements. Lavinia and Annette were helping Laurelle in the kitchen. Everything was under control. And, oh, yes—Maurice Benoit was back, and Grandfather Jim had suggested that he and Brent and Maurice should go with Adeline and Happy, whose clothes had already been changed, to look at the colts. She supposed that the children would have to see something of the funeral. But she thought perhaps the less, the better.

Clement nodded and went into the big bedroom which, like the adjoining *salle,* had its own front door. When he came out, dressed in his best clothes, the others were already on the gallery and the pitifully small cortege was just entering the yard. Directly behind the hearse was Dale Fontenot's handsome Packard, with Dale driving, and Michel and Clarie Dargereux, both still in a daze, but both decently clad in black, in the back seat. After that, came Bennett's shrieval Ford, in which the Professor was, somewhat surprisingly, riding beside Tobe; and, bringing up the rear, another Ford whose occupants Clement did not immediately recognize. Then he realized that one of them was Baer Scholtze, whom he had seen the night before in the group of witnesses waiting to be called before the coroner and the district attorney while August Scholtze was being interrogated, and whom Dale Fontenot had identified for him. It was therefore not difficult to decide that the driver, beside whom Baer was seated, must be August Scholtze. Clement's heavy brows instantly drew down in a scowl and, a moment later, to the stupefaction of everyone in sight, he had gone stamping off the gallery and striding to the rear of the cortege.

"W'at you doin' yuh on this place, *hein?*" he demanded truculently.

"Ain't this here where the funeral is going to be at?" asked Scholtze, his tone matching Clement's in belligerency. "I am here because I feel for attending the funeral. The girl she works for me."

"I already hear, me, w'at that young girl does fo' you, yes," replied Clement, in mounting rage. "An' I guarantee you, nobody who got on his conscience w'at you boun' to have is goin' make good character, no, by showin' off how he comes to this funeral. So I tell you plain, me, get out. I mean right now you got to get out."

"What the hell itches you, *Dummian?* Everybody should feel for showing respect for the dead. So have sense already. I don't know what crazy idea you got in the foolish head yet, but nobody ain't asked you you should invite me by the house. I brought some flowers and want to stand by the grave from a girl what works for me since more as two years." He nodded to the otherwise unoccupied back of the tonneau, where a cross of white tuberoses and carnations fastened to a moss-stuffed framework of wire had been laid.

"You get you' goddam' car an' you' goddam' flowers away from yuh, you hear me, yes?" grated Clement. "This ain't no public *cimetière*, no, like you makin' out, no, not fo' one small-small minute. This yuh's my proppity, an' I tell you once mo', me, an' for the las' time, you got to get off my proppity."

"But for Sweet Christ, why?"

"It ain't no law fo' me to tell nobody, no, why they got to get off my proppity. But if you so goddam' anxious to know, it's biccoz I think, me, from all w'at I hear, if anyone kill that po' young girl, it would be you. So all you tryin' to do, I expec', is make like you got only kin' ideas 'bout her, an' maybe stand by the grave an' let people see you cry, cry, cry fo' the sorrow in you' rotten heart!"

Furious, Scholtze turned toward the boy beside him.

"Get out, *Dummkopf*," he snapped. "Get out so I could get out, too, and show *Herr* Loud-talker a good lesson yet." When Baer made no move to comply, Scholtze, whose old model touring car had no door in the driver's side, wrenched his big body from under the wheel to climb over the solid panel.

"Don't do it, *Onkel*," he urged. "Look!" He pointed to the priest who, in his turn, had left the gallery and was now approaching Scholtze's car.

"What the hell I care how many priests they got?" Scholtze said through clenched teeth, struggling to free his big body from its confinement. "It ain't no cop-cop gonna say I kill Titine, not when he's got standing on his gallery a bastard what's been running around with her till it's a scandal for the snakes already. Benoit is good enough to invite, but me, August Scholtze, I ain't. Wait! I show you who is good enough, cop-cop!"

"But he got a right to make you get off his land, *Onkel*," protested Baer, as Onezime stood quietly beside them, waiting for the right moment in which to speak a soothing word. "I know you never kill nobody already. But if you go for trespass and hit him when he says git off from his land, they throw you on the jailhouse sure and maybe yet send you by Angola."

Slowly, grudgingly, Scholtze squirmed his big body back into position behind the wheel. "Get out *und* crank the handle, Baer," he said.

"We go." He turned to face the still glowering Clement and the quiet priest. "But I don't go on account I feel for being afraid of no cop-cop, *verstehst?* You *und* the Army couldn't to scare me into running off." The motor sputtered into life as Baer expertly spun the crank handle, and August raised his voice to make sure his words were audible. "It's got something else I tell you, *auch.* I go just on the outside of your gate on the public road. I stay there, too. *Und* if *there* you feel for making me move on, *Kleiner, there* you will find me."

He shifted the gear pedals expertly with his feet, reversed, spun into the opposite direction, fragments of crushed shell spurting sideways from beneath his tires, and guided his vehicle on its asthmatic course out to the highway. There he drew up by the side of the road, just outside the gate, switched off the ignition and watched to see what would happen next. Clement, with Onezime, still completely calm, at his side, turned back toward the gallery where everyone else was still waiting.

"Who we got fo' pallbearers, us, outside of me an' Odey?" asked Clement. Maurice and Dale both raised their hands in a gesture of acceptance. "Tha's two mo'," Clement noted. "Mist' Fontenot an' Mist' Benoit. Now we got to have two mo'."

Sheriff Bennett stepped forward. "If you'll let me, I'll consider it a privilege to be of service. I'm not a Catholic, but I understand this is not a strictly formal burial service. . . ."

"Thanks, Mist' Tobe," replied Clement. "An' I guess it's no use askin' Mist'—" He paused uncertainly.

"They call me Professor," explained that individual. "No, I'm very much afraid I'll have to say no. It's not the sort of service one is happy to render in any case, but since I was Titine Dargereux's neighbor and friend, I, too, would consider it a privilege to render this final service to her mortal body. However, it's all I can do to stand without some sort of support. I twisted my ankle going down the courthouse steps, and didn't even wait to have it strapped up before coming out here."

"I know it mus' be hurtin' you plenny bad," Clement said, not unsympathetically. "An' Mist' Dargereux, him, he's the father, he got to be a mourner, yes, an' not no pallbearer." He glanced uncertainly at Brent Winslow. "I know good we got no right to ask some ol' gentlemens like you, to help carry the coffin, but it's only a few steps, an' we would appreciate it so much if—"

"Of course, I'll act as pallbearer," interrupted Winslow. "For a short distance, and with five such stalwart companions, I imagine I am still equal to the demands of the occasion."

The hearse driver pulled out the coffin, his practiced hands finding a hold beneath the end nearest the hearse door, until the first pair of handles came into view. Clement and Odey, ranging themselves alongside the casket, grasped these and moved forward until the middle handles could be reached. Tobe Bennett took hold of one, motioning Brent Winslow to take the other; this would be the one bearing least weight; Dale and Maurice took the last two handles and, lifting the burden clear, walked to the gallery steps, mounted them and thus proceeded to the *salle*. Directly behind them came the Dargereux, hand in hand, each clinging to the other as the sole familiar concept amid this bewildering concatenation of strange happenings. When the solemn little procession had reached its destination, the hearse driver opened the casket and stood respectfully to one side while Onezime sprinkled with holy water the body thus revealed. Then, as the Catholic participants in the gathering, led by the priest, began the recitation of the Rosary, the driver returned to his somber black vehicle, with its glossy plumes of carved wood, closed the door, mounted to his seat and started briskly back for Crowley, feeling that he had discharged his obligations. Meanwhile, Onezime, suppressing his lack of ease at officiating when not permitted to wear the vestments usual for such an occasion, proceeded with the solemn recital of the antiphon and *De Profundis*.

Brent Winslow had obviously been thankful to sink into one of the waiting chairs as soon as the coffin had been put in place. With chagrin, he recognized that he had been unequal to the effort he had just made. This was not only because of his advanced years; the sedentary life he had led, while making experiments to improve the quality of rice, instead of working in the fields, had taken heavy toll of his physical endurance. Holding a hand over his eyes, he did his best to hide from the others the rapidity of his shallow breathing; but this did not go unnoticed by Clement, who turned to Odey as soon as the prayers were ended and the Dargereux went forward to kiss their daughter's dead face, before the coffin was closed.

"We got to fin' us another pallbearer some place, us," he murmured. "The ol' gentleman hardly made it up to yuh, no, so how he's goin' carry the coffin over that ground through the yard an' to the other side of the orange trees, him? We got to wait a li'l minute, us." He looked toward the Professor, who shrugged helplessly.

"It would be no problem if only I had not met with this unhappy mischance. But with the best will in the world, I would prove a broken reed."

"Wait, now," Clement spoke up with sudden decision. "I got an ide-yuh, me. I be right back."

He hurried out and across the gallery to the gate, where the Scholtze car was still indomitably parked. August was standing beside it.

"Goot. This is *aussgezeichnet*, I bet you my life yet!" he exclaimed as Clement approached. "Here it got no trespass law neither, so if you got something to say, say it, *und* I take it from there. *Ganz gewiss* I take it from there."

"I got this to say, me, an' I hate like hell to say it, this I must tell you. We got only five people as could be pallbearers an' we need one more, yes, fo' to carry it from the house to the place where my people is buried, them."

"And so, after you order me off your property like I was a *Schwein-hund* of a hobo what asks for a handout, you got to come ask August Scholtze to help, *ja?*"

"No *ja*, never," Clement burst out. "You I still won't let on my prop-pity, not if the house is on fire an' you got the only water fo' to put it out. But the boy, the young boy, he could help; him I ask, me, will he help so a young girl has a decent *enterrement?*"

Eagerly, Baer moved to comply, but a sweep of August's thick arm sent him back against the car.

"Baer I don't allow to go," he announced with finality.

"*Aber Onkel, bitte doch!*"

"*Halt's Maul!*"

Clement puckered his lips and spat noisily into the roadway.

"It ain't no name fit to call you, now," he flung over his shoulder as he turned back toward the gate. "So you can put it on you' rotten con-science, fo' true, how you kept the young girl from havin' a pallbearer to carry the coffin, on top of everything else you done her. I got too much riss-peck fo' dogs, me, to call you son of a bitch."

"Hey wait, you," Scholtze called after him. "I make you one trade. To a *Schafskopf* like you I couldn't explain nothings, you already feel for having your mind made up, yet. So I do this: I let Baer go with you, but only if he can take my flowers and put them on the grave. I don't do no good to try to tell you why; you couldn't understand it."

For a moment Clement paused, considering.

"All right, so come, yes, an' bring the flower cross," he agreed.

Chapter Seventeen

PROSPER HAD TUMBLED INTO BED MONDAY NIGHT WITHOUT A THOUGHT about the fresh impetus which the press must, by this time, have given to the widespread excitement roused by Titine Dargereux's tragic death. The various items in Anne Marie's note had more than sufficed to increase his perturbation: the funeral, which had taken place at his cousin Clement's, had been the occasion of "a terrible scene"; Prosper's mother and Onezime and Odey must be staying overnight at the farm because "everyone was very much upset . . . all sorts of new wild rumors were flying around." Lavinia had said nothing about the funeral when Prosper had talked with her, over the telephone, the previous afternoon; he had not even known that the tentative plans for it had actually gone through, much less that his mother had attended. He could understand why she had done this: it was her way of showing the world that she did not consider there had been anything shameful about her only son's association with the dead girl, or that he was even remotely connected with Titine's untimely end. To a lesser but also to a very significant degree, it was her way of showing that she believed in the Cajun principles of solidarity and that, as her mother-in-law had emphasized, these held that a woman accepted her husband's relatives as her own and that he did the same with hers; therefore, since Clement Primeaux had taken a certain stand, Lavinia Villac would take it, too, or at least uphold him in it. Of course, similar motives had prompted the immediate appearance on the scene of Onezime and Odey; Onezime would have officiated at the funeral as a priest, Odey as a pallbearer. But who on earth—Prosper asked himself—would have created "a terrible scene" amid such unity of purpose and action? What were the "new wild rumors flying around," which the group of lighthearted young girls, foregathered for the festivities so erroneously labeled a slumber party, would doubtless discuss with avidity throughout most of the night?

Prosper did not sleep very much himself and, when he dropped off into fitful slumber, this was riddled with agitated dreams. At the first sign of dawn, he gave up the idea of getting any rest and, having showered and shaved, flung on his clothes and went down to the kitchen and made coffee for himself. Anxious as he was to learn more about what had happened at the Primeaux farm the day before, he was thankful that he still had the house to himself.

The telephone was still silent, the house still empty, except for himself, when he left for the mill. Paula was there before him and the Monday afternoon papers had already been laid neatly on his desk. He snatched up the Crowley *Signal* and took in the headlines at a glance:

TO SIFT DEATH OF
GIRL ENTERTAINER
AT THE CLAUDIA

Landry Promises Relentless Search for Slayer
of Swamp Singer Last
Saturday Night

Without reading any further, he tossed the *Signal* aside and picked up the Lafayette *Advertiser*:

SOCIALITE TO BE
QUIZZED ON DEATH
OF ENTERTAINER

Dist. Atty. Landry Promises
Sensational Development
in Probe

He threw down the second paper and called to Paula. "You've seen these, haven't you?" he inquired abruptly, as she came into the office, notebook in hand.

"Yes, of course."

"Is that all you have to say? Can't you tell me what you think of them?"

Paula pursed her lips slightly. "Well, I suppose they're only what we've got to expect. Of course, newspapers always go out of their way to be sensational; even when a publisher's friends are involved, it doesn't seem to make any difference. I do think, though, that the least the *Advertiser* could do would have been to say 'Socialites,' instead of 'Socialite.' "

"Why?"

"Well, Dale Fontenot certainly is a socialite. But I suppose the Benoits would be considered in that category, too, don't you?"

It had not occurred to Prosper that the reference could be to anyone except himself. Somewhat to his chagrin, he felt a wave of relief upon learning that Paula had interpreted the reference as applying only to Dale.

"Not that I ever thought Maurice and Didier really belonged there myself," Paula went on. "Especially, Maurice. And of course, after yesterday—"

"What do you mean, after yesterday?"

"Haven't you heard?"

"I sure haven't. What did he do?"

"He went out to your grandfather's place and then to your cousin's," Paula said primly. "He asked Mrs. Winslow for flowers. He offered to make himself useful in any way he could at the—the services. He even acted as a—as a pallbearer. Afterward, though, he made a holy show of himself. He went back to Lafayette and got drunk and babbled to everyone who would listen to him. Several of my friends who live there called me up and told me some of the things he'd said, but they're very coarse and I'd rather not repeat them to you, if you don't mind."

"No, I don't mind. I can hear them later. Anyway, I think I can guess what they were." So Maurice had made a great display of sympathy! He had not gone to Titine's funeral like Lavinia and Onezime and Odey, to bear witness to their faith in someone near and dear to them. He had gone with the idea that such an action on his part would indicate that he was in the clear and thereby cast more suspicion on others! Prosper felt reasonably sure that, as far as the family was concerned, this *beau geste* would be a boomerang. Whether the authorities would regard it in the same light was something else again. . . .

"According to Malvina Walton, Maurice has such a dreadful hangover that he can't come to the courthouse today," Paula was continuing. "At least, Didier says he's sick, but of course everyone knows what that really means. Probably he *is* sick, disgustingly sick. What's more, Mr. Benoit has been to Tobe and said he didn't see any reason why Maurice and Didier should be required to hang around in the courthouse, waiting to be called, when you're allowed to come to the Claudia as usual. Mr. Benoit says they're needed at Pecan Grove just as much as you're needed here. Of course, that isn't so. We're at the very height of the rice season and cane grinding doesn't begin for six weeks yet. Besides, you can get to the courthouse from the Claudia in five minutes, if they want you, and it takes the Benoits a good half hour or more, even driving the way they do, to get there from Pecan Grove. Tobe pointed all that out to Mr. Benoit. But he said Mr. Landry would excuse Maurice for today anyhow. I understand they're going to start in on the Professor, in just a few minutes now. In fact, I think they may have already begun. They wanted to get under way earlier than usual, because they didn't get as far as they expected yesterday, and they feel they must make up for that. After all, as they say, this isn't just some minor crime they're investigating. It's a possible murder."

Paula was right; the grapevine was almost infallible. The interrogation had already begun and the Professor was now seated, as Scholtze and Paula had been on Sunday evening and Monday morning, at the end of a long table, facing Theo Landry and Tobe Bennett, who were ensconced at the other end. The witness' appearance was bizarre. His rusty garments hung about his skinny frame as though they had been draped on a mannequin made of jointed broomsticks; yet somehow there was nothing about this animated clothes rack which suggested physical weakness; on the contrary, it gave the impression of wiry strength. His clean-shaven face was a network of wrinkles, and the brows above his deep-set eyes were wispy. A sparse fringe of gray hair encircled the tonsurelike baldness of his finely modeled head. His hands were surprisingly smooth, and the knuckles of his long tapering fingers were unknotted. Unlike Paula, he did not keep them clasped as he responded to questioning; he tapped noiselessly on the table and, from time to time, lifted his hands lightly; the well-correlated movement was suggestive of imaginary piano playing. Despite this finger play, however, he was courteously attentive to his questioners; not once did he burst into violent speech, as he had the day before, when he forced his way into the room and announced that nothing would keep him in the courthouse. Moreover, his diction was as meticulous as if he had been the dean of a New England college, though the accent was unmistakably that of the Middle West.

"I live in what is known as the Stewpan Cove Community, between Bayou Warehouse and Bayou Patou, not far from Cypremort in the parish of St. Mary," he said with precision, in answer to the first question put to him.

"And your name?"

"I am called the Professor. That is the only name by which I am known hereabouts."

"I realize that. But for the record we must have your legal name."

"The only name I have—in fact, the only name I've had for more years than you might credit—is 'Professor,' and that is the only name I will give."

"I'm afraid I must insist."

Countless wrinkles sprang into being as the Professor smiled in high humor. "That, sir, is assuredly your prerogative. I can no more stop you from insisting than you, in your turn, can stop me from withholding from you any other name than the one I have already given. The rack and thumbscrew went out of fashion with the Great Charter of Runnymede; and the rubber truncheon or piece of garden hose which some urban police departments still employ in what is known as the third degree. . . ."

"You seem to forget that contempt of court is punishable by imprisonment or fine or both."

"But this is not a court, is it? No one has put me under oath. And, even if it were a court, my dear sir, no one—"

"Soon or late this case will come before the courts, if you'll stop your speechmaking long enough to let me get in a word or two. Then you'll be called as a witness and put under oath."

"And if I refuse to give any other name at the outset of your questioning, I'll be sent to jail for a few hours or possibly even a few days, and you'll have no chance to question me further about certain matters vital to your case of which it is conceivable I might have presential knowledge."

Theo Landry chuckled. "I give up," he conceded. "After all, I don't care two hoots in hell what your real name is and I do care a great deal, and so does Sheriff Bennett, about learning what you know concerning the goings-on of Saturday night." He turned to Mrs. Walton. "Put him down for the time being simply as 'Professor,' identifying him also as pianist among the musicians employed by August Scholtze at the Salle des Tuileries cabaret." He faced the Professor once more. "I assume you do know something about what happened last Saturday night in connection with this girl, Titine Dargereux?"

"I do, indeed. It was my custom to call for her each evening about half after eight, and—as they say hereabouts—carry her to the Tuileries."

"When you say 'call for her,' do you mean at her door? That is to say, at the house where she lived?"

"That would be quite impossible, Mr. Landry, as you would realize if you were more familiar with the area. Stewpan Cove is on what is known throughout this section of the country as an 'island.' This does not mean, as I was taught in school, a body of land entirely surrounded by water, but a section raised far enough above the level of the encircling swamp or marsh to be habitable. Sometimes it is known as a *chenière*, because oak trees can find there a footing which is denied them elsewhere in the surroundings. It may be a large area of high ground, like Avery Island or Weeks Island; or it may be barely large enough for half a dozen cottages where dwell the trappers, fishermen and moss-pickers who find their livelihood in—"

"Spare us the rest of your lecture, if you will. All of us live in this part of Louisiana and are familiar with its physical aspect. Let's not lose sight of the question I asked, which was whether you called for Titine at her door."

"And as I said before, that would be quite impossible. There is no wheel road—indeed, there could be none—to Stewpan Cove. I always waited for her at the point where the main road crosses over Bayou Mauvais Bois. During dry spells, she would walk out along the footpath beside the bayou; if not, she would paddle out to the road in her pirogue. She would change to other shoes at Scholtze's."

"And you would meet her there at about eight-thirty?"

"That is correct, sir."

"Did you so meet her on every evening during the latter half of last week?"

"No. On Thursday and Friday there was no need; the Salle des Tuileries was closed because it was being redecorated, and even more barbarously in garish scarlet and silvery radiator paint than before. And, on Saturday night—"

"Yes, on Saturday night—?" Landry prompted at last, when there seemed to be no indication the Professor would continue of his own accord.

"On Saturday night—on Saturday night—she was not there."

"Do you know why she was not there?"

"Not of my own knowledge, sir. No."

"Was any explanation given you by anyone at all?"

"Yes, but I am unable to vouch for its truth, nor can I call it false."

"Well, for Pete's sake, get on with it. What was this explanation and from whom did you get it?"

"From Clarie Dargereux."

"Who is she?"

"Titine Dargereux's mother."

"Well, out with it. What was it she told you?"

"Titine should have been waiting by the roadside when I drove up, for this has been a long, dry spell, and not only the bayou bank, but many otherwise impassable parts of the swamp were high and dry. After a few minutes' wait, when there was still no sign of the girl, I walked along the bayou bank to the section of Stewpan where Titine lived and, though the house was dark, I knocked on the door. . . ."

"How did you know which house it was?"

"I had been there often. As a matter of fact, when I was wont to bring her home, after work—after the cabaret closed, that is—I would walk from the road to her home with her. She was not afraid, to be sure; but in the dead of night, like that, it was reassuring to have someone along."

Landry chuckled, and the Professor, raising his eyes, regarded him with something that might have been compassion.

"You laugh because I am no man of brawn, no manner of protector against perils of the night, no Caesar whose word but yesterday might well have stood against the world, though there be now none so poor—" He paused a moment, as though savoring the expression "—so poor to do me reverence? That is not seemly, Mr. Landry. It is not worthy of you."

"Of course, I didn't mean it that way, Professor. On the other hand, you must admit—"

"It is you who now stray from the course of your questions," the old man reminded him. "You asked how I knew the house, and I told you."

Landry looked at Bennett and Davila and shrugged.

"Don't pass that buck to me," grinned the coroner. "You're the D.A., and questioning witnesses is your pidgin. Get on with it."

"Perhaps we'll come back to the other part later," Landry observed. "For the moment, we'll hew to the line. You said you knocked at the door, though the house was dark?"

"I did, indeed."

"And what happened then?"

"Mrs. Dargereux opened the door a crack. The family had already retired, as is the custom in that part of the country, where the mosquito bar over the bed affords the only protection from the minute vampires. And Mrs. Dargereux said Titine had left early, more than two hours

before, saying she needed much time to make ready for the grand opening. The girl's parents had assumed, quite naturally, that she was going
to meet me, and were surprised—though not alarmed, as I understood it—
that this had not been the case. She had carried a paper-wrapped bundle
in which she said there was a pair of gold slippers she must return."

"That was all she said by way of explanation?"

"That was all her mother told me, sir. Titine did not make this explanation to me."

"All she took then, according to her mother, was a paper-wrapped
bundle in which slippers were wrapped. What about her accordion?"

"Normally, it was kept in the back of my car, well wrapped in oilcloth,
to spare her the necessity of carrying it back and forth between the roadway and the house. It is both bulky and—"

"All right, we know what an accordion looks like. Was the accordion
in the back of your car at the time?"

"I am unable to say, sir."

"What do you mean, unable?"

"Precisely that. I assumed it was there, and so did not look. Yet later,
just before August Scholtze left for Crowley, saying something to the
effect that this matter must be settled, I went down to bring up the
accordion, and it was not in the back of my car, though its oilcloth
covering was."

"When had it been removed?"

"Ah, that is precisely what I cannot say. All I am prepared to vouch for
is that the accordion was not in my car at approximately nine o'clock
that night; but whether it had been removed before I ever called for
Titine, about an hour earlier in the evening, or after I parked the vehicle
at the Salle des Tuileries, I am in no position to assert."

"We'll come back to that later if need be. Meantime, after Mrs.
Dargereux told you what she knew about the girl's early departure, what
did you do next?"

"I apologized for my intrusion, bade Mrs. Dargereux a good night and
walked back to my car, after which I drove directly to the Salle des
Tuileries."

"Was Titine there when you arrived?"

"No, sir. She was not. But this did not surprise me. I knew, of course,
that no arrangements for an early rehearsal had been made and that if
Titine left her home at about six o'clock, as her mother said, it was not to
come straight to the Tuileries. As I came in through the grocery, I saw
Baer wrapping some bulky package or other, and asked him if Titine

had arrived, and he shook his head in denial. So I hurried up the stairs, and when Gus saw me, he asked where Titine was. I had to tell him I had no idea. To tell you the truth, gentlemen, I had assumed she was with him. They had had a very violent quarrel the night before—Friday night, that is—and these quarrels between them were usually followed by equally stormy reconciliations, so I thought—"

"We may come to what you thought in a little while. For the present, we're anxious to establish, first of all, what actually happened. So I ask you now, what did Scholtze say or do when you told him you did not know where Titine was?"

"He flew into a rage, of course. Everyone who knows August Scholtze at all, knows he is of a choleric bent. He was apparently swearing a great deal in German, but as I am not familiar with the Teutonic idiom of profanity, I am unable to report exactly what he said. When his first fury had spent itself, he said opening night or no opening night, something had to be settled once and for all, it could no longer go on like this. He then directed me to take charge in his absence, to see that, even without a vocalist, the orchestra played music, to keep my eye on both the waiters and the customers, so as to prevent the small peculations to which some persons are prone when exposed to temptation—naturally, that was not what he said; his words were something to the effect that I should watch out lest any of these steal him blind. He also said that if anybody made trouble, I was to call Baer; he would tell Baer himself to come upstairs and be bouncer if a bouncer were needed, and then he left, saying he would drive to Crowley and return as soon as possible."

"Did he say why he was driving to Crowley, rather than to some other destination?"

"No, sir. He did not."

"Was it at this time, or about this time, that you went down to look for the accordion which you assumed to be in the back of your car?"

"It was, indeed."

"Have you heard anything from any source that might suggest why Crowley was the place he had in mind?"

"I have heard many things from many sources, most of them contradictory and different."

"But there must be one of them which, more than the others, strikes you as being nearest to the truth?"

"As Pontius Pilate said to the mild Saviour: 'What is truth?' . . . indeed, there are many truths. There is an old French battle epic, a *chanson de geste*, about one of the victories of the Duke of Marlborough.

If you played the music of its simple melody and asked me the name of the piece, I might say '*Malbrook s'en va t'en guerre.*' I might say 'We Won't Go Home Until Morning,' I might say, 'For He's a Jolly Good Fellow,' I might say, 'The Bear Came Over the Mountain,' and every one of these seemingly contradictory answers would be the truth. The same musical jingle has been used in all the songs whose names I have given you."

"Oh, for the love of Mike and all the other archangels, spare us your lectures! This will have to be another of the points we'll take up later, if we don't die of old age or break our necks tripping over our beards before we get to it. . . . If I understood you correctly, you said you ordinarily called for Titine every evening and brought her back home after the Tuileries had closed. That is about what you said, isn't it?"

"Every night when the club was open, not when it was shut down for renovation, or for such holidays as Good Friday and the like."

"Every night when she was working. Was this her idea, or was it yours?"

"Originally, it was August Scholtze's idea. At least, he was the first one who asked me if I would see to it that Titine was brought to work from her home, and got back safely when the night's work was finished."

"Why should he ask you particularly to do that?"

"He knew I lived in the same general neighborhood. Would that not be reason enough?"

"How long have you lived there?"

"A little more than a year."

"Where did you live before that?"

"In a little house on Bayou Sally, as it is called, though I understand the correct pronunciation would be *Salé.*"

"And before that?"

"In New Orleans. That was before the war."

"You were a pianist then?"

"I was; and, anticipating your next question, I was still called only Professor. I went by no other name."

"Where were you employed then?"

"In various cabarets. In what are now called night clubs."

"And in brothels?"

"At times, but not often. May I call your attention to the fact that most of those establishments had mechanical pianos—quarter-in-the-slot abominations—and did not encourage their clientele to sit about listening to music?"

"And how long have you been in the employ of Scholtze?"

"Ever since the war. During the war, the old Tenderloin in New Orleans was closed and, after prohibition, the speak-easies did not go in for floor shows, even the more luxurious ones like Tony Denapolis' Little Club on Dryades Street. I had known Scholtze in the old days, when he was a bouncer at The Vineyard, before he set up on his own out here in the country."

"The Vineyard . . . The Vineyard . . . were you employed there for some time?"

"From time to time; off and on. Those places didn't want to keep the same people, and they were always looking for some new sensation like Armstrong and Bunk Johnson on the trumpet, and Papa Celestin on the piano. Then, in between times, they would call on me until some other craze took over. I didn't mind, because even when I wasn't working, they would let me come there in the forenoon and practice music—real music, I mean, and not the horrible 'Smiles' and 'Everything Is Peaches Down in Georgia' and stuff like that, which was all they would permit me to play at night."

"Why did you leave there?"

"They put the lid on, as the saying goes, during the war, when Washington decided the Tenderloin was bad for the soldiers. And, after the war, as I told you, the speak-easies were not interested in music. Scholtze had saved a little money, and made a lot of money out of it by laying in a stock of good whisky before Prohibition went into effect. He cut this and sold it for fabulous prices and, through the connections he had made as a bouncer for The Vineyard, he arranged for other sources of supply. I met him one day on Basin Street, and he said he was starting a night club of his own, but not in New Orleans; he said the competition was too keen, and too many people had to be paid off. He had found this place not too far from Cypremort, a grocery and former liquor store with a second story that used to be a dance hall, and said if I would get up a small band for him, so that he could have dancing and music every night, he would offer me the job."

"And that is how you came to St. Mary Parish?"

"That is how, sir."

"But you moved from Bayou Sally to the Stewpan Cove Community, you told us."

"That was after August had found Titine. I never was told where or when they met, but he saw at once she would be a splendid drawing card, and he bought her a fine, beautifully inlaid accordion, instead of the battered old instrument she had been using; and he bought me the little house where I am living now, so I could bring her to work and take her home. . . . He said he didn't want the Tuileries to get a bad name—a really bad name, you understand—and so Titine must continue to live with her parents, even though, after a while, she had a very nice room in his living quarters, too."

"So that, in effect, you were a sort of guardian for her in his behalf?"

"I think perhaps chaperon would be the better term, sir."

"Were there ever nights when you did not bring her home from work?"

The Professor looked down at his tapping fingers and then lifted his eyes to let his glance pass from one member of the group at the far end of the table to another.

"The girl is dead now," he said gently. "Perhaps she has been done evilly to death through some deed of darkness. In any case, the words I speak can harm her no longer. Yes, there were nights when she did not return to Stewpan Cove."

"Where did she stay on those nights?"

"Of my own knowledge, I would not know. August would simply tell me not to wait for Titine, and I would leave in some bitterness, thinking of what was written in *Poor Richard's Almanac* of Samson, that he had a strong body but a weak head, or he would not have laid it in a harlot's lap. . . . They were not really in love, those two. They had merely ensnared one another so that neither could escape from the other's jealous possessiveness. . . . That, sir, is one of the truths which I believe implicitly."

"Let us get back to Saturday night. Scholtze left the Tuileries, telling you, or at least letting it be known, he was going to Crowley. What time was it that he left?"

"Approximately nine o'clock."

"And he returned?"

"A little after three. There were still quite a few patrons at the tables."

"Did he say whether or not he had seen Titine?"

"He did not."

"You did not ask?"

"It was none of my business to ask. If she was coming and he wanted me to take her to her home, he would tell me."

"And he did not tell you?"

"As I told you a moment ago, he did not."

"Did he mention meeting anyone else?"

"No, sir."

"Did he tell you to go home alone?"

"Quite a bit later he told me not to wait for anyone, but to go to my house."

"And you did?"

"Yes, sir."

"One more question on this point. Before leaving, he said he would send Baer up to you in case you needed the young man's services as a bouncer. Did he do so?"

"I must assume so, since August had hardly left the place when Baer came to the desk where his uncle usually sat, and took a chair which he leaned against the wall. He said nothing about having seen his uncle. But in any case, it was not unusual for him to come upstairs as a sort of ex officio guardian of the peace on his own volition."

"Was he called on to eject anyone or otherwise carry out whatever a bouncer might be called on to do?"

"No, sir. Everyone was very orderly, considering the amount of liquor that was being consumed. From that aspect, it was more like a family beer garden in a German settlement than a speak-easy night club."

"Were there any ladies among those present?"

"No. Just some women who were in and out during the course of the night."

"In your opinion, could Baer have functioned as a bouncer?"

"Oh, indeed yes! He's only a youngster, eighteen or nineteen, but he is tremendously strong. You should see him lift a cask of needled beer to his shoulders and walk upstairs with it. He would have had little difficulty on that score in quelling almost any disturbance that might occur at the Tuileries. Besides, his uncle had taught him some of the tricks of the trade, such as wrapping a salt cellar in a napkin and wielding this as a weapon."

"Was his behavior perfectly normal throughout the night?"

"Ye-e-es, except . . . actually, I cannot be sure of this, but once he excused himself and said he would be right back. Without Titine to sing any songs, one of the Jourdain boys sang a number now and then. He hasn't much of a voice, but we were hard put to it, you see, to offer entertainment without Titine's vivid presence as she walked among the tables, singing in that husky sweet voice and accompanying herself on the accordion. He had just sung 'Auprès de Ma Blonde' in French, with some Cajun variations in the way of extra verses. Even in the original French, the last line goes 'Qu'il fait bon dormir.' And while the Jourdain boy was singing about this, Baer asked if he could be excused and, of course, I told him to go ahead; nobody was likely to make trouble while that song was being sung—they were all joining in on the refrain. So he went and, when he came back, he kept his face turned away from me; naturally that piqued my curiosity, and I made it my business to get a clear view of his features two or three times before he could turn away."

"And what did you see? Were there any evidences of his having been in a fight?"

"Oh, no, nothing at all like that, sir. On the contrary. Though his eyes were puffy and red, I would almost be willing to take a Bible oath the boy had been weeping uncontrollably, weeping as though his heart would break, weeping so that he could not erase from his features the plain evidence of a tearing, devouring grief."

Chapter Eighteen

THE PREVIOUS AFTERNOON'S CLOUD-SCUD HAD COAGULATED INTO AN UN-broken, sullen overcast. By morning, a weeping drizzle of rain had begun, increasing in volume and fury as the day wore on. Crowley's streets were all but deserted, the only figures visible being those of pedestrians hastening toward indoor shelter. Occasionally, small automobiles went splattering along, their isinglass curtains securely fastened, but obviously inadequate to shield the wayfarers from wind-lashed sheets of rain.

Within the crowded courthouse corridors, where those who ordinarily would have lounged about the sunlit square had taken refuge, yellow incandescent lights accentuated, rather than relieved, the gloom whose somber semidarkness matched the all-pervading smell of mildew given off by damp walls, damp clothing, stale tobacco remnants of discarded quids and stubs, and close-packed humanity.

Booted farmers, drovers and others, clad in streaming oilskin raincoats, stamped the clinging mud from their feet and tilted their heads forward to let rivulets of water run from broad hatbrims in minuscule cascades; then they went about their normal occupations. Some wandered down to the parish agricultural agent's offices, others to the clerk of court's office, where they rubbed elbows with attorneys who were filing divers documents, most of them typed on long foolscap and bound with eyelets into powder-blue covers.

Still others sought the sheriff's staff of assistants, or the assessor, while the remainder simply lounged in groups of tobacco chewers or smokers, silent for the most part, except for an occasional eruption of plaintive profanity about the weather which would delay the harvest, possibly long enough to let overripe heads of grain shatter in the field, bringing an entire year of toil and planning to nought.

Only one or two troubled to walk up to the second floor, where the witnesses, who had been summoned for interrogation about Titine Dargereux, were waiting in the corridor outside the room ordinarily used by the jury. Within, beyond the closed door, were District Attorney Landry, Dr. Davila and Malvina Walton; but the sheriff's office was represented only by Chief Deputy Guerra. Despite the inclement weather, Tobe Bennett had left, after the interrogation of the Professor, for a tour of the Iota area with the parish registrar, to give those who lived there an opportunity to register and pay poll taxes without having to take time out from harvest labors to journey to Crowley for this purpose. The guardian at the door was Deputy Barousse, who wore shoes that still creaked despite the dampness that seeped into everything.

Joe, after receiving whispered instructions from Landry, called to his subordinate.

"Get Baer Scholtze in here," he ordered. "The boy's out there somewhere. I saw him earlier this morning."

"On second thought, let's recess for a few minutes first," Landry suggested. "Mrs. Walton's got a right to rest and I'd like to stretch my legs and have a small black."

During the quarter hour that followed, Baer sat uncomfortably alone in the single chair at his end of the long table, with Barousse watching him ponderously from the door. At the end of this time, Landry, Davila, Mrs. Walton and Guerra returned, filing in and taking their places. Landry picked up a sheaf of legal-length paper, leafed through it to the point where he came to the transcript of Scholtze's testimony and rapped out a sharp question.

"Can you account for everything you did and everywhere you went last Saturday night?"

Baer ducked his bullet-shaped, close-cropped head and squirmed miserably.

"I ask you excuse," he rejoined. "Please. I do not understand so good. Please explain me how you mean, yes?"

"I mean can you tell us where you were and what you did Saturday night?"

"Sure, I work by my *Onkel* August's store."

"Anybody see you there?"

Baer beamed in obvious pride. "*Everybody* sees me," he replied.

"Did you go anywhere else on Saturday?"

"Not after I come to work again."

"What do you mean 'again'?"

"*Nu*, the store is open in the afternoon, *nicht wahr?* So I work in the afternoon. I work also in the night, when the dance hall is open, and I got to carry the cases up the stairs; sometimes I got to help *Onkel* August stop a fight. So I work."

"And between the afternoon and night jobs, what do you do?"

"So I sleep, ain't it? I sleep."

"That figures, all right. And on Saturday, when you left the store in the afternoon and before you came back at night, you slept, and I assume this was in your uncle's quarters which are connected with the grocery store and the Tuileries night club. Right?"

"No, that ain't right."

"You mean that's *not* where your uncle and you live?"

"No, I mean Saturday I do *not* sleep."

"Oh?"

"Saturday Titine asks me would I take her to the Tuileries early because she says she got to practice or *Gott weiss was*. She come on the store with her mama like lots of peoples do on Saturday morning to buy groceries, flour, coffee, sugar, tin cow, and everything for the week. So somebody has a car, and everybody what can piles in so they come shop, *nicht wahr?* She comes with her mama *und* she says the Professor is gone, that is why she can't ask him, when she finds she must got to come early, so will I come by the bridge six o'clock *und* wait for her, so she can come early by the club and practice."

"So it was you! You're the unknown swain who called for her early. Have you got a car?"

"*Nein.* But I drive my *Onkel* August, his car."

"Did he know about it?"

"*Wer weiss?* He never ask, *und* I never told him. It is nothing new I should use his car, but not on no long rides, no. Just for short trips."

"Where was your uncle all this while?"

"He sleeps. He always sleeps before he has to open up the club, the Tuileries, so he can stay up all night."

"So while he slept, you took the car, and you drove to the bridge where the Professor usually meets Titine about eight-thirty, but you got there about six; and then what?"

"And then I wait until she comes out."

"Wait long?"

"Not long. I even say, already, she must got to have been walking for the road before I come there, so soon she comes after I get the car turned around."

"And then you drove her to the club?"

Baer's delft blue eyes became cloudy with querulous bewilderment.

"*Aber nein!*" he said. "*Ganz gewiss nicht!*"

"Does that mean you did *not* take her to the club?"

Baer nodded in dumb misery.

"Well, where *did* you take her then?"

"I didn't took her nowheres," the boy mumbled. "She jumps in the car with her bundle—"

"What bundle?"

"How I know? It is a bundle, wrapped around in paper about so long *und* so big around, *und* it is tied with a white string."

"Could it have been her accordion?"

"No, no, it was too little. I even ask where is her accordion and she said she left it in the Professor's car Wednesday night like she always does, and he will bring it, *auch* like always."

"Well, you did drive off *somewhere*, didn't you?"

Again the boy's eyes clouded and he wrung his big hands, the fingers interlaced, until the knuckles cracked.

"We drive maybe a couple miles, *und* all from a sudden she says she loses her pocketbook, it must of fell in the road when she got in my car. She says she will get out and I must drive back fast like everything, before it gets too dark, and bring it to her. So I do it."

"You mean you found the pocketbook?"

"I never found nothings," he complained, still wretchedly bewildered by this complex of events. "I turn around *und* hurry back, but what you think? When I am yet half a mile away already, I see how comes another car from up the road to where Titine stands, and the car turns around and Titine jumps in, and the car goes away *hui!* like the wind! I think well maybe it is some customer what knows her and he gives her a ride on the club, but she never got to the Tuileries all night."

"How about the bundle she brought with her?"

"That also she takes out when she sends me back for the pocketbook I can't find."

"You never saw her after that?"

"Never, never. Only I help carry the coffin yesterday, and I put a cross out of white flowers on the grave. *Aber mein Herz ist schwer* even before the funeral. She is such a pretty girl, and when she says will I come get her Saturday evening I am so happy, I think maybe she might want to be my *Schatzi,* maybe I could put my arm around her, kiss her even, *und* then she runs away. Why she runs away? I never done her nothings, not nothings at all, but *mir nichts dir nichts* she runs away."

Theo Landry regarded the boy curiously, the wide shoulders and thick arms, the deep chest and the great hands, and yet the mien was that of a woebegone baby, about to burst into tears when it realizes the moon is beyond reach.

While the others watched this play of naked emotion, a child's tantrum in what had the physical aspects of fully developed manhood, Baer's expression abruptly changed. The pale, straw-colored eyebrows contracted in a berserk scowl; one of the big fists knotted and was brought down on the table with a crash that caused Mrs. Walton to flinch away, and brought Guerra half out of his chair.

"But someday I show them, *ja,* I show them all; most special of all I show that *Hundsvieh* what comes up in his car. Oh, I hear all about those gold slippers, *und* I stuff one gold slipper down his goozle *und* one I stuff down hers. I could wait till I find out who he is, him *und* his *gottverdammt noch a' mal* gold slippers!"

Chapter Nineteen

THE BAD WEATHER HAD INCREASED, RATHER THAN DIMINISHED, THE NUM-ber of rough rice buyers, farmers, brokers, bag salesmen and others who frequented the small and dingy wooden structure, situated between the office of the Crowley *Signal* and Forshag's Filling Station, which served as local headquarters for the Southern Rice Growers' Association. The manager had announced that approximately five thousand barrels of rice would be offered for sale that day—some of it the new long grain variety just perfected by Brent Winslow—and, for the most part, the habitués were merely killing time until the bidding opened. Three o'clock was the hour set for this and, as it approached, more buyers and farmers drifted in.

Sacked samples of the sale rice stood in rows on the counters along the walls, and interested buyers examined these samples, critically watching handfuls of the grain as it trickled back into the paper bags, and taking note of the items marked on each bag: the lot number, the variety and quantity offered for sale, the producer's name and the area where the rice was grown. Meanwhile, the current market and the bad weather were the main topics of conversation, coupled with the usual hard luck tales of the farmers', whose hopes for a good crop and high market were, apparently, never realized. ("Juanette had been waiting for her new piano since last year, but the poor child realized, of course, that such a thing was impossible with the price of rice what it was then; now I had to pay all that money for a new tractor and, unless the price is right now, my rice is gonna stay in that warehouse. I said I was gonna hold it and I am. I don't have to take the high bid unless I want to.")

The interminable game of dominoes that went on at Association headquarters, sale or no sale, was also in full swing. No one could say how long this had been progressing; the players changed, but the plaques never remained idle as long as the office was open. The men gathered around the tables were talking less of the market and the weather and more about the *cause célèbre* now under investigation at the courthouse.

"I'll lay six, two and even," offered a wide-shouldered, flat-stomached Texan, looking up from beneath the brim of his Stetson, "they catch the guy that killed that babe—I've forgot her name; six they get him by tonight; two they tap him by tomorrow night, and even they corral him this week. Any takers? . . . Hell, there goes my only play. Now I got to go to the bone yard again."

"Too bad, too bad," commented one of the other players. "I'll bleed for your hard luck. No, I won't take you. Everybody's got a hell of a good idea it's bound to have been one of two people. One'd be that bootlegger that's been keeping her. If I was betting, I'd make him favorite in running for the rope. And the other—"

"Yes, go on. What about the other?"

"The other'd be this Villac party that runs the mill where they found her Sunday."

"You crazy lak a *poule d'eau*, talkin' like dat, I guarantee you, me," a bystander scoffed. "Tha's a decent riss-peckable *famille*, an' if it wasn't for *M'sieu* Winslow, Villac's *gran'père*, we could all of us be starvin', us, an' you, too. W'y? Account if we ain't got that Blue Camellia, all we'd have 'round here, us, would be red rice, or either rice w'at wouldn't stand up, no, in the kin' of weather we got today; and if we got no rice you couldn't come 'round yuh, cheatin' us on the price, an' gettin' you' own self hr-r-rich like a bastard, no."

"Nuts to you, *copain*. That fine family stuff is what makes me sure he's the one got most to gain. Ain't he fixin' to go up the middle aisle with the doll from Lafayette whose daddy is a New York zillionaire or something? And I hear how he's in some kind of a bind with Little Miss Round Heels. What's the one sure way to fix things so she won't mess up his new play-pretty deal? Put her out of the way for keeps. . . . Well, at last, a play. Three at the other end and this double six makes a sweet and sassy fifteen, don't it?" He slapped down the tile with a sharp clack.

An altercation at the rice sampling counter switched the interest of those present into a new channel, while some of the jostling crowd broke away, stepped into the streaming rain and joined more congenial ac-

quaintances at the courthouse where, in the jury room, District Attorney
Landry had just begun to question Ten High.

"Let me ask you again," he was saying, "how many times you made a
'complete kiver-to-kiver round,' as you call it, of the Claudia Mill
Saturday night?"

"When I first come on, Mist' Theo, I went from the top to the bottom; I even looked under the loading dock and the office floor joists
from outside. And, like I told you, I never seen nothing out the way.
After that, right at two in the morning, I made another round just like
it, from the top floor to underneath the loading dock, and I never seen
a thing out the way then, neither."

"But you did make other rounds?"

"Just walking through, sure, like everybody does, and punching in at
the station boxes, every hour, after Mist' Prosper called it a night and
went home. I did that on the hour, every hour, till Old Man Hector
Ashford, the Sunday watchman, relieved me."

"And what time would that have been?"

"Like always, eight o'clock straight up!"

"While you were on the top floor, either in your two thorough inspection trips or during your hourly rounds, did you at any time look
into any of the four bin openings?"

"No, Mist' Theo, I didn't."

"Why not? You did say, didn't you, that ordinarily you flashed your
light into the bins on your last round to check up on how much rice
was in each?"

"That's weekday nights. There wouldn't be no reason for me to do it
on Saddy nights, seeing as how the mill would be closed Sundays. There
wouldn't be nobody working there, or either unloading rice or anything.
So it's the Sunday watchman who checks the bins and marks on the
board how much about is in each one, so the foreman, coming in on
Monday to start work for the week, knows how he stands. The Sunday
watchman could do this any time during the day or either the night.
Old Man Ashford done it about noon, las' Sunday, and that's how come
he seen that gol' slipper stickin' out."

"At any time during or between your thorough or routine tours did
you notice anything out of the ordinary going on at the mill?"

"Well, sure, they was all running 'round in circles about some missing
carload that got picked up by the wrong train or something before I come
on, and—"

"We know about that. Was there anything else?"

"Not that I know of."

"Better think about that. Remember, we've talked to other people who were there. Miss Bennett for one."

"There wasn't nothing out the ordinary about her being there. She works in the place; this time of year she's there at night right often; matter of fact, she's there oftener than not."

"What about her aunt, Miss Eaton?"

"That's not out the way, neither, Mist' Theo. Miss Eaton don't hardly ever miss comin' when Miss Paula's workin' late."

"But you and Miss Paula did both go out to the millyard where Miss Eaton was blowing the horn of her car sometime between nine and ten on Saturday night, didn't you?"

"Sure we did, but—"

"And while you were all out there in front, talking to Miss Eaton in her car, anybody in this living world could have slipped into the mill through the back entrance, the one from the loading dock, and hidden, without your knowing the first thing about it. Isn't that right, Ten High?"

"We-e-ell, yes, I reckon they *could* have, but it don't seem like anybody'd want to do a—"

"Somebody did, though." The district attorney's expression had become grim. "Either Titine Dargereux went into that mill by herself, got up to the top floor and stumbled into one of the bin openings in the dark, or someone took her up there and pushed her in. One way or the other, one or more persons got into that mill Saturday night, the mill you were supposed to be guarding as watchman, and you didn't know beans about it. Those are the facts!"

"But it wasn't the way you make it sound, Mist' Theo. I did like I always do. Sure, I stopped in for a cup coffee, and while I'd be sitting in the office, till Mist' Prosper come back and closed everything up, anybody could have sneaked up there or in there. But I'm the watchman. I'm supposed to keep my eye out for fires and see nobody don't steal nothing. I give you my affidavit nobody couldn't have got in there and toted off nothing!"

"But you do admit—which isn't really necessary, since it is obvious one or more persons did so—that others might have got into the mill without your knowledge?"

"We-e-ell, it ain't right, the way you make it sound."

"However it sounds, those are the facts. Now—one more question:

was there anything else about that night that you know, and that you think we should know?"

"No, Mist' Theo. Not that I know of."

"You're positive?"

"Positive."

"Then let me refresh your memory." He turned to Mrs. Walton. "Be sure you get every word of this question, and every word of Ten High's answer," he directed. "I'll speak very slowly, so you can't miss. Ten High, is it or is it not a fact, that some time in the neighborhood of eleven-thirty or very shortly thereafter, Gus Scholtze came to you in the mill-yard and asked you to let him look through the mill, that he slipped you some money—a bribe, mind you—to let him do so, and that you did in fact lend him a flashlight so that he could go through the mill, un-watched and unattended?"

The watchman started to speak, but the gobbling sound that he emit-ted was quite unintelligible. He swallowed convulsively and finally said, in a croaking half-whisper, "I never thought there was nothing wrong about it, Mist' Theo, and he wasn't in there more'n five-six minutes, so help me Christ!"

"But you evidently meant to conceal this vital bit of information from us. Why?"

"Oh, you know why, good's me. It wasn't what I was supposed to do, but men been doing things they wasn't supposed to do ever since that apple business with Eve in the Bible. I bet you done plenty little things like that you wasn't supposed to do, when you was younger and raising hell with the other students at L.S.U."

"Whatever your opinion of my conduct may or may not be, I have never admitted an unauthorized person to premises where, within twelve hours, the body of a dead girl was found. Now tell me exactly—and this is the part I want Mrs. Walton to be certain of, so speak slowly and distinctly—what happened."

"Well, this was about twenty-thirty minutes after Miss Paula and her auntie went home, Saddy night, near's I can remember. I seen this here car drive into the millyard, and I could tell by the sound even it wasn't Mist' Prosper's Olds and, anyway, that was still parked where he left it when he went to the Archers' house—I think that was where he said he was going to meet one of the Benoit boys. Anyway, I went out to see who it was coming in at that hour of night, and it was this Scholtze."

"You recognized him?"

"Yeah. He's got plenty customers he serves right here in Crowley. I seen him lots of times."

"Tell us what happened and what was said after he got out at the mill Saturday night."

"He asked for Mist' Prosper, saying was he here and so on. I told Scholtze no and he asked did I know where Mist' Prosper would be, and I told Scholtze, like I just told you, how Mist' Prosper had gone to the Archers' to see could he meet one of the Benoits; I didn't know which one, but I was pretty sure it was Maurice. So Scholtze asked how long before Mist' Prosper'd be back, and I told him nobody could say that, account he was also trying to chase down this stray carload of rice, and so then he asked had anyone else come to see him that evening, and I said no, not's far's I knew."

"And you still say that, as I understand it?"

"Yes, sir, and I'll say it forever, because it's true. He asked me next, as near as I can rec'lect, was I certain sure nobody wasn't in the mill waiting for him, and far's that went, I could swear on a stack of Bibles there wasn't nobody waiting for him. Then he says did I care if he looked around, just to make sure, and I said, 'You're goddamn right'—excuse me, Miz' Walton, I wouldn't go to cuss in front of you, but that's what I said—'you're goddamn right I mind. Nobody ain't supposed to go through the mill!'"

"Yet your objections were overcome, weren't they?"

"We-e-ell, it was like this, Mist' Theo. He says he just wants to make sure this girl that was supposed to sing for his big opening night show wasn't hiding here. He says he and this girl had a big bust-up, and she's trying to get back at him; he thinks she's gone off the deep end for Mist' Prosper, by she's always sayin' why can't he be more like Prosper Villac, and what a kind gentleman he is and such as that. So he thinks she's come here maybe, to get Prosper to either hide her or either help her get away. Well, I knew good's anything she ain't there, and when he says it's worth ten bucks for him to go through and see for himself, I said go ahead, if that's what it takes to get you in the groove. . . . Like I said before, he wasn't in the mill more'n five or six minutes, just long enough to give a quick look around, and then he comes barreling back out, a mile a minute, and says I'm right, it ain't nobody up there now, and to don't tell nobody he went to look. So I said hell, I won't tell nobody, but for him to be sure not to tell nobody, else I'd get in trouble. And that was all."

"You saw no one or talked to no one else that night?"

"Oh, sure. Mist' Prosper come back it musta been gettin' on to'rds 'leven, near's I can reckon it, and he said for Miss Paula to go home. So she telephoned to her auntie and, while they was waiting for Miss Eaton to come get Miss Paula, I heard Mist' Prosper say something about double checking later that night to make sure the stray rice car really was on the westbound Red Ball, and Miss Paula says she would take some papers with her and work at home on them the next day, which was Sunday. She had a bundle of papers, at least that's what it musta been, by I couldn't see what they were, wrapped up in paper and tied with a string like that, and soon's ever her auntie come by, she got into the car with her and drove off. This musta been not too long past 'leven, close as a body could cipher it."

"That was the last time you saw her that night?"

"I never seen her again, not till Monday evening when I come on, by I don't work Sundays."

"And how long did Mr. Prosper stay at the mill after that?"

"I couldn't rightly say."

"Why not?"

"Well, it was like this, near's I rec'lect. He said something about it was sure a relief to have found that missing car, or some such, and that he had telephoned Miss Paula about it earlier. I expect he did, too, that bein' the natural thing to do, but I got to admit I never heard no phone ring, or nothing, nor neither did Miss Paula say ary word about having got no phone calls. But it 'pears to me, she hadn't hardly more'n got out of sight—at least the lights of her auntie's car hadn't got out of sight, I sh'd say—when Mist' Prosper says he's plum out of cigarettes, and would I take his car and run up to Keller's and get him a couple of packs. I done it."

"Then, after you got back, how long was it before Mr. Prosper left the mill?"

"That's the funny part, Mist' Theo. He was done gone by the time I got back, so I put the cigarettes on his desk and locked the office door. I knew he'd be back sometime, by his car, that I had used, was standing where he always parked it in the millyard."

"Well, did you see him after that?"

"No, but he sure Lord did come back sometime whilst I was making my two o'clock round."

"How do you know?"

"His car was gone, when I come back to the ground to look under the floor joists and such like, and when I unlocked the office to see, I saw the cigarettes was gone from his desk, too."

"Is it possible he might have remained somewhere in the mill till you made your kiver-to-kiver two o'clock round?"

Ten High shrugged. "Anything's possible," he conceded. "Just like you said, that young girl got into the mill without I saw her, and Miss Paula got at least one phone call without I heard no ringing, so it could be he was looking 'round the loading spur when I come back with the cigarettes, and seeing his car back, sat in it, napping kind of, till sometime between two and two-thirty—it takes me near about half an hour to make that round—when he lit out to check on his car. I wouldn't know. But I'd bet a purty he never done it."

"Very well then. That will be all the questions I'll ask you for now. But bear in mind you're still under subpoena, so don't leave the jurisdiction of this court until you're formally released."

"What's all that mean?"

"It means don't leave town until this case is over. I might want to call you again, when the grand jury meets, and later when court's in session maybe. It means if you do decide to leave, you'll be a fugitive, and can be arrested and brought back. It means—"

"Okay, okay. I understand, Mist' Theo. And I ain't leavin'. I got a job, I make a living, and I ain't lost nothin' nowhere's else."

He rose, nodded and left by the door which Barousse opened for him. Landry shuffled his papers and looked at Guerra.

"Now that we've got Scholtze's visit to the mill checked and re-checked," he said, "I think we might look a little more thoroughly into the difference between Scholtze's statement and Paula's about the degree of their acquaintance. Get one or the other back here—whichever you can locate first. I should think it would probably be Paula. Maurice Benoit has been excused because he's 'sick.' Do we need anyone else here?"

Chapter Twenty

IN WELCOME CONTRAST TO THE TURMOIL WHICH HAD PERVADED IT SATUR-
day and Monday, comparative quiet reigned at the mill on Tuesday
morning. No cars went astray, no dissatisfied patrons argued about prices
and Paula was back at her post, her usual efficient self. She had managed
to meet Malvina Walton during her coffee break, and gleaned a few
more stray bits of gossip, none of them particularly disturbing; as a matter of fact, once she had told Prosper about the disgusting behavior of
Maurice in Lafayette the night before, she seemed disposed to work,
rather than to chatter, which suited Prosper perfectly; he would ask his
mother to tell him about the "terrible scene" at Cousin Clement's, when
he went home to dinner; he knew she would do this dispassionately and
accurately.

As it turned out, Onezime was the one to do it. The morning had
not been as uneventful at the Monrovia as it had at the Claudia, and
Lavinia had been delayed by foreign visitors from Spain and Java, whom,
ordinarily, she would have brought home with her to share the midday
meal. This time, Henry Blanchard, her right-hand man, recognizing the
various handicaps under which she was operating, had stepped into the
breach and asked them to his house; she had telephoned to say she would
be along presently, and that they could either begin dinner without her
or have it a little late. Onezime and Odey had decided on the latter course
and were seated in the living room, enjoying a leisurely drink and a
brotherly visit, when Prosper came in. Anne Marie was nowhere to be
seen; presumably, she was off to an early card party, but Prosper could
not entirely still the suspicion that she was avoiding him, not altogether
by accident.

"I found a note from Anne Marie pinned to my pillow when I came in last night," he said without preamble. "I've already filled in some of the gaps that it left wide open. But not all of them. She referred to a 'terrible scene' that took place at Clement's yesterday afternoon. Can either of you explain just what she meant by that?"

The priest and the teacher exchanged glances and the former set down his glass. "Why, yes, I think I can," he said quietly. "When the cortege— a very short one, of course—came into the yard, Clement recognized the occupants of the last car as August Scholtze and his nephew Baer. He left the gallery, walked straight past the hearse and the other cars and asked Scholtze what he was doing there. Scholtze was civil enough at first; he said he hadn't expected to be invited to the house, but he wanted to go to the grave—he had brought an enormous cross of white flowers to put on it. Clement ordered him off the premises—by that time, both men were so angry that they had raised their voices and we couldn't help hearing everything they said. Scholtze went out to the highway and parked there and, later on, Clement had to eat humble pie, because we were one pallbearer short; he went out and asked to have Baer fill in the breach. At first, Scholtze refused his permission, but finally gave it—on condition that the 'flower cross' could be put on the grave."

"You've left out something very interesting, Onezime," Odey interposed. "Of course, you can't quote everything Clement and Scholtze said, word for word. In the first place, it would take too long. In the second place, some of the expressions they used would be unbecoming to your cloth. In the third place, I doubt if any of us, except Clement, could revert successfully to the patois we spoke when we were children. Indeed, it's a source of surprise to me that Clement, who did go to high school, under protest—at least, he didn't actually graduate, but still—"

"Uncle Odey, do stop talking like a professor and tell me what Clement and Scholtze said that you thought was very interesting," Prosper interrupted.

"Well, Clement said he had too much respect for dogs to call Scholtze a son of a bitch and Scholtze said he thought Clement was inconsistent, to say the least, in ordering him, Scholtze, off the property, on the ground that he was the probable killer of Titine, when Clement had 'standing on his gallery a bastard what's been running around with her till it's a scandal for the snakes, already.' . . . A scandal for the snakes! —that's a very disagreeable expression, but it's a very effective one. I'm not sure that in one of my English classes—for the older students, of course—I couldn't suggest its use to telling advantage."

"Scholtze was referring to your friend Maurice Benoit, Prosper," Onezime said mildly. "As a matter of fact, Clement and Odey had already remarked that his presence, at such a time, was rather surprising under all the circumstances. But of course we know he's a very good friend of yours and, doubtless, he was just taking the occasion to stand by you, like the rest of us."

"It wasn't in the least like the rest of us," Odey said impatiently. "How can you say such a thing, Onezime? None of the rest of us ever saw Titine Dargereux, much less had an association with her that was a scandal to—"

"Listen! I think Mother came in just then," Prosper interrupted. "I don't believe she wants to hear any more about this—she probably had about all she could take yesterday. And I've heard enough now to fill in all the gaps that hadn't been taken care of already this morning."

There was no doubt of it, Maurice had laid himself open to very grave suspicions, and Prosper felt guilty because he was not sorrier for this. Moreover, while he knew that the unseemly happenings of the day before must have been very trying to anyone whose code required that everything should be done "decently and in order," he realized that his mother's recoil from them would be less violent than if it had not been tempered by the realization that the more guilty Maurice appeared, the less fixedly the finger of suspicion pointed in the direction of her only son. Making every allowance for this feeling on her part, however, and for the fact that her powers of self-control enabled her to appear calm and collected under almost any circumstances, he did not expect her to look actually happy when she entered the living room. But the smile which now illumined her face gave it that rare beauty which he so seldom glimpsed; and, after briefly and joyously greeting her two guests, she came over to Prosper and kissed him.

"Captain Bob telephoned just as I was leaving the Monrovia," she said. "That's why I'm even later than I expected to be. The first copies of the *Advertiser* were just coming off the press and one had been delivered to his office at City Hall. You didn't tell me your engagement was going to be announced this afternoon, Prosper. Captain Bob says there's a beautiful picture of Vicky in the society section and the finest kind of an article with it—a long one, telling not only about her education and so on, but about her father's pre-eminence in the field of design and my father's successful experiments with rice breeding. Of course, it's always the girl, rather than her fiancé, who's featured in such announcements, but you're mentioned as having served 'with distinction' in the Rainbow Division as an officer of the Cavalry Troop from Jennings and graduated with honors from L.S.U., and being the co-owner with me of the Monrovia and the Claudia and the 'highly efficient manager of the latter.' There's not a word about—about the recent trouble. Captain Bob is sending over half a dozen copies right away by messenger, so that we won't have to wait for the regular delivery. And he said that, just as soon as he'd finished telephoning, he was going to start making a flower arrangement and take it personally to Vicky."

"I'm sorry I forgot to tell you about the announcement in the *Advertiser*," Prosper answered, returning her kiss. "Vicky told me, over the telephone, Sunday night, that she wanted it to come out the next day, and I persuaded her to wait. That is, I thought I did. But if it's given all that prominence, I bet the little scamp wrote it herself and got it to the *Advertiser* office with her picture yesterday, before she wrung a consent out of me to have it appear today. They couldn't have spared so much space without some advance notice."

"Well, however it happened, it's out now and I'm delighted," Lavinia went on. "I waited to ask whether you and Vicky have any other plans before calling her, but if you haven't, I'd like very much to invite her and her father here for supper tonight. And my father and mother and Grandfather Jim. I hoped," she added, turning to Onezime and Odey, "that you'd both stay over. I heard you saying something about leaving right after dinner."

"Well, yes, we did," Onezime admitted. "I feel, in a way, I ought to get back to my parish as soon as I can. But it would be very late now before I could get to the Delta, and I've already told Father Gubler that I'd let him know when I *did* get back. I don't suppose one more day . . . how about you, Odey?"

"Oh, I took the precaution of arranging for a replacement for the entire week," Odey said rather smugly. "I'd like very much to meet the LaBranches, father and daughter both. I never have. I've thought that, possibly, I might interest Moïse LaBranche in starting a scholarship."

"I wouldn't be at all surprised if you could. Well, everything seems to be working out just as I hoped. Go on in to dinner, the rest of you. I'll be with you directly. But I want to call Father and Mother right away."

"Just a minute—"

"Oh, Prosper, you don't mean to say that you *did* have other plans!"

It had been on the tip of his tongue to tell her he had meant to get away from the mill early, since everything there was running so smoothly

again, and to go to Krauss's Jewelry Store in Lafayette before closing
time and buy Vicky the ring he had promised her. But when he saw
the swift darkening of the radiance in his mother's face, he could not
bring himself to do so. He would explain to Vicky and Vicky would
understand. That was one of the most wonderful things about her—she
understood, so readily and so pleasantly, with so little explanation.

"None that can't be changed," he told his mother. "Go right ahead
and make yours, any way you want to."

The little party was a complete success from everyone's point of view.
Lavinia suffered a momentary disappointment when Anne Marie came
in, after her bridge party, and said she was staying just long enough to
change her clothes. She was going to the Benoits' and, no, she didn't
think she should break the engagement, that late. *Break the engagement*,
Lavinia inquired with lifted eyebrows. Oh, Mother shouldn't take things
so literally. Anne Marie didn't mean she was engaged to be *married*.
She meant she had a date. She thought Mother objected to that new
term, "dating"—that was why Anne Marie had talked about an engagement. And this was to be a formal occasion, with guests from New
Orleans, not just a supper that had been dreamed up on the spur of the
moment, for a lot of relatives. Yes, she knew the LaBranches weren't
relatives yet. But they were going to be, and Vicky had been at the
Villacs' to supper, dozens of times already. There was nothing very exciting about that. As far as the real engagement went, Anne Marie didn't
think that was exciting, either; under the circumstances, she thought it
was very poor taste to announce it just then. No, of course Mr. La-
Branche hadn't been to the house before, Anne Marie knew that. But,
after all, he was just a doddering old man and probably a snob into the
bargain. He would look down his nose at everyone else. . . .

"You're not by any chance a little out of sorts, are you, Anne Marie?"
Lavinia asked quietly.

"Of course not. Why should I be out of sorts?"

"You didn't behave very well Sunday night, you know, either to Dale
or to Prosper. I think you're sorry now, on both scores. Being out of
sorts might be your way of betraying it. Because it isn't like you. Everyone's always admired—and envied—your lovely disposition. I have myself.
Well, run along, dear, and have a good time at the Benoits'. I hope
Maurice has sufficiently recovered, by this time, not to embarrass his
parents in front of their guests from New Orleans. And that nothing

will be revealed in the interrogation at the courthouse tomorrow that will give them and him any cause for anxiety."

It was very seldom that mother and daughter spoke to each other in this vein. Such clashes as occurred in the household—and these were, fortunately, few and far between—were generally between Prosper and Lavinia. After a rather disrespectful retort, Anne Marie left the pantry, where her mother was getting out the best china, and Lavinia did not see her again until she had slammed the back door behind her and was running out of the house toward her parked car, looking, as she always did, like a beautiful young angel who had strayed into an exclusive dress shop and emerged wearing the latest fashions instead of flowing white robes, complete with halo and wings. Evidently, she was driving to Pecan Grove herself, instead of being escorted to the party, which was as uncharacteristic as her ill temper. But Lavinia did not give the matter much thought, nor did she feel troubled, though it crossed her mind that Anne Marie was leaving very early and that the girl should have put on a wrap to protect her better from the rain, which was still falling. Lavinia was too happy and too busy, with her preparations for the family supper, to think of much else; and when Prosper came home, his good spirits would have been contagious, even if his mother's had been low. The fact that Paula had been recalled to the courthouse was not troubling him; she had not been gone more than half an hour, and nothing had gone wrong during her absence. On her return, she said she had not been asked any disturbing questions. He attached even less importance to the fact that Scholtze had also been recalled, later in the afternoon, and that Dale had been summoned, too; this could all be shrugged off as inconsequential, according to the grapevine. What really mattered to Prosper was that he had talked with Vicky and she had confessed that his suspicions about the announcement were correct. Was he going to scold her? He could hear her catching her breath, with a little laugh, as she asked the question over the wire, and he laughed, too, and said he would probably not only scold her when they next met, but shake her until her teeth chattered; then they had laughed together. She had been wonderful about the ring, too; of course, she did not mind waiting for it; in fact, she thought it would be fun for them to choose it together. Her father was a little sorry Mrs. Villac had got ahead of him; as Prosper knew, he had meant to have the first family party himself. But he would have one later in the week and, meanwhile, he was delighted to accept Mrs. Villac's kind invitation. The Winslows and Grandfather Jim were also delighted. Mary Winslow wondered if Vicky would like some rooted cuttings of rare flower specimens; of course, she knew the LaBranches could buy anything they chose, but they might feel pleased with a gift, even though Captain Bob had probably forestalled her with anything she could offer. Brent thought the next variety of rice, which he hoped to have on the market by spring, should be called Princess Victorine; he would make the suggestion that evening and see if it were pleasing to Vicky. Grandpa Jim wanted to know if she rode; it was her huge Dalmatian that he seemed to hear people talking about, but a girl with her background surely knew how to ride. He had just the mount for her and he would like to offer her that. . . .

The good will which preceded the party pervaded it throughout. Anne Marie's prediction that Moïse LaBranche would act like a snob, which Lavinia had not believed for a minute, was unfulfilled. Completely at ease in any kind of gathering himself, he had the happy faculty of putting everyone else at ease, also, without any effort whatsoever. He selected topics of conversation congenial to all his fellow guests. Vicky was equally adaptable and equally co-operative. She was genuinely delighted with the offer of the cuttings, even more delighted with the prospect of having a new variety of rice named for her, and most delighted of all with the offer of a horse. Yes, she had ridden from time to time, most of her life, until she came to Lafayette; but with so many other things to do, she had not ridden there yet; could she come out to the Winslow farm, the very next day, and try her mount? She had no inhibitions about showing her pleasure; she threw her arms about both Winslows and then about Grandfather Jim as she voiced it. With equal enthusiasm, she talked to Onezime about the Delta and with Odey about L.S.U. She had never been south of New Orleans and only once or twice to Baton Rouge, on which occasions she had seen nothing of the University; they must plan for some trips. And, by the way, why couldn't she and Prosper be married then and there? What was the good of having a priest in the family if you didn't make use of him? Oh, very well then, not tonight! But he could come back, couldn't he?

By the time Callie, whose style in serving did not bear close comparison with her faithfulness and general efficiency, announced that soup was on, everyone was in a mellow mood. Vicky herself fairly radiated happiness and Prosper was beside himself with pride at the favorable impression his sweetheart was making. They gathered around the hospitable board and stood silent while Onezime said grace, asking God's blessing upon a happy betrothal.

A few blocks away from the Villacs', August Scholtze rang the bell of a small neat white house and waited impatiently for admittance.

Chapter Twenty-one

THERE WAS ALWAYS GENERAL REJOICING AT THE CLAUDIA AND, INDEED, at all the rice mills in the locality, when circumstances permitted closing at a reasonably early hour during the busy season. The days that this happened were few and far between, which made it seem even more of a blessing to everybody than if it had been a frequent occurrence. But, on the Tuesday when his engagement was announced, there was probably no one, except Prosper himself, who was as pleased at the prospect of an evening free from such responsibilities as Amanda Eaton. The Foreign Missionary Society of the Third Evangelical Church, an organization of which she was president, was holding a special meeting, preceded by a spaghetti supper that evening, and it was very important that she should preside. Nevertheless, her feeling of responsibility toward her niece would not have permitted her to attend this important event, if she had not seen Paula safely home first.

Paula was equally glad that she was going to have an evening to herself. She worked long hard hours and did a conscientious job; when she could really relax, she enjoyed doing so. Her idea of really relaxing was to get out of the simple serviceable clothes she had worn all day, take a hot bath into which bath salts had been liberally sprinkled, and put on lounging pajamas, the vogue for which had just reached Crowley and which she had been among the first to embrace. Anyone who had not seen her in her hours of ease would have been amazed at the extravagant lengths to which a woman, normally as conservative and frugal as Paula, would carry such a taste. Once rid of her workaday garments and refreshed by a leisurely, hot, scented bath, she wanted a drink and a cigarette—in fact, several drinks and several cigarettes.

Amanda accepted the idea of the daily baths, though she had been brought up to believe that one or, at the utmost, two a week were plenty, and would have approved more wholeheartedly if it had not been perfumed. Somewhat more reluctantly, she accepted the idea of the lounging pajamas, though she would have preferred what she still called a wrapper rather than a negligee. But she disapproved so highly of the drink and the cigarettes that only when she went out could Paula remove her bootleg gin from hiding and open a whole package of Lucky Strikes. To be sure, her breath betrayed her secret weaknesses on less propitious occasions, and Amanda scolded, or merely sniffed, according to her own mood at the time. Both habits annoyed Paula intensely; she was thankful that the missionary meeting would spare her such irritation.

Because of Amanda's urgent wish to arrive at the vestry in time for the spaghetti supper, she did not even insist, as she usually did, on seeing Paula through supper before she left the house. Her niece was therefore free to soak in the tub with a gin and orange where she could reach it easily and, when she was attired in her latest and most extreme creation, to stretch out at ease on the living room sofa with the makings for further drinks, an ample supply of cigarettes and sandwiches, and her favorite magazine, *True Confessions,* on a near-by table. She was deep in an especially lurid Confession when the doorbell rang.

Callers were very rare and almost invariably unwelcome. Paula concealed the bottles of gin and Mission Orange under one of the sofa cushions, put the plate of sandwiches, the ash tray and the cigarettes under the sofa itself, and walked rather hesitantly across the living room; then, in a gingerly fashion, she opened the front door, which led directly into this. Though the opening was hardly more than a crack, it sufficed for her to identify her caller, and she threw her weight against the panels, in an attempt at quick closing and bolting. But August Scholtze had foreseen that something like this would happen and he was too quick for her; he had already thrust a foot into the opening and the next instant he was inside.

"That is not the sort of welcome you gave me in France, already, *Liebchen,*" he rumbled down at her with a wry grin. "But now you could shut the door. I'm here and your *Tante* ain't. That I know."

"What do you want of me?" Paula demanded with what she hoped was businesslike crispness. Sometimes, the gin affected her speech very quickly; at other times, this did not happen so soon and, fortunately, tonight was one of those times. Her severe manner was strangely at variance with her appearance and Scholtze did not immediately answer. He was looking her over from head to foot, genuinely puzzled at the radical departure from what he believed to be her normal mode of dress. He had not forgotten how impeccably neat she had always looked in the uniform she wore abroad while in the Graves Registration Service; and he knew, as did almost everyone, about her complete "correctness" as a secretary—a correctness by no means limited to her skill as a stenographer or to her general efficiency in assisting the manager of the Claudia in the mill's administration. But the woman who confronted him, as she stood with her back to the door, was wearing black satin lounging pajamas, lavishly embroidered in gold. An array of gold bracelets, which clanked at her slightest movement, encircled her lower arms and her wrists, and large gold loops hung from her ears. Her loosened hair was confined in a long red snood, and her bare feet were thrust into scarlet sandals.

"Maybe it disappoints you, but I don't want nothings from you except to talk a *bischen*," he said after a considerable pause.

"We have nothing to talk about, you and I. So please be good enough to leave at once. I mean get out!"

"*Aber* we do got something to talk about, and I don't feel for standing up while I talk. So if you feel for it, stand by the door yet, dressed up like you was a *Dirne* waiting to see if comes any callers. Go ahead and stand by it. But not me. *Ich nehm' Platz, gnädiges Fräulein. Mit Erlaubniss.*"

He was already walking across the living room toward the "mission" sofa of fumed oak, upholstered in dun-colored leather, and flung the closing words over his shoulder.

"Will you get out, you hulking beast?" Paula called after him. "Or shall I telephone my cousin, the sheriff?"

"Call him all you feel for. I got no feelings against him listening to what we got to say."

"I haven't anything to say to you."

"Maybe yes, maybe no. But I got somethings to say to you, and till I say them, I don't get out. Maybe I don't get out even then, yet. Maybe I stay till comes your *Tante* back by her house, so she can hear what I got to say, too. So anyhow, you could just as easy be sitting down as standing up already, *nicht wahr?*"

"If it will make you leave sooner, I'll sit down. Too bad I can't send you back to your swampish girl, but you saw to that, didn't you? And that's *all* I've got to say to you."

Scholtze shifted his relaxed pose to lean forward, his elbows on his knees, his big hands clasped so that the thick, sausage-shaped fingers were interlaced.

"To me you got nothings to say, but you already said too *verdammt* much when they question you by the courthouse yesterday and also today. You got it in your lying mouth to say you couldn't even swear yet as you would know me if you seen me! You got the *unverschämt* gall yet to say we ain't never had nothings but the barest acquaintance."

"I was ashamed to admit even that much, if you must know. And what of it?"

"This of it. When I was in that room, the night before, I already told them I know you; I said I know you a lot better as only by sight barely. So when you tell them difference, what happens? They call us both back, *und* again already you tell them the same thing. I stick by my story, too, but the difference is I am telling truth. And I got this much to say to you, *Schatzi*—"

"Don't you dare call me that!"

"*Aber warum nicht?* You was my *Schatzi* once . . . but never mind." For a moment, he ruminated on the idea of telling her that she never would have been that, but for the sad dearth of more attractive possibilities in the available personnel of the Graves Registration Service. Then he remembered that she had, in her way, tried to be kind, besides being conveniently complacent. There had been others at her headquarters who sneered at him, saying he had strayed into the wrong army, that his place should have been on the other side of the trenches; and Paula had patiently explained, more than once, that he was the son of a brewmaster, that he had grown up in the section of Cincinnati still known as "Over the Rhine," where German was more nearly the daily speech of the residents than English. It was as unfair to condemn him for the thick guttural overlay of patois in his speech as for his close-cropped bristle of blond hair, pale lashes and a generally Teutonic cast of countenance; he had been among the first of those whose numbers were drawn in the famous goldfish bowl, and he had seen twice as much service as those who were deriding him. . . . "All I got to say to you is Ten High never got by trying to lie, *und* you won't get by, not neither," he went on. "The only one as will get by is me, because I felt for telling truth."

"Rubbish! You might have told the truth about something that happened long ago in France, but you didn't tell the truth about what happened to Titine Dargereux Saturday night, or how it happened that girl's accordion was hidden at your house."

"How should you know about the *verdammt* accordion yet?"

"As far as that goes, how do you know what I said or didn't say when I was questioned by the district attorney?"

"I find things out when I feel for knowing them. How I do it—*das ist keine grosse Sache*. Maybe you do feel for being sorry now, about how you was a push-over that time in France, but you didn't feel for being sorry then; you felt for being glad when it happened already. *Ganz gewiss! Und* you been feeling for having it to happen again, only here you are too scared somebody finds out about it. Look what you got on, making out as *vielleicht—wer weiss?*—somebody is coming, and *doch* scared to have somebody to come. Even me, you would take right now, if you wasn't scared, but *ohnehin* you won't let yourself think even the truth yet, by the truth is more bitter as gall, the truth that you know nobody ain't coming. Only a fool would even try to fool hisself."

"You tell the same old lies you tell every girl you defile by even looking at her," Paula flung back. "Oh, you could fool me in France. Could? You actually did. But not here, not where I meet men whose shoes you aren't fit to lick, men who are courteous and considerate and kind, even if they can be bewitched by the scarlet temptations of a vampire like the Dargereux girl. Only to you, she wasn't a low creature, because you are one yourself. To you, she was—"

"Shut the mouth, already. You are saying more as you want to say. *Es macht nichts aus* what you feel for to think. All I am saying is don't lie no more. You are too *dumm* to lie. Even smart people can't get away with they should lie to the law, *und* you ain't smart. *Also*, if you lie you get caught worser and worser yet. So I come here to tell you to don't lie. Suppose you do tell them I know you from France already. So who feels for caring? Not me! And *ganz gewiss nicht* your fine gentleman from a boss of a Prosper Villac. Not by he is too particular. If, like I think, he is the one give Titine those gold shoes, yet, which I make her give back already, I bet you anything he don't give them for nothing. So he don't take it too particular, this fine, good gentleman. But it stands on the *Advertiser* this afternoon how he is going to marry with Moïse La-Branche's daughter. So now he is glad to have Titine out of the way—to put her out of the way. Why not? He can't have no swamp girl mixed up with no fine marriage yet."

"Shut up and beat it! I tell you again I would die before I would admit having ever known you—intimately. They can kill me, they can charge me with whatever they want. But you can't and they can't make me admit that."

Scholtze heaved his massive bulk upright. As he did so, he dislodged one of the cushions on the sofa and the bottles of gin and Mission Orange were revealed. He picked up the former and inspected it disdainfully.

"I already knowed real good something stinks, something that ain't no *Kölnisches Wasser* by a hell of a sight," he said, "but never in my whole life yet would I feel for finding rotgut what is made in bathtubs around your house. Ain't you got no *Schande* at all? Couldn't you know this here is poison, what them *Italienishe* alky cookers makes in stables? If you got to drink, drink *doch* something as is anyways clean, even if it is cut with water, which is likewise *auch* clean. If you feel for having some, I even give you all you can *sauf*. I would bring it when your *Tante* ain't by the house, like tonight. That you would like, *nicht wahr?*"

Paula wavered. She would, indeed, have liked reliable gin very much and, despite his violence and his insults, Scholtze had come uncomfortably close to the truth when he said that maybe she was disappointed, but that all he wanted was to talk to her; she would have reveled in a chance to repel improper advances. If he came again, even once, she might have such a chance. If he came several times . . . well, of course, that was not to be thought of. Again, she ordered him to get out, though less vehemently than before.

"All right, I don't come myself, I send Baer with the booze," he said, not unpleasantly. But when she shook her head, though she tried not to do so too decisively, he shrugged his shoulders.

"*Schon gut, Liebchen. Wie du willst.* I already done what I come for," he spoke with an air that was little short of casual. "I try all as I know how to keep you out from trouble like you gonna have if you try to lie. *Wenn's dir nicht passt, kannst mir am Buckel steigen.* From what I hear they got a party at Villacs' house tonight. Somebody says to me how the old man feels for having his daughter get married with Prosper real soon, by his heart has got a *Fehler*—the old man's heart, I mean, *ganz natürlich* —and he feels for seeing her settled down. So your fine gentleman had to work quick. Watch what I tell you, you with your black and gold dress like a *Dirne* waiting for company and your *grossartig* talk about fine gentleman bosses yet. I bet you they get married by each other inside a week. . . . A cow, yet, would have more sense as to lie when it stands like that! *Also, kuss' die Hand, gnä' Fräulein. Hab' die Ehre!*"

The pleasant atmosphere which pervaded the Villacs' dining room throughout supper continued the rest of the evening. Lavinia was asked to play and, once seated at the piano, went readily from one selection to another, among them Debussy's *"Clair de Lune"* and Mendelssohn's "On Wings of Song." Then, turning on her bench, she reminded Odey and Onezime of the songs they and their cousins had sung when she had first known them as children: *"Caillette"* and *"Hier Après Midi"* and *"O Ma Petite Bergère."* Did they remember these still? They admitted that they did; both were music lovers, both had good voices, and both were well versed in Cajun lore; without too much persuasion, they began to sing and, presently, everyone was taking part in the choruses. Grandpa Jim was the next to indulge in reminiscences; at the first *boucherie* his family had attended, he had entertained the other guests with some rollicking ballads about Paul Bunyan; of course, his voice was gone now, but perhaps some of those who were present on that occasion and who were present again now would substitute for him. Not only his obliging neighbors, who had quickly and delightedly learned the ballad long before, but his son-in-law and daughter, who had known it before, and his granddaughter and his great-grandson, who had learned it since, all joined in. It was the turn of the LaBranches, who had contributed so much to the earlier part of the evening, to be listeners now; everyone felt the balance to be a happy one. It was not until the time had come to say good night that regrets about anything were voiced. Then Vicky did so, with sincerity, but without any loss of the lightness which had characterized her mood throughout the evening.

"I'm sorry Anne Marie couldn't have been here, too—Anne Marie and Dale, and that this couldn't have been the time that they announced their engagement, too. But of course this party at the Benoits'. . . . You know, Father says he's heard old New Yorkers insist there was a strict rule that, once you had accepted an invitation to a seated dinner, there was only one valid excuse for breaking the engagement—your death; and, in that case, your family had to supply a satisfactory substitute."

"I don't think we take dinner parties quite so seriously here. But thank you, Vicky, for being so understanding about it."

"That's one of her strong points, understanding," Prosper said proudly.

"Now, maybe. But it took me a while to learn, didn't it? I didn't understand Louisiana or you, either! And now I love you both better than anything in the world—except Father, of course. But then he is part of Louisiana and Louisiana is part of him. He remembered that just in time to teach me!"

She distributed good night kisses impartially and went down the steps to the waiting car with her father and Prosper. Then, quite without self-consciousness, she embraced Prosper before she and Moïse drove away. Beaming, Prosper went back to the assembled family.

"Didn't I tell you she was wonderful?" he asked. "But she's right—if only Anne Marie and Dale—"

And happily, none of them guessed that Anne Marie and Dale had also been together that evening or how or where.

Chapter Twenty-two

ANNE MARIE HAD NOT ACTUALLY TOLD A FALSEHOOD ABOUT HER ENGAGE-
ment at the Benoits'; they were giving a formal dinner that night, in
honor of friends from New Orleans, to which she had been invited. But
she had omitted to state that this dinner was to take place fashionably
late; and her mother's passing impression that she had left the house
unnecessarily early was even closer to the mark than Lavinia suspected:
Anne Marie had allowed time to drive to Sapphira before turning back
and going to Pecan Grove.

She had covered the ground countless times already, of course, but
usually in someone else's car and almost never when she was at the
wheel; she was not an especially good driver, nor did she enjoy handling
an automobile. The rain was now falling in torrents and she was having
trouble with the windshield wiper; more than once, she was obliged to
draw up beside the road and try to tinker with it. She was not very
successful with things like that and, every now and then, she gave up the
effort and simply sat still, hoping that the downpour would abate. Since
it did not, and since she had made no allowance for delays of this sort,
eventually, she had no choice but to go ahead more or less blindly,
hoping that she would not miss any of the turns she should take or get
stuck in the mud. She was thankful when she recognized the familiar
landmark of the Salle des Tuileries, though never before had she looked
at it, in passing, without extreme distaste; and she was tremendously
relieved when she saw the great bulk of the Louisa sugarhouse looming
up before her. Sapphira's sugarhouse would be next and, though she still
could not see her way clearly, she knew she must now turn to the left,
not to the right, toward Cypremort Point. But the private bridges which

spanned the bayou were very close together, and several of the plantations on the farther side shared a bridge among them; moreover, the approaches to all these passages were so rank with palmetto, and the bridges so over-hung with the mossy branches of dead and dying cypress, the tangle of muscadine and the jungle growth of swamp myrtle that, even at high noon on a sunny day, they were obscured. She was taking a bold step in going alone to Dale's house and she was all too well aware of this; if, by mistake, she strayed into a neighbor's yard instead of his—by herself—at dusk—in the pouring rain—her presence might very well arouse unwel-come curiosity.

It was not until she reached the clearing which constituted a yard, beyond the growth of palmetto, and recognized it as being unmistakably Dale's, that she was relieved of her major anxieties. She drove her car straight up to the side of the dripping gallery and leaped out as quickly as possible. Nevertheless, the water from an overflowing eaves trough streamed down on her before she could get under cover, drenching her head and the upper part of her light wrap and spattering her tulle skirt. As she lifted her hand to the old-fashioned knocker, it was with the acute realization that she was very far from presenting the glamorous figure which she had sought to achieve while she dressed, and which usually represented so little effort on her part.

No light was burning on the gallery and only two or three dim ones in the house. She had, of course, reckoned on the possibility that Dale might not be at home, but she had decided that this was a slight one. Increasingly, as his courtship dragged on without success, he had become something of a recluse; unless he knew that Anne Marie was to be one of a party, he was apt to remain at home, reading until all hours, rather than spending those same hours in dancing, drinking and playing cards. She had taken the precaution of inquiring whether he had been invited to the Benoits' party, and found that he had not; now that Didier felt he was making some progress with his suit, he did not voluntarily invite competition from his most formidable rival. Moreover, Anne Marie felt almost equally certain that, if Dale *were* at home, he would be alone; when he entertained, she was always included among the guests and he did not encourage "droppers-in." He had good servants: an ebony giant of a man named Tiger, his bright-skinned wife, who Dale had insisted should be called Leona, and their numerous offspring, to whom they al-ways referred as "so many head"; but excellent quarters were provided for them at the rear of the back yard, which was a large one; when not on duty, they were at some distance from the Big House, and Dale followed the local custom of having his main meal in the middle of the day, letting the servants leave after they had prepared a light supper and put it in the refrigerator, where he could help himself to it, whenever he felt so inclined. Very possibly, he might be doing that now, which would account for his delay in snapping on more lights and coming to the door. Nevertheless, the delay was so long that Anne Marie raised the knocker again and rapped harder. This time, from one of the dormer windows, a voice, which she thankfully identified as Dale's, called to her out of the darkness.

"Just a minute! I'll be down as soon as I can!"

The longed-for lights began to appear, first in the upper and then in the lower hall, next in the double parlors and, finally, on the gallery. Then the heavy, old-fashioned bolts of the front door were drawn back, and it opened to reveal Dale, wearing a crimson dressing gown of brocaded silk, hastily thrown over his pajamas. As he recognized his surprising visitor, he instinctively drew the dressing gown a little more closely around him.

"For heaven's sake, Anne Marie! What on earth are you doing here? Is anything wrong?"

"No, nothing's wrong except that I had an awful time getting here and I'm wet through."

"Well, how did you happen to come in the first place?"

"Because I wanted to see you, that's all. Aren't you going to let me in?"

"Why, of course! But you see, I wasn't expecting anyone and, as I didn't feel very well, I thought I'd spend the evening reading in bed. I'll light a fire right away, so you can get dried off while I go back upstairs and dress."

"What do you mean, you're not feeling well? You're not really sick, are you?"

"No, no! Just a little tired and—well, rather low in my mind. Not that I ought to be, but sometimes I am and, very often, when I feel that way, I go to bed early and read. I can get into another world quickly like that and forget all my own problems. Good Lord, you *are* wet through! I didn't think you really meant it! I thought you'd just got caught in the rain for a moment and were talking figuratively."

She had stepped inside as soon as he opened the door and was standing beside him, rivulets streaming from her curls, her drenched wrap clinging to her shoulders. She looked up at him, pathetically.

"Just put your hand on my head and you'll see whether I really meant it. My hair's as wet as if I'd been in swimming with no cap on. Couldn't you give me a towel, or something, that I could dry it with? We can hang my wrap up by the fire, as soon as you've built one; but my dress is wet, too, and I'm on my way to a dinner party. I'm afraid I'll have to ask you to lend me something else to put on, so that I can get that dry, too."

Somewhat to Anne Marie's surprise, Dale did not follow the suggestion that he should put his hand on her head. If he had only done that, everything would have been very simple; because next he would have raised his other hand, also, and they would have rested on either side of the central part, and then they would have slid gently down to her cheeks and tilted up her face, and the next minute he and she would have kissed and made up. Instead, he turned away rather abruptly, walked the entire length of the hall and threw open a door at the end of it.

"I don't believe you've ever been in this room," he said. "I've kept it closed, since my mother died. But if there's anything in the house you could put on, while your own clothes are drying, it would be here. You're welcome to look in the chests and armoires. I think the fireplace still works all right, but I'll make sure. It's been cleaned out, though. I'll have to get some kindling and coal and then I'll be right back."

He left, carefully closing the door behind him. Anne Marie took off her wet wrap, hung it over the back of a chair, and opened the door of a huge *armoire à glace*. It was full of clothes, in such orderly array that they might have been prepared for speedy selection among all the different kinds available—afternoon dresses, evening dresses, springtime prints, summer muslins, autumn *tailleurs,* winter woolens. The *robes d'intérieur* were grouped together at one end; Anne Marie took a lace-trimmed challis, figured in small bright flowers, from its padded hanger and, standing in front of the cheval glass, held it up to herself to judge its size. It would fit very well, she decided—not perfectly, but then a *robe d'intérieur* was meant to be loose and flowing. She had just struggled out of her blue tulle and was getting into the sprigged challis, when Dale knocked at the door.

"Here we are," he said, entering the room with a bundle of kindling in the crook of his left arm, and the handle of a well-filled coal scuttle in his right hand. "You'll be fixed up in no time now." With hardly a glance at her, he went straight to the hearth and, bending over it, laid a fire with the ease of long practice and watched it until he was sure it would burn brightly and not merely smolder. Then he brushed his hands together and straightened up.

"I'll be back in a few minutes and take a second look at it," he said.

"Meanwhile, I'll start another fire in the front parlor and get dressed. Did you find a towel all right? No, I don't suppose you knew where to look for one, since there's no connecting bathroom." He walked over to an old-fashioned washstand and opened a deep drawer below the marble shelf dominated by an enormous bowl and pitcher, which, in turn, were flanked by a smaller pitcher, a mug, a soap dish and a toothbrush holder, all in matching, highly ornamented china. From the drawer, he extracted two huckaback towels, heavily fringed and embroidered in large initials outlined in red. "I can get you something more modern, if you prefer," he said. "There are plenty of Turkish towels in the house. But I thought maybe you'd like to use these—they're very soft."

"I'd love to use them. But, Dale, why do you have to light another fire? It's warm, anyway, and this one's burning beautifully. And why do you have to go and dress? We can talk while I'm drying my hair. I've got to be on my way just as soon as I can, or I'll be late for my dinner party. And it won't take me long to say what I want to—that I'm sorry about Sunday night."

"I'm sorry, too. So why don't we let it go at that?"

"You're sorry about what?"

"Sorry I displeased you. Not sorry for what I did. I'd do the same thing right over again."

"I wasn't talking about what you did. I'm talking about what I did. I'm sorry I displeased *you,* sorry that you thought I was unreasonable."

"You didn't displease me. You disappointed me."

"Well, whatever I did that you didn't like, I'm sorry about."

"Anne Marie, it isn't a question of whether I *liked* it or not. It's a lot more basic than that. I'd rather not talk about it, if you don't mind. And if the only reason you've come all the way out here, by yourself, in the pouring rain, was to tell me you're sorry you displeased me Sunday night, I don't see why we need to settle down for explanations and arguments anywhere. In fact, I shouldn't think, since you're in a hurry to get to your party, that you'd want to be bothered with me while you're drying your hair. I'm sure you can do it much faster if you don't try to talk at the same time."

He had started across the room as soon as he handed her the towels. Now, he was already at the door, with his hand on the knob. Anne Marie spoke almost desperately.

"It wasn't the only thing I wanted to say to you. It was the first thing. There's something else, a lot more important."

"Well, what is it? I'm listening."

"Dale, I've made up my mind. I want to be engaged to you—right away. I'll be happy to marry you as soon as you like."

This time, Anne Marie was sure, there could not possibly be any doubt as to what he would do. He would rush to her side and take her in his arms. Instead, he continued to stand beside the door with his hand on the knob.

"I don't believe you really mean that," he said steadily. "Perhaps you haven't heard that I was called to the courthouse this afternoon, to tell Landry and Davila and Bennett what I told your family Sunday night—of course, it was no more of a secret after that than if I'd stood on a street corner with a megaphone. I'm a suspect in this case, which may very well be a murder case, just as much as anyone else who's been called in—or who's going to be called in. In other words, I'm in the same category as August Scholtze—and as your brother. The only person who's completely in the clear is Didier. He's the man for you."

"But, Dale, you weren't even at the mill Saturday night!"

"That's true enough. But, as far as I know, it hasn't yet been proved, to the satisfaction of the authorities, that I wasn't there. Of course, I've told them that I was at home, reading. But I don't know whether or not they believed me. It's rumored that they've caught two witnesses in lies already. If that's so, they're doubly suspicious of everything that's said to them and taking extra care to check and recheck."

"Well, I think it's very insulting, if they're doing it in your case, and I think it will be very insulting if they call in Prosper as a witness. But that wouldn't make any difference in what I've just said about having made up my mind and wanting to get engaged to you. Why should it? Vicky's father has announced her engagement to Prosper."

"Yes, and Vicky telephoned Prosper Sunday night, to tell him that, whatever he'd done, she loved him and that she wanted the whole world to know it. If you'd told me something like that Sunday night—"

"I'd planned to tell you Sunday night!"

"You planned to tell me before you heard about the gold slippers. And then, you *changed* your mind."

"Oh, Dale, I'm sorry, I'm awfully sorry! Do you think if I weren't, I'd have come out here to tell you so and ask you to forgive me?"

"No. And I don't want to say anything unkind, Anne Marie. I've loved you very much, for a long time. But I haven't quite figured out why you changed your mind—either the first time or the second time, the first time being Sunday and the second today. If you loved me so much that you wanted the whole world to know it, whatever I'd done, the way Vicky loves Prosper, you wouldn't have let a little thing like a pair of gold slippers get in your way. You didn't love me that much—you know you didn't. And I don't believe you love me that much now. How could you, with only two days in between what you did Sunday and what you're doing tonight? You couldn't change that fast."

"I've thought it over, I've realized what a terrible fool I was. Dale, please! Oh, what's that noise?"

Her plea ended in something very like a scream. Someone else was pounding at the front door, banging the knocker harder than she had less than an hour earlier. Dale crossed the room quickly and put his hand over her mouth.

"Keep quiet!" he said compellingly. "If you scream like that, someone will think *you're* being murdered. Someone else is at the door, that's all. I'll have to go and see who it is. Perhaps there's an emergency of some kind. Or, perhaps, it's just a neighbor dropping in for a visit. In any case, there's no reason why you should be frightened and no one needs to know you're here. Lock the door after me, when I leave, if you want to, and turn out the lights. The fire'll keep the room from being completely dark. But don't try to come out or call. I'll get back to you as soon as I can."

The knocking had begun again, louder than ever. Dale dropped his hand to Anne Marie's shoulder and pressed it reassuringly. Then, before she could stop him, he was gone. He heard her whimper, "Oh, Dale, I *am* frightened!" as he hurried to the door. But he did not hear her lock it, because the knocking was drowning out every other sound and, since there was no transom, he could not see whether she had turned out the light. Calling, "Just a minute!" as he had before, he ran toward the front door and opened it.

The Professor, wrapped in a long black cloak, was standing on the threshold.

Chapter Twenty-three

"I TRUST MY VISIT IS NOT INOPPORTUNE," HE SAID, WITH HIS USUAL FORmality. "Had you already retired for the night? When I saw another car outside, my first impulse was to withdraw. But then I recognized the Oldsmobile of our mutual friend, Prosper Villac, and I realized that he would not consider my visit an intrusion. In any case, I wished to take this opportunity to return the twenty dollars which you so kindly entrusted to me. I kept hoping for a chance to make the purchase you had in mind, but I was neither able to go to New Orleans myself nor commission anyone I could trust to do the delicate errand for me and now, of course, the chance is gone forever."

He stepped inside the door, shedding his long cloak as he did so; evidently it was not raining as hard as it had been, for, though this was damp, it was not drenched, as Anne Marie's had been. Having folded it carefully, he felt for his wallet, removed this from his hip pocket and extracted a twenty-dollar bill which he proffered to Dale. This done, he glanced in the direction of the double parlors as if hopefully expecting that he would be invited to enter, that he would find Prosper ensconced somewhere thereabouts with a drink in his hand and that when he, the Professor, had enjoyed one, also, they might have a little classical music, as had been the case when he called on Dale before.

Dale accepted the twenty-dollar bill mechanically, assured the Professor there had been no hurry about returning it and, leading the way into the front parlor, invited his unwelcome guest to be seated. Meanwhile, he was wondering what on earth he should say or do next. He inwardly cursed the local custom which encouraged parents to give their offspring identical—or almost identical—cars, if they could afford to do so. He had stopped in to see Vicky that afternoon, after leaving the courthouse and reading the announcement in the *Advertiser*, to take her flowers and extend his best wishes in person. She had told him there was to be a family party at the Villacs' that night, and Dale did not dare pretend that the car parked beside the gallery was Prosper's. If he did, sooner or later—sooner, rather than later—the Professor would learn about the celebration of the engagement, wonder why on earth Dale had deceived him, and attribute some wholly incorrect and, doubtless, damaging significance to the deception. Besides, if Prosper had been in the house, he would presently have put in an appearance; his failure to do so would have meant other misconstructions. Dale must try to explain the car in some other way. But, even if he could think of something plausible, that still would not help Anne Marie. She could not remain locked up in a dark room and Dale had no delusions about the probable length of the Professor's visit; the poor lonely old man would stay as long as he could. Meanwhile, Anne Marie would not be getting to her party, the Benoits would telephone the Villacs to ask what had become of her, both families would be thrown into a state of consternation when it was discovered that she was missing and there would be the devil to pay, generally. Somehow, he must get Anne Marie out of the back door and on her way to Lafayette, unbeknownst to the Professor. He might be able to manage it when he went for the drinks—on the other hand, he might not. The Professor was almost sure to hear footsteps, subdued voices, the sudden starting of an unexplained car; it was even possible that he might follow Dale to the rear of the house and ask if he might be of any help in getting the drinks.

While all this was passing through Dale's agitated mind, it also suddenly occurred to him that the Professor would consider him dressed unconventionally, to say the least, to act as host for a young lady whose reputation was not only unsullied, but unassailable. Even more violently than he had inwardly cursed the identical cars, Dale cursed himself for not having managed, somehow, to get back upstairs and fling on some clothes, any kind of clothes, rather than pajamas and a brocade dressing gown. He could not imagine any kind of a costume more likely to suggest a secret and shameful assignation to a suspicious mind, and he did not see how the Professor could help having a suspicious mind, after his experience in dance halls, night clubs and worse. As far as that went, Anne Marie's costume would not help any, if she burst upon the scene —which Dale believed her quite capable of doing if she lost her head— still wearing the challis negligee. She might, conceivably, get back into her dress, which was only damp, for, being low cut, it had escaped the worst of the deluge; but Dale had an uncomfortable feeling that it was one of those mysterious feminine garments which no girl could get into without some help, since it fastened in the back. Her cloak must still be soaking wet. Her appearance in her own dress, inadequately hooked or snapped or buttoned or whatever was done to make two sides of it come together, would be almost as damaging as the challis.

He had, however, underestimated Anne Marie's resourcefulness, once she had recovered from her chagrin and fright. The door of the long-disused room opened, as he had been afraid it might, just as he started for the pantry, with the Professor in his wake. But when this happened, it disclosed the vision of a beautiful girl, clothed in the height of fashion—of some thirty or forty years earlier. She had on a stiff pink satin dress made with a many-gored skirt reaching to the ground, a tight-fitting bodice, a *décolletage* which was discreet, though generous, and enormous puff sleeves. Her hair was gathered into a great golden knot on top of her head, and this was surmounted by a quivering upright bow of velvet ribbon. In one hand, she carried a gauzy painted fan, and over one arm was flung, with apparent nonchalance, a narrow velvet cape with a high shirred collar. She came forward, wreathed in smiles, and without the slightest sign of embarrassment.

"I just don't know how to thank you enough, Dale," she said sweetly. "It was really most inconsiderate of my host to suggest, at the very last moment, that he thought it would be fun to have his guests dress up for a Gay Nineties party. There wasn't a thing in our house I could use. Mother never went in much for elaborate evening clothes, I'm afraid, and anyhow, she's slimmer than I am, to this day. If I hadn't remembered what you'd told me about that armoire full of beautiful old dresses, I'd have been simply lost! I'm a little late, so I've just left my own clothes scattered around, wherever they happened to fall, but I'll send for them tomorrow. They won't be in your way till then, will they? The only thing I feel badly about is getting you out of bed when you're coming down with the grippe." She turned toward Dale's startled companion and included him in her charming smile. "Don't keep Dale up long, will you?" she entreated. "He's got—oh, I don't know how many degrees of fever! You're the Professor, aren't you? I know once he starts listening to your playing, Dale won't want you to stop. I haven't had the pleasure of meeting you before, but I've heard that no one, absolutely no one, can make a piano sing the way you do. I'm so sorry I can't stay to hear you tonight. Some other time very soon, I hope!"

She was gone, in a rustle of silk and a flash of buckled slippers. The Professor looked after her with mingled admiration and amazement. Then he drew a deep sigh.

"What an apparition of elegance and charm!" he exclaimed. "It is not often, nowadays, that we see its like anywhere. She should have come in a golden coach! But I assume that the Oldsmobile I saw outside is hers and, if this is the case, that she is Prosper Villac's sister."

"Yes."

"She does not in the least resemble him," the Professor said thoughtfully.

"No, she looks like her mother—or rather, as her mother must have looked once, only, I believe, even lovelier. Prosper takes after his father's family—that is, there's a general resemblance. I haven't a very clear recollection of Claude Villac—I was still a small boy when he died and we weren't here much in those days. I never saw his cousin Felix, as far as I can remember. But I've heard that he was the best looking of the Villac-Primeaux tribe—slender, instead of stocky like the rest of them, and merry instead of stolid, with very fine teeth and eyes and what's generally known as 'a way with him.' All that would add up to a description of Prosper, too."

"Yes, yes. He and his sister share the quality of charm, if nothing else. A pity that Prosper should be involved in such a dreadful scandal, and just at the time when he is about to be married."

"It's worse than a pity, it's a tragedy. But his fiancée and his mother are standing up very well under it." Dale realized that he had not included Anne Marie in this statement, but it was now too late to rectify the omission. "Shall we sit down and have our drink?" he asked. "And perhaps you'd play for me, too, before you leave."

"Nothing would give me greater pleasure. But I'm afraid I must confine myself to one selection. My employer has again gone to Crowley on some private business and especially charged me not to be late in arriving at my post."

"Will it delay you too much—or seem like an impertinence—if I ask you one or two questions? Just for my own information, of course."

"Permit me to say, Mr. Fontenot, that I do not believe you could ever do or say anything that would seem like an impertinence. I shall be happy to answer whatever questions you may see fit to put to me. And while doing so, let me drink to your health and happiness!"

He leaned back in a large armchair and began to savor his bourbon in leisurely, appreciative sips. Dale sat down opposite him.

"I couldn't help wondering whether, in your testimony yesterday, you said anything about my offer of twenty dollars with which to buy a pair of gold slippers?"

"Positively nothing. No question was asked me concerning them and I saw no reason for introducing the subject on my own initiative. Toward the end of my interrogation, I mentioned the fact that, on the fatal night, Baer had burst into uncontrollable weeping. After that, all the questions asked me concerned him, though there was nothing I could say that threw any light on the sad subject under discussion."

"Then I'm afraid you may be recalled. As you must have heard, I told the Villacs and Primeaux Sunday night, at a private gathering, about my offer. I did so with the best possible motives."

"Of course, of course. You do not need to assure me of that. You reasoned, and quite rightly, that if it were known you were making the gift, indirectly, through an elderly man who stood *in loco parentis,* so to speak, that neither you nor anyone else would be suspected of an ulterior motive."

"That *is* the way I reasoned. But, as I told Anne Marie a few minutes ago, we don't know that the authorities are going to reason the same way. I was called to the Crowley courthouse this afternoon and told to return tomorrow morning. Doubtless, you'll be called, as soon as you get to the Tuileries, telling you to go back there tomorrow morning, too."

"And, if I am, I shall simply tell the truth, as I have consistently done so far. I shall corroborate everything you have said. And that will be the end of the matter."

"I'm afraid not. If Bennett and Landry and Davila believe you and me, as I'm rather hopeful they will, they'll naturally go on searching for the person who did give Titine the gold slippers and under what circumstances. They won't rest until they find out. And, when they do, it may be very unpleasant."

"Yes, you're probably right." The Professor sighed again and took a last draft of his drink.

"Well, I regret that there seems nothing you and I can do to alter such unpleasantness. And I must be getting back to my work, though I have little heart for it now. . . . Shall I play Chopin's "Raindrop Prelude" for you before I leave? It seems appropriate for a night like this."

Anne Marie's feelings, as she made her hurried trip from Sapphira to Pecan Grove, were compounded almost equally of chagrin and relief. Dale's cool reception of her and his distant attitude throughout her stay

in his house had, of course, been a great blow to her pride; but she did
not believe for a minute that he would remain aloof for long and, meanwhile, she thought she had considerable cause for self-congratulation in
the adroit way she had managed to extricate herself from what might
have looked like a compromising situation and, at the same time, to
provide herself with a costume which was sure to cause a sensation at
the Benoits' party. Of course, she would not tell quite the same story there
that she had at Sapphira; she would say she had had a sudden yen for
dressing up and that, when she found these beautiful clothes, she simply
could not resist the temptation to gratify it then and there. The inference
would be that the pink satin had belonged to her mother, and that she
had discovered it hidden away, though perfectly preserved, in some
obscure corner of a closet of the Villacs' house. But there would be no
real falsehood involved, because she would not actually say this. . . .

The rain had abated and she was able to make good time. She would
be a little late, but the Benoits had no scruples about serving cocktails
and the consumption of these could be counted on to take up the greater
part of an hour. As she never drank spirits and this was well known
among her friends, her tardiness could, and doubtless would, be attributed largely to the fact that she found it both pointless and tiresome
to sit around while everyone else enjoyed them. Besides, in urging
Didier not to come for her, she had told him she wanted to do one or
two errands on her way to the party, and that it would make her nervous
to think he was sitting around outside while she did them; he could
take her home in his car and send hers back to Crowley the next day.
He had not welcomed the suggestion, because he wanted two rides with
her, not one, but he had accepted it. Now he could easily be imagining
and telling others that her errands had taken longer than she expected.

Unfortunately, the course of events at Pecan Grove was no smoother
than it had been at Sapphira. Anne Marie made her grand entrance with
all the éclat she had planned. But she was hardly inside the living
room where, as she had anticipated, the other guests were all contentedly sipping cocktails, when a handsome elderly woman, obviously
one of the guests from New Orleans, since she was a complete stranger
to Anne Marie, set down her drink and looked fixedly at the newcomer.
Then she gave a scream which was half admiration and half sharp surprise.

"Oh—am I seeing a ghost or something? My dear child, *where* did those
clothes come from?"

"Why—I just happened to find them, that's all," Anne Marie answered, startled in her turn.

"Yes, but *where?* Because I could swear that dress you're wearing was in Lily Brockenborough's trousseau! She was the one who had the fortune, you know," the speaker went on, turning to address the company at large. "All her clothes were made in Paris, by Worth, and when she came from Virginia to New Orleans as Eugene Fontenot's bride, she caused a sensation! She had a different dress for every occasion—every luncheon, every dinner, every ball—and each appearance she made seemed to eclipse the one before it. She was the talk of the town. If I'm not mistaken, the dress this pretty child has on is the very one she wore to Comus in '94—or maybe it was '95. Yes, it must have been '95, because I was in the Court that year and had an unobstructed view of everyone who came on the floor. Lily Brockenborough! Why, she was the toast of the town, just as she had been in Richmond!"

A buzz of interested comment followed this announcement. It soon appeared that the handsome elderly woman who spoke first was not the only person present to remember the beautiful Virginian who had married Dale Fontenot's father; several others recalled her with equal vividness and, now that they were reminded, thought that the pink satin dress looked familiar to them, too. In the midst of this general chitchat, Didier, who had met Anne Marie affectionately at the door and was standing beside her, spoke to her in a way that seemed to her rather heated, despite the fact that he had lowered his voice.

"Is that really one of Mrs. Fontenot's dresses?"

"Why—well, yes, it is."

"How on earth did you happen to wear it tonight?"

"Didn't you or Maurice or someone say something about making this a Gay Nineties party?"

"I never did, and if 'Rice had, I'd be sure to know it. Obviously, Mother didn't, either—otherwise, you wouldn't be the only one here in such an outfit. When did you get it?"

"Just this afternoon."

"You mean you called Dale, after I'd told you he wasn't invited to this party, and asked him to bring you one of his mother's dresses?"

"No, it wasn't exactly like that."

"Well, what was it like?"

"Didier, can't we talk about this on the ride home, if you think we have to? Your mother's signaling that she wants everyone to go in to dinner."

The dinner was excellent, but Anne Marie was not able to do it justice. Didier dropped the subject of the borrowed dress, but she realized he was doing this only temporarily and she began to dread the ride home. Maurice was in no mood to add to the gaiety of the occasion, either: his hang-over had been a bad one, he still had a raging headache, and he had received an unwelcome message from the assistant district attorney to the effect that he would not be excused a second time from coming to the courthouse; he was expected to be there promptly at nine the following morning. This summons was not calculated to improve general malaise. With the younger element so little disposed to add to the gaiety of the occasion, it was natural that the elders should take over and, once started on the subject of the fabulous Lily Brockenborough, for the Orleanians to go on and on talking about her and the period when she and other belles had reigned. To Anne Marie this was not only very annoying, but very dull. Since she could tell by Didier's glowering expression that she could not avoid a scene with him sooner or later, she decided that it might just as well be soon. She did not, however, realize how far gone he was in anger, until she was actually in the car with him on the road to Crowley.

"Did you go all the way to Sapphira this afternoon and get that dress?" he demanded.

"Don't take that tone with me, Didier."

"Never mind about my tone. Answer my question!"

"I don't know that I'm obliged to account to you for my actions and I don't propose to make a habit of it. But I'll answer you this one time. Yes, I did."

"You went all the way from Crowley to Cypremort in the pouring rain, to borrow a dress that you didn't need any more than a cat needs two tails? You've got more dresses already than you know what to do with, more than any other girl around here, unless it's Vicky."

"I told you I somehow got the idea that this was to be a fancy dress party."

"Yes, and I've told you that you imagined that. I'm giving you the benefit of the doubt. I'm not saying that you told a deliberate lie."

"Don't you dare talk that way to me, Didier Benoit!"

"I won't, if you stick to the truth. You went to Cypremort because you wanted to see Dale Fontenot, and you knew perfectly well he wouldn't come to see you after the way you acted Sunday night."

"Well, what if I did?"

"Just this: Sunday night, you as good as told me, after I brought you your supper and we were by ourselves, that you were ready to be engaged to me. I ought to have known that this was only to spite Dale, that it was Dale you really wanted. But I didn't. I thought right along I had a fighting chance, and Sunday night I went home, thinking I'd won out. If you'd been playing fair, you would have let me know, the next morning, that you were afraid you'd given me the wrong impression. But you didn't do anything of the sort. The only word I've had from you was to ask whether Dale was invited to our house tonight and then to say you had some errands to do on your way there. *Errands!* A trip to Cypremort to make up with Dale on the trumped-up excuse of borrowing a dress!"

"There wasn't any trumped-up excuse. Since you're so bound to hear the truth, the whole truth and nothing but the truth, I'll tell you that I went to Cypremort to let Dale know I was sorry I hadn't behaved very well on Sunday. But I arrived there soaked to the skin, and he took me into his mother's room and told me to help myself to anything I could find there. The idea was just a negligee of some sort, while my own clothes were drying. But I realized how late it was getting, so, instead—"

"*A negligee of some sort!* And I suppose he built a fire for you and that you and he had a nice cozy visit together! It's a lucky thing for you Dale hadn't already gone to bed with the birds, the way he does lots of times! Or that someone else didn't arrive and find you and him, both more or less *en négligé,* with no one else in the house!"

Anne Marie pressed her lips together hard. She realized it was quite likely that Didier might find out that something very like this had happened. But she was determined not to tell him this now.

"So you ended up all safely engaged to Dale?" Didier asked sarcastically. This time, she had no choice but to answer.

"No, I didn't."

"You mean to say—"

She knew only too well what Didier guessed she would have to say, if she said anything. She continued to keep her lips pressed together, wondering if they would ever reach Crowley. Scott and Duson were behind them now, but they had not even reached Rayne. They had at least eight miles more to go. Didier give a short ugly laugh.

"If anyone had told me, Sunday afternoon, that you couldn't have either of two men who've been in love with you for years, just by lifting your little finger, I'd have laughed in his face. And now, forty-eight hours later, here you are without either one of them in reach. Dale won't forgive you because you didn't trust him—and I don't blame him. And

I shan't forgive you, because it's evident I can't trust you. If you start two-timing me at this stage of the game, there's no telling what you'd do later on. I can't very well let you out by the side of the road, looking as if you'd come from some kind of fancy house ball. But I can tell you right here and now, this is our last ride together!"

It was very late when they finally drew up before the "prettiest house in Crowley." As Lavinia had reminded Prosper, she was "old-fashioned about such things"; she did not actually sit up until her daughter was in for the night, but, on the other hand, she did not turn out her light or go to sleep and she always left her bedroom door open. Anne Marie was not required to go in and give her mother an accounting of the evening's outing, but it was her habit to do so, and both of them enjoyed these intimate visits, regardless of the hour. This time, however, Anne Marie simply called to Lavinia from the hall; it was late, she was terribly tired, they'd see each other in the morning. . . .

"Oh, do come in, dear! I want to tell you about our family supper. It's a shame you missed it. We all had the best time! And we're all in love with Vicky."

"All right, I'll be back in just a minute. My shoes are killing me. I'll have to get some slippers."

She would have to go back, she would have to tell her mother something, she would have to think of a way to get the pink satin dress back to Dale before it was discovered. But, after all, what would be the use in trying? Lavinia would hear all about the Benoits' party within twenty-four hours, and it would not be much longer before she realized that both Dale and Didier had stopped coming to the house. Anne Marie might just as well tell the whole story herself. She flung herself down beside her mother's bed and sobbed her heart out.

Chapter Twenty-four

NEITHER DALE NOR THE PROFESSOR WAS DETAINED LONG FOR INTERROGA-
tion Wednesday morning. Dale was questioned first; his straightfor-
ward story, repeated almost word for word at the courthouse as he had
told it at the Villacs' Sunday night, rang so incontestably true from
beginning to end, that the Professor's was not really needed to confirm
it, except for the record. As soon as he had finished, he drove over to
the Villacs', where he was warmly welcomed by Callie, who opened the
door for him.

"Miss Anne Marie, she goin' be powerful glad to see you, Mistuh
Dale," Callie announced, ushering him into the living room. "Seems
like she all upstirred this morning. She in the bed still, she say she
done cotched a bad cold. Her eyes, they runnin' all right, but look to
me more like she cryin' than like they streamin', 'count of sickness. She
don't sneeze, she don't cough, she just cries."

"Do you think she'd feel able to come down and see me for a few
minutes? I wouldn't want her to, if it wouldn't be good for her. Mrs.
Villac's at the mill, I suppose, so I can't consult her."

"Ain't no need you should consult Miss Lavinia, Mistuh Dale. Us
can tell you it won't do her no harm to see you. It'll do her a heap of
good."

Dale had been prepared for at least a half hour's wait, but inside of
ten minutes, Anne Marie was on the threshold of the living room. She
looked at him doubtfully, almost timidly, as if uncertain how she ought
to greet him. Without hesitation, he came forward and took her hand.

"Let's sit down and talk for a few minutes, Anne Marie, shall we?"
he said quietly. And when she nodded, her lips trembling a little, he

put his arm around her waist and guided her to the nearest sofa. Then, still encircling her with his arm, he went on speaking in the same quiet way. "I've been thinking about last night," he said. "And I'm very much ashamed of the way I acted."

"Oh, Dale, you—you haven't anything to be ashamed of! I've treated you very, very badly and—"

"Let me do the talking for just a minute or two, will you, dear? You made a great effort to come all the way to Cypremort to tell me you were sorry for what happened Sunday and, instead of welcoming you, I repulsed you. I told you I wasn't displeased with you, I was disappointed in you. I can't take that back, because it's true, any more than I can truthfully say I might have acted differently Sunday night; I know I couldn't have. But I'm afraid most people, no matter how much they love each other, disappoint each other sometimes. You must have been terribly disappointed in me yesterday. So I'd like to suggest that we go back to where we were Sunday afternoon, before the news of Titine's death reached us, and carry on from there. Wouldn't you like to?"

"You know I'd love to, more than anything in the world. But I can't, until I tell you what happened after I left Cypremort."

"All right, tell me, if it'll make you feel any better."

"It'll be terribly hard, but I'll try."

It was not as hard, after all, as she had expected, not nearly as hard as it had been to tell her mother both what had happened at Cypremort and what had happened at Pecan Grove. And all the time she was telling him, Dale sat with his arm around her, every now and then pressing her waist a little, in a way which somehow gave her great encouragement. It was not until she quoted Didier's final taunt that he interrupted her.

"Didier's a good friend of mine and he does love you, too, Anne Marie," Dale said. "Don't make any mistake about that. However, he and I don't always look at things the same way—we never have and probably we never shall. Of course, I think mine is the right way and his is the wrong way, but that's just my opinion. Anyhow, I want you to forget not only what happened Sunday night here, after we heard Titine was dead, but what happened last night, at Sapphira and Pecan Grove. Will you, to please me?"

"I'll try," Anne Marie said again.

"All right. I don't want you to say anything more now. But, next Sunday, I'll come to see you again. That'll give you several days to think things over. And, perhaps, you'll have something more to say to me then

—something I'll be awfully glad to hear and that I hope you'll be glad to say."

He leaned over and kissed her cheek. "Meantime," he said, "I wouldn't be in the least surprised if you saw Didier again after all. He's thinking things over, too—don't you believe for a minute that he isn't. And he was quite right in assuming that he had a fighting chance—until now. I hope I'm not being unfair when I say I consider that he forfeited that last night. And if you don't think I'm presuming too much, I'd like to ask you not to give him another."

"Of course I shan't give him another."

"Another thing—the Fontenots don't go in much for what my mother used to call lavender lies and I don't believe that, by and large, the Villacs do, either. I understand about the jam you were in last night. But, again, I hope you won't think I'm presuming too much if I say—"

"You're not presuming about anything. You're a perfect angel, Dale."

"Oh, no! Don't say that! If for no other reason than because angels belong in heaven, where there's no marrying or giving in marriage. That wouldn't suit me at all."

He kissed her again, this time on her mouth, but quickly and lightly. Then, after tightening the pressure on her waist again, barely long enough to make her conscious of it, he rose and smiled down at her.

"Good-by until Sunday, darling."

"Good-by and—and I don't know how to say the rest."

"This time, you mustn't try. And I must be on my way."

He was gone before she could protest, out of sight before she could believe that at least part of what had occurred was not a happy dream, coming after a nightmare. As he approached the courthouse, he saw that the Professor was just coming down the steps. Dale stopped his car and called to the forlorn old man.

"You didn't run into any unpleasantness, did you?"

"None at all. It was just as you said you hoped it would be. The authorities did not doubt my word about the unspent money for the slippers, any more than they doubted yours. At least, that was my impression. Of course, I did not hear their opinion voiced, nor did I see the transcript. They're still pursuing the subject of the accordion. I'm not so sure they believe my story about that, though it's quite as true as the other: I did not see it from the time Titine last performed at the Tuileries, namely a week ago tonight, when, as usual, she left it in my car, until it was produced in a battered condition during the course of an interrogation. But that question's in abeyance for the moment."

"So you're free for the rest of the day?"

"Completely."

"Then why not come and spend it with me at Sapphira? We could have lots of music and as much bourbon as you feel like consuming."

"I cannot imagine anything more agreeable. I might say in passing, however, that our young friend, who is now undergoing interrogation, may not get off as easily as we did. But then, perhaps, he did not face questioning with as clear a conscience or in as confident a mood. He was summoned by Guerra just as I was leaving, and his countenance was marked by that false flippancy which, in itself, is usually a giveaway."

The Professor had formed a correct estimate, regarding both the impression which he and Dale had made and that which Maurice Benoit was now making. His general air of jauntiness and the manner in which he answered the first routine questions did nothing to predispose Landry and Bennett in his favor.

"Let's get on with the hog-sticking, Theo," he said breezily, in response to the warning that any effort to withhold information was a serious offense. "I'm not about to hide anything I know."

"I thought it fair to acquaint you with all the situation implies," Landry said stiffly. "But we will now proceed with the hog-sticking, as you so elegantly term it. . . . Were you or were you not acquainted with the late Titine Dargereux?"

"I was acquainted with her."

"Slightly or fairly well?"

"Fairly well."

"One might, perhaps, say very well?"

"One might, of course."

"I asked that question seriously. I should like to have you reply to it in the same way."

"All right. I knew her very well."

"When did you last see her?"

"On Saturday."

"About what time?"

"About six in the evening."

"Was that the only time you saw her Saturday?"

"No, I'd seen her earlier in the day, too."

"By chance or by a previous appointment?"

"The second time was by previous appointment. Earlier that day I'd driven down to Stewpan Cove to give her a present I knew I couldn't

give her that night, or any other night for the matter of that. Not without having this big hood Scholtze blowing his stack."

"What kind of a present?"

Maurice hesitated. "I know it sounds dopey," he said at length. "It was
a pair of high-heeled gold slippers, the same ones she was wearing when
her body was found. I suppose she was buried in them, if they put
shoes on people's bodies in a coffin."

"Wouldn't you consider that a rather unusual sort of gift?"

"Not if that was what a person wanted. She wanted them more than
anything, she said."

"Was that declaration made to you personally?"

"Hell, no! The time I heard her say it, a dozen others must have heard
it, too. Of course, for all I know, she might have said it at other times
to maybe just one person."

"Are we to understand, then, that, having heard this girl make what
apparently was a public declaration of her desire to possess gold slippers,
you simply decided without further ado to gratify her wishes in this
respect?"

"That's a potful of fancy-Dan wordage. If it means did I send off to
a mail-order house for a pair of the damn things, so as to give them to
her, the answer is, 'Yes, I did.'"

"And you delivered them Saturday morning at Stewpan Cove, or in
that general vicinity?"

"I did, with all the herein aforesaids and whereases you'd like to put
in."

"Don't take this down," Landry said in an aside to the stenographer,
and then turned toward Maurice. "Look, my fine friend, if you think
this is an occasion for airy persiflage, let me disabuse you of the notion
right here and now. A girl has been murdered; at least she has come to
a violent end. We are trying to find the last person to have seen her
alive. At this moment, so far as we know, that last person was you, when
she got into your car on the Cypremort Road. At least, we have not yet
found anyone who will admit to having seen her after that moment. If
you think that to be a laughing matter, a topic for jests, keep the notion
to yourself. That's not a request; that's a direction, even if it is unofficial."
To the stenographer, he added: "From here on, take notes again."

"Of course, I realize everything you've said. That's why I'm whistling
in the dark. No one knows better how dark it is. Sorry. I'll be good."

Mollified, Landry turned to the male stenographer, who had now
been substituted for Mrs. Walton, because the nature of the investigation

seemed increasingly to indicate that such a change should be made. "Take down everything from here on again, Bob," he said. Then, facing Maurice, he asked, "Then it was Saturday morning when you delivered your gift? Incidentally, about what time?"

"About eleven. I was on my way to Dale Fontenot's place to look at some young bird dogs. He'd promised me a puppy and I was picking one out to have Sullivan Brock, up in Mississippi, train for me."

"And was it when you gave her the slippers, about eleven that morning, that you and she arranged to meet that same evening in the manner in which this was finally done?"

"That's right. She said she simply had to go to Crowley before she went to work at the Tuileries grand opening that night, and there was nobody she could trust to take her there without a lot of explanations. Would I do her this one more favor?"

"And you said?"

"I told her sure I would. All right, so I was on the make. Who isn't? Who, outside of some monk like Dale Fontenot, maybe. I wasn't trying to ruin some innocent li'l prairie flower, growing wilder by the hour. Everybody knew she could be had, if she liked you, and I was figuring, if I did her a favor, on top of giving her a pair of cheap gold slippers, she'd like me. That's plain enough."

"Did she say why she did not want you to call for her at the Stewpan crossing in the first place?"

"I don't remember if she said that in so many words, but I know I got the idea from what she did say she wanted no one to know where she'd gone, or who with. So she'd get this lunkhead Baer to call for her, and she'd get rid of him, and I would pick her up and drive her to Crowley. She said she'd take it from there."

"And so that evening—?"

"I waited at the bend of the road where she had told me to, and where I could see that flivver of Scholtze's coming. When it stopped and she got out, I waited till it turned around and got out of sight down the road, then started my Reo and drove to where she was with this bundle wrapped in paper in her arms, and she jumped in and I drove off to New Iberia and from there to Lafayette and Crowley."

"At any time, did you ask or did she volunteer the information as to what was in this bundle?"

"Yes. I asked, and she said."

"Well?"

"Well, it seems like I wasn't the only one, by a hell of a ways, to get the idea of booning her with a pair of gold slippers; you know—here's your heart's desire, so now *you* give. All but Dale. I give him credit. He wanted her to have the damn things just because that's what she wanted, and he gave the Professor the money to buy them for her. I heard all about how he said this, in front of a houseful of people, at the Villacs' Sunday night, from my brother Didier and, what's more, I'd bet the last button off Gabriel's coat he made the Professor promise not to tell her who the slippers were from. That's the way he is."

"But the Professor didn't buy those."

"I know. By that time she already had another pair."

"From—?"

"Why ask me? Don't you know?"

Tobe Bennett spoke up, interrupting. "Hold on, Theo. I know about the other pair, and I haven't said anything because, if we can find out what became of them, we'll know who killed Titine. I've been keeping that quiet in the hope somebody'd make a slip."

"Naturally, all I know was what she told me while we were driving to Crowley," said Maurice. "I'd seen that morning she'd been cuffed around by somebody; she had a swollen lip and a bruise on her chin, but I pretended not to notice. After all, you don't say to a girl, 'Who's been beating you up?' or 'Where'd you get that shiner, baby?' But when I asked her what's with the bundle she's lugging around, she said it was another pair of gold slippers she was taking back to the—the one who gave them to her."

"Did she say who it was and why she was returning them?"

"Yes. She said it was Prosper Villac, and she was bringing them back because this big gorilla Scholtze said he would kill her if she didn't. He was the one that beat her up on Friday night, and she was scared witless what he'd do to her if she didn't give back the slippers. Also, that was why she was so glad to get the pair I gave her, Saturday morning, because Scholtze didn't know about those, and she'd damn well see he never found out, or words to that effect. I felt pretty relieved to hear that, I can tell you. Scholtze is one guy I wouldn't choose any part of."

"So she was coming to Crowley to see Prosper Villac and return the slippers he had given her. Did she do so?"

"How would I know? I asked her did she want to go to his house and she said no, that would make trouble for him and she did not want to do that, when he had been nice to her. So I said if she went to the mill, she might not see him at all, because he might not come in there that night—I didn't know then what I heard later, that there was some sort of foul-up about a carload of rice. By this time, we were coming into Crowley, on the old Spanish Trail Route. As you probably know, there's a little grocery store right there and Titine said if I'd stop, she could telephone and find out, right then, the best place to meet Prosper, so she could be on her way back to the club pronto. She went into the grocery store and, when she came out, she was all nerved up and jittery and said maybe I'd better take her back to the Tuileries, if I could, because she wasn't going to be able to meet him before ten."

"Prosper told her that?"

"I suppose so, but she didn't say and I didn't ask her."

"And what happened next?"

"I told her I couldn't take her back to the Tuileries then, because I had to put in an appearance at the Archers'; but I would try and take her back later if she wanted me to. She said no, she guessed she'd better get rid of the slippers before she went back to the club, even if it would make her that much later. Scholtze was going to be wild, anyhow, but it would be worse if she still had the shoes when she did get there. So she asked me to drop her about three blocks from the mill."

"And you parted there? You did not see her again?"

"I did not see her after I left her on that little dirt road about three blocks from the mill gate. I asked her if she was sure she'd be all right by herself and she laughed. She got out of the car and said in that funny way she had, 'Thanks for the buggy ride,' and that's the last I saw of her."

"Just one or two questions more, Maurice. Did you see Prosper Villac at the Archers'?"

"Sure, I did. After I let Titine out, I went by the mill to see if he was there. He wasn't, so I went on to the Archers'. He came in late, with apologies all over the place, telling everybody about this car of rice that had got itself lost and then found. It was actually kind of ridiculous the way he kept explaining about that car of rice to show why he was late. Oh, it was important to him, of course; I expect if it had been my car of rice, I'd have been in a sweat, too; but I think telling about it once or twice would have been all I'd do, even then."

"Did you mention Titine to him?"

"Yes, after I got him outside, where nobody'd hear us."

"What did you tell him?"

"That I knew about the slippers *he* had given her and that Scholtze had told her she had to give them back."

"What was his reaction to that?"

"He said something like, 'My God, I wonder how many more she's told about those goddamn slippers?' and how he sure picked a fine time to get himself tangled up with a tramp like Titine. So I told him to take it easy, how there hadn't been any time, from the Golden Age of Babylon on, when most men didn't go overboard, sooner or later, for one of Titine's kind. Of course, I didn't know then that he was right on the verge of getting engaged to Victorine LaBranche, or I'd have understood better why he was so hot and bothered—though, as a matter of fact, I don't think he actually knew it himself; he was just hoping, because he'd had an encouraging telephone message. Anyway, I tried to calm him down and he finally told me to say he'd been called away, and he would see what he could do about getting this Titine out of town to her job at the Tuileries."

"You didn't tell him you knew Titine had arranged to meet him at ten?"

"No, I thought if he wanted to play it cagey and not let on that he had a definite date with her, that was his business."

Bennett interrupted again.

"If Theo doesn't mind, there are a couple of questions I'd like you to clear up. First, was Titine wearing those slippers you gave her when she got into your car?"

"No, she wasn't. She was wearing black shoes and not new ones, either."

"Did she change at any time while she was in the car?"

"Just before I let her out. She said she was going to get as much pleasure out of them as she could, because she'd have to change back to her old ones before she showed up for work, or Scholtze would raise the roof again."

"So that bundle she was carrying did have two pairs of slippers in it?"

"It most certainly did. First, two pairs of gold ones, and then a pair of gold ones and a pair of black ones."

"Well, that's all I wanted to ask," the sheriff said, with a sigh, turning to the district attorney.

"In that case, Maurice, you can leave," Landry informed his witness. "Naturally, I want you to repeat what you told us to the grand jury, if we ever ask for an indictment, and at the time of a trial, should it come to that."

"Like I said," Maurice agreed, with a hint of renewed jauntiness. "I have nothing to hide. Call me any time."

"The last person known to have seen her alive," Bennett said musingly, after Guerra had closed the door behind the departing witness.

"Now hold it a minute, Tobe," protested Landry. "You know as well as I do he couldn't have been that."

"Not if he smuggled that girl into the mill while Ten High and Paula and Aunt Amanda were all out in front at the Eaton car?"

"In that case, yes. But I don't believe he did, and neither, I suspect, do you. Lookie here, Tobe. I've gone along with you this far in not calling Prosper Villac to testify, even if I don't buy this notion that you're doing it only to see if that other pair of gold slippers can be traced, but that string's run out, now. We know the girl came here to Crowley to give the slippers back to Villac; at least, we know she said that was her purpose in coming; and the next thing we know for sure is that her body was found the next day in Villac's rice mill. How the hell can you expect me *now* to pass up an interrogation of the man?"

"All right," agreed the sheriff heavily. "All I ever told him was I'd have it put off as long as possible—I owe his family at least that much, even if I didn't feel in my bones he's not a killer. Don't forget, his daddy got himself killed doing something I asked him to do—something I'd have got killed doing if Claude hadn't gone out in my stead. I'll step down to my office and phone Prosper to come over. It won't take him five minutes."

"Let's adjourn for fifteen minutes. I could do with a small black. I'll wait here for you and send across the street. You'll have some, too, of course."

Chapter Twenty-five

JIM GARLAND WAS WHAT WAS KNOWN LOCALLY AS A CHARACTER. HE HAD not accompanied his daughter and son-in-law, Mary and Brent Winslow, when they first pioneered on the prairie; but he had joined them shortly afterward, bringing two immigrant cars, filled with purebred cattle and horses, far superior to any hitherto introduced to the region. If he had not been so genial of temperament, envy might have outweighed the admiration these evoked, but he very quickly made himself a general favorite and, as the years went by, his popularity increased rather than diminished. In his younger days, before coming south, he had gone in for harness racing; and when Crowley achieved a race track, shortly before the World War, he was one of the prime movers in the undertaking. Though he handled a car well enough, from preference he still drove a dashing horse hitched to a light and elegant sulky and this outfit was as familiar a sight in the locality as he was himself. Though the Winslows had always kept a good deal to themselves, hardly a day passed that he was not seen here and there about town; he had any number of irons in the fire and countless cronies. It was said that he had tucked away a very tidy fortune, what with his blooded stock and other business ventures, not to mention his phenomenal luck—or skill—at poker and dominoes. He spent almost nothing, living in a small house on the Winslows' property, which he had steadfastly declined to enlarge or elaborate, though they had done both with theirs. Someday, he would leave a good deal of money; the miracle was that this day had not come long before.

He had been greatly pleased with Vicky's enthusiastic acceptance of the mount he offered her, and eagerly anticipated her promised visit.

He had heard Prosper teasing her, jokingly, about her lazy habits and, therefore, he did not expect her much before noon on the day following the party; to his surprise and delight, she drove up to his door shortly after nine, her great dog leaping out of her smart little car in her wake. She was carrying a crop and wearing a white shirt, open at the throat, boots and dark riding breeches. Her appearance, like everything else about her, was intensely pleasing to the old man.

"Am I too early?" she inquired gaily, as she went up the short walk. "I was so excited about the horse, I couldn't wait! And am I dressed right? I have everything to complete this outfit, and I'll put it all on sometime, so you can see how I look that way. But it's such a lovely warm day and I thought, out here on the prairie—"

"You couldn't be too early to suit me and you're dressed exactly right. You're one of those girls that always is, aren't you? Come along, we'll go straight out to the stables—or would you rather stop in and see Mary and Brent first?"

"It would be nice to do that, wouldn't it? I mean, perhaps, they'd be expecting me to."

He noticed that she had not given him a direct answer, but that was not displeasing to him, either. Of course, she would rather have gone straight to see her horse, but she knew that, out of courtesy, she should say good morning to Prosper's grandparents first. It would have been a disappointment to Mary, Jim Garland realized, when he saw the coffee service all ready on the living room table, if the girl had not done so, and if she had not reminded Mary about the rooted cuttings which, it presently appeared, were prepared for her; and she listened with attention, and with interest which in nowise seemed feigned, while Mary explained that it was in this very room Brent had made the experiments in the breeding of rice—using his wife's sewing table as a testing board—which, after long discouraging years, had brought him fame. He worked in a separate room now, which he would like to show her some other time—the room where the new variety named for her was under observation. Perhaps, after she came back from her ride. . . . She hesitated, but only for a moment. Yes, of course she would like to see that, too; and she had thought, as long as she was out this way, she would go to the Primeaux farm, too. She had not met them yet and she wanted to. They would not mind, would they, if she made the first call?

"They'd be very much honored. But you know—"

Mary stopped, flushing. She could not say of her nearest neighbors, who were also among her dearest friends, "But you know, they haven't had your advantages." She could not explain that Clement, hard working, honest, and so shrewd in his own way that he had become extremely prosperous, was the only one of the cousins definitely to resist education, and that he had married a girl who had even less schooling than he did. She wondered, momentarily, if Vicky's adaptability, of which she had already received a favorable impression, would be equal to making such a visit a success. Then, very quickly, she decided that it would.

"I'll ring them up and tell them you'd like to come over as soon as you've had your ride," she said, and stood in the back doorway, her arm linked in her husband's, to watch Jim Garland and Vicky, with Levvy beside them, as they walked toward the stables and disappeared among the trees. When she caught sight of them again, the girl was already on horseback, and the old man was observing her, with obvious satisfaction, as she put her mount through its paces. After that, Vicky galloped away, out of sight and, half an hour later, reappeared and drew up beside the kitchen door, flushed and merry.

"He's marvelous," she told Mary, leaning over to pat the horse's neck. "I suppose I ought to take him back to Grandpa Jim now, but I can hardly bear to leave him. I'll have to, of course, until we can get a box stall ready for him. It never occurred to either Father or me that anyone would give me a present like this, and we haven't done anything about renovating our old stable. Naturally, we will, right away now. Meanwhile, I'll have an excuse, won't I?—for coming out here every day to ride—that is, every day I feel easy about leaving Father. He enjoyed his outing last night very much, but he was pretty tired this morning. He said he'd really rather spend the day in bed, resting quietly, and I knew he meant that. But if he'd felt like having me keep him company, or if he'd been in any pain, of course I wouldn't have left him. . . . Would you and Mr. Winslow help me think up the right name for this prize winner? I hear you're awfully good at things like that and I'm very bad. Prosper doesn't like Levvy's name at all, and I wouldn't want to make a second mistake. . . . Well, I'll be back from the stables to get my cuttings and see the workroom and then I'll be on my way to the Primeaux'. The next time I come, I hope you'll let me go through your flower garden, bed by bed. Gardening's another thing I'm very stupid about. I've never been in one place long enough at a time to have one of my own. But all that's going to be different now."

"I'd like to have you stay, and if there's anything I can teach you about gardening, of course, I'd be very pleased and proud. But I know Laurelle and Clement are waiting for you, and my flower beds will be prettier a few weeks from now, when I have more chrysanthemums ready for *Toussaint.*"

Again Mary watched the girl out of sight, with a deep feeling of relief and contentment. Whatever else happened to Prosper, he would find joy and fulfillment in his love. To Mary, as to most women, that was more important than everything else put together. . . .

Her momentary uneasiness about Vicky's visit to the adjoining farm had found its counterpart there, but this had been quickly dispelled. Vicky did not seem to notice that the *salle* had not been especially prepared for company; she was outspoken in her admiration of the grass rug that almost covered the wide boards of the floor, the large wooden rings from which the heavy draperies were hung and the typical early Acadian furnishings which she had never before seen put to practical everyday use and adapted for the adornment of a house that was still lived in. Encouraged and delighted by her enthusiasm, Laurelle and Clement took her into the best bedroom as well, then to the kitchen and, finally, to the small separate room dominated by the great loom.

"Yuh is where my sister Mezalee, her, the one w'at's a *religieuse,* use' to weave," Clement said proudly. "Maybe you know 'bout Mezalee bein' at the *Sacré Coeur* at Gran' Coteau, no?"

"Yes, I know. I've had the sweetest letter from her and I'm going to see her tomorrow. . . . But you still use this, don't you?" Vicky inquired, turning to Laurelle.

"Some I do, me, but not like Mezalee, no, not so much nor neither so good like her," Laurelle told her. "Could I show you how it works? I mean this here loom, how it goes?"

"I'd love to have you."

Again Vicky watched an unfamiliar practice with eager attention as Laurelle shuttled the weft thread through from one side to the other. "That's something else I have to learn how to do," the visitor said, "when I come out to the Winslows' to learn about gardening, I'll come on over here and learn how to weave. Is it a bargain?"

"We would be so proud, us, fo' to have you do it," Laurelle and Clement assured her together, and Laurelle added, "I ain't but just the other day got finish' with one striped blanket, like we always gives to a bride. I made it, me, fo' one *cousine* w'at live in Breaux Bridge, her, but she don't get married up till nex' spring, no. I could easy make another one biffo spring, and Mary, her, she been tellin' me how you fix it up to get married with Prosper right away soon, yes. So you got to take that blanket, so soon like I get it out of the chest where it's put away, just like it was made special fo' you. You will take it for a bride blanket, won't you, yes?"

"I'd be thrilled to have it. May I really take it with me—right now? I think perhaps I ought to be getting back to Crowley."

"We been hopin', me an' Clement, how maybe you stay by our house fo' dinner. It's mos' cooked by now, an' we got a big blackbird jambalaya with tomato-pas'e gravy, so we can all pass a good time when the children, them, comes home from school. Anyway, I would love it, an' also Clement, fo' them to meet with you, yes."

"And I'd love to. Well—" Vicky had concealed her disappointment, the previous day, when Prosper telephoned that he would not have time to come to Lafayette, and still fall in with his mother's plan for a family party; this had meant a postponement in buying the multicolored ring and they had decided to select one in Crowley, today, during his dinner hour. She had expected to be back from her visits to the two farms by then—indeed, her early arrival had been timed with this in view. But, as she looked from Laurelle to Clement, she realized that her refusal to stay would mean more than disappointment to them; it would mean she thought their dinner would not be worthy of her.

"Of course I'll stay," she said quickly. "I can telephone, can't I, to say I'll be a little delayed?" Yes, indeed, she was assured, and taken to the old-fashioned wall instrument, which she had to be shown how to use, thereby giving them all a good laugh. Prosper was not available just then, Paula told her briefly when the connection had been put through, and hung up without any further comment. Vicky tried the house next and Lavinia answered; Prosper had not come in yet; some urgent business that he had not found time to tell her about must have called him away temporarily; but she was sure he would be back soon and, as soon as he came, she would give him Vicky's message. She hoped Vicky could stop in to see her and Anne Marie later in the day. Had the morning been pleasant? Lavinia was delighted to hear it. . . .

"Everything's all right," Vicky said, hanging up the receiver. "Could I help with dinner, Laurelle? Cooking's still another thing I don't know much about and I'm badly in need of lessons!"

"This yuh ain't no day fo' no lessons. Comes some other day, yes, you can learn. But this yuh day is fo' pleasure, I guarantee you, me. You done seen the house, an' the big loom, them, an' we ain't got no fine stock an' no fine horses, not like they got by the Winslow place. W'at we do got, though, us, is one fine orange orchard w'at is bigger an' even better as the one they got by Winslows," Laurelle said with pride.

"Clement, why you don't take our new *cousine,* her, out by the orange trees? An' while you gone, I'll be finishin' up this yuh dinner we goin' have."

"If it wouldn't take up too much of your time, Clement. I know I've broken into a working day."

"I would like it plenny-plenny, me, if I got mo' workin' days interrup' this yuh way," Clement assured her with complete sincerity. "So come on, an' we go see them orange trees."

They left the kitchen and went through the yard, with Levvy still patiently tagging along. But the morning had not been as exciting for her as for her mistress, and she was beginning to feel the urge for more freedom of action. They had hardly reached the grove when she bolted suddenly, and then bounded away through the laden orange trees to the unseen space beyond, in pursuit of a cottontail's bobbing white powder puff. Vicky called her repeatedly and with increasing sternness; then, as the errant dog was still lost to view, she spoke apologetically to Clement.

"She hasn't been a bit like herself these last few days. I'm afraid I'll have to chase after her. Will that be all right?"

"Sho' enough will it, but I think maybe we better both go, account on the other side of the trees is our li'l *cimetière,* yes. I never meant fo' us to go over to it, but now—"

They ran ahead, side by side. Levvy had already lunged through the open gate of the picket fence which surrounded the small enclosure when Vicky caught up with her, clutched at her collar and snapped on the leash which had hitherto seemed superfluous, but which, nevertheless, had been prudently kept in the pocket of the riding breeches. After speaking still more severely to the Dalmatian, Vicky looked up apologetically at Clement.

"I'm awfully sorry. I didn't mean to intrude, I wouldn't have for the world."

"I know, an' it ain't no need fo' you to say nothin' 'bout it. You ain't w'at you say intrude, no, by you like you was in the fam'ly already. It's just only—" Involuntarily, his eyes strayed in the direction of the raw grave which he had dug only two days before, and on which the white tuberoses of the great cross Baer had put there were now brown and wilted. Then, still involuntarily, he looked past this to the urn filled with beautiful flowers which stood in front of an adjacent tombstone. Vicky followed his gaze and faced him squarely; if she flinched inwardly, her expression revealed no such shrinking.

"You mean because Titine Dargereux is buried here?" she asked. "I heard all about that, of course. And I hope you won't mind if I tell you I think it was a wonderful thing for you to do—to give her a grave beside the brother you loved so much, because some of the circumstances surrounding their deaths were similar. That is, I understand she wasn't entitled to burial in consecrated ground because she'd been—well, remiss about her obligations to the Church; and your brother Felix was a suicide, wasn't he? So he wasn't entitled to such burial, either. It's all tragic and—a little mysterious to me still. But when you enter a family, you share its tragedies and its mysteries, don't you? And you've been good enough to say I belong to your family now. So, since I'm here anyway, would it be all right if I went with you to see the rest of the graves?"

"You got no idee, never, no, how I feel good when I think you do this, like you really was one of us, the same as the fam'ly would be from a child. See them three leas' li'l crosses? Tha's where we think an' believe, us, are graves from my two li'l brothers, an' also a li'l sister. I think maybe you already know why nobody can't be certain sure, no, how tha's where they were buried. On the other side, where those fine big tombstones is at, my *maman* an' my daddy is buried, where we knowed good, us, it was consecrate' ground. We got to tell you about *maman* someday, us, account she was a real fine lady w'at give up fine clo'es, an' fine houses an' fine people an' fine mos' ever'thing else, to come out yuh on the prairie with my daddy, biccoz she love him so much, her, she never cared, no, how it wasn't no other house fo' nobody knows how many miles, nor no roads an' neither no good crops, with wild ponies an' scrubby ol' range cattle runnin' every place. An' I got to tell you frankly, me, she also never was sorry she give up them things fo' w'at she got, no."

"I'm sure she wasn't. I'm sure he made up to her for everything she left behind. I know Prosper would to me. There's no tragedy about them, is there? Or any mystery, either? But your brother—wasn't there anyone who loved him, wasn't there anyone who'd have given up everything for his sake . . . or shouldn't I have asked?" she added quickly, as she noticed the masklike look which had suddenly banished all expression from Clement's pleasant face.

They had passed Titine's new-made grave and were standing in front of the plain neat tombstone, marked only with the simple lettering:

FELIX PRIMEAUX
1871-1905

but saved from starkness by the fragrant flowers in front of it. Clement glanced down at the flowers instead of meeting Vicky's direct gaze. "I expec', me, the time was bound to come when you would be wonderin' in you' mind 'bout that," he said. "So it's good, yes, you ask me instead of maybe some other peoples. I got to admit, me, how somebody loved him enough fo' true, to fo'get 'bout fine clo'es, fine houses an' mos' ever'thing, her, to marry with him. But he wasn't like my daddy, him; he got his mind made up like a stone, yes, he wasn't good enough fo' her, no. Tha's w'at her folks thought, too, them. An' I tell you frankly, even if I hate like the devil, him, hates holy water, to admit it, that I expec' Fleex wasn't good enough for her. Don't make no mistakes, no, 'bout how I feel, me. I loved him, too, better as I loved *maman* or either my daddy, them. I even had my own li'l boy baptize' Fleex, after my brother, yes. But the truth's true, an' nothin' else ain't so. Anyway, Fleex, he went off, an' I expec' she was thinkin', her, how he wasn't never comin' back, no, so, after a long, long while, she married up with somebody else, her, a good man, I got to admit, an' also he loved her plenny-plenny, too, him."

"And was she happy with this other man? I wouldn't have been."

Clement raised his head at last and regarded Vicky thoughtfully. "I guarantee you, me, you wouldn't. Not you, no. My mind keeps tellin' me you' plenny like my *maman*, plenny mo' as this other lady we been talkin' 'bout, us. Again I got to ask you to please don't make no mistake," he went on, obviously choosing his words with great care. "She's a fine-fine lady, her. I got no idee to say one li'l word against her, by she is so good, like the angels wouldn't be no better, them. Why I say that, me? I tell you frankly, you' bound to guess—an' maybe you done guess already who she is, that fine lady. An' if you know, you, who we talkin' 'bout, I got it in my mind as it wouldn't be too bad, no; it could even be good . . . but we better be gettin' back by the house, us. Laurelle might have ever'thing on the table, an' she don't like it, no, to let the food get cold when she been workin' to cook it."

"May I ask you just one more question?"

"Sho'. Ask so many like you want. But I ain't sayin', me, no, I promise to answer."

"Someone told me there are always fresh flowers on your brother's grave. Is it all right to ask who puts them there?"

"Well, like I tol' you, I never promised to answer, me, an' that there one is like that. I got no answer fo' it, no."

"I'm sorry. Forget it, won't you please?"

They walked slowly back toward the house, Levvy, now thoroughly subdued, held firmly on her leash. They had not quite reached the yard from the orange grove when Laurelle came rushing out to meet them.

"Judge Martin, him, been callin' you two-three times, not only yuh, but plenny other places, too, yes," she said. "He say to tell you frankly you better go home by you' papa's house, account he ain't feelin' so good, no."

Chapter Twenty-six

AFTER RECEIVING BENNETT'S TELEPHONE MESSAGE, PROSPER SAT VERY still for a few moments, staring straight in front of him. No other call upon his courage—not even the one he had answered that black night beyond the wire at Saint-Mihiel—had evoked such dread as this one. It was easy enough for a decent man like Tobe to say cheerfully, "Just stick to the truth. Nobody's ever made a lie stand without some clever lawyer tripped him up in it, sooner or later." Tobe had never done anything which would force him to confess to a tawdry liaison with an even more tawdry wench, almost on the eve of his betrothal to a fine girl. Vicky would stand by him; of that Prosper was as certain as he was of his own name; but even this conviction gave him scant solace now. For she, too, would be mired by his shabby surrender to lust; he could not dignify it by any other name, he could not dismiss it lightly, as Maurice had done, by telling himself that almost every man yielded, sooner or later, to elemental desire. In his abject misery, he could liken himself only to some common traveling salesman, out on the road and registering at a cheap, small-town hotel, who commissioned a grinning bellboy to "dig up a pint of hooch and a woman." It would be at Vicky, even more than at him, that the Pharisees would leer, Vicky about whom it would be whispered along the bayous that she sho' had to be easy satisfied, her, with a shopworn article, to marry with Prosper Villac, him, yes. . . .

Vicky . . . he must get hold of her before he went to the courthouse, he must tell her that he could not meet her, at his dinner hour, and go with her to choose the multicolored ring, as they had so buoyantly planned. By now, she would be out on the prairie, trying the new mount which Grandpa Jim had given her, happy, carefree, delighted with her present and giving delight to those who watched her as she put the horse through its paces. This meant that, when he telephoned the Winslow farm, he would not get her direct; he would have to speak first with either his grandfather or his grandmother, whichever one answered the telephone; and, even if he did not actually say so, they would know he was on his way to the courthouse, the minute he explained that he would not be able to meet Vicky; as matters stood, nothing less urgent would cause him to cancel such an appointment. . . .

It was his grandfather who happened to be nearest the telephone when it rang, and Brent Winslow was normally a man of few words; but the silence with which he listened to the message was unnatural, and Prosper knew that he was stricken, for the moment stricken beyond all speech, at the knowledge that his only grandson, the only male heir to his kingdom of discovery, was so suspect that interrogation had proved unavoidable.

"I'm sorry, I can't give Vicky your message myself," Brent said at last. "She's had her ride, and she left, about half an hour ago, for the Primeaux'. She said that, as long as she was out in this direction, anyway, she'd like to pay them a visit. You'll have to call her at their house. Or I'll do it for you, if you'd rather."

"No, I'll do it myself. Thanks, Grandfather. And I don't need to tell you that—"

"No, you don't. You better get hold of Vicky, right away."

But he could not. Happy, who had just that minute come in from school, and who regarded the telephone as a bauble provided for his special amusement, seized it before his sister could stop him and further delayed matters. When Adeline had summoned their mother, Laurelle said that Clement and Vicky had just gone out to the orange grove for a minute, but she was sure they would be right back. She would have Vicky telephone Prosper as soon as they came in.

Laurelle, of course, had not reckoned on the unexpected visit to the cemetery, precipitated by Levvy's mad dash after a rabbit. The call which came through to the Claudia almost immediately was not from Vicky, as Prosper had anticipated, but from Tobe.

"I'm sorry to hurry you, son, but Theo's getting impatient. He did take a fifteen-minute recess to give you plenty of time to get over here. But it's most half an hour since—"

"I know. I apologize. I wanted to get in touch with Vicky and I thought I could do it quickly. But I'll leave the message with Paula."

Well, here was one more thing that Vicky would have to understand, if she could. The purchase of her ring had been delayed and she had been nice about that; now it would have to be delayed again, and she would not even receive a direct message about it; she would have to hear, impersonally, from his secretary, and of course she would know what had caused this second delay, whether Paula told her or not. And he would have no way of explaining, with terms of endearment, no means of comforting her.

"I was expecting Miss LaBranche to meet me here at dinnertime," he told Paula, as he left the office. Paula interrupted him.

"She telephoned, while you were out at the rough rice warehouse with Wayland Foster, to say she'd be late. I told her you weren't available just then."

"I'm sorry you did that—I'd have come a-running. Anyway, now I've tried to reach *her*, to tell her I can't keep the appointment at all. But she's left my grandfather's and gone over to the Primeaux'. According to Mrs. Primeaux, she's out around the place somewhere. When she returns my call, will you please tell her I'm terribly sorry, but I've had to change my plans? Or, just in case there's some slip-up and Mrs. Primeaux didn't understand what I was trying to get over—the connection wasn't very good—would you mind waiting here until either you've heard from Miss LaBranche or she just arrives?"

"Don't worry, Mr. Villac. I'll take care of the situation."

"Thanks. I know you will. And, by the way, you may have more than one situation to take care of. I don't expect to be back here this afternoon."

The sense of dread which had been so strong when he received Bennett's first call was even more overpowering now. But if Paula noticed anything unnatural in his voice or manner, she gave no indication of it. She had scarcely glanced up from her machine when Prosper spoke to her and she answered; now, she went on quietly typing. The telephone rang several times and, each time, when she picked up the receiver, she was prepared to hear Vicky's voice and give her Prosper's message. Then, half an hour later, Laurelle telephoned.

"Could I speak with Mr. Villac?"

"He isn't here just now. I'll take a message."

"Miss LaBranche can't meet him like she' supposed to, no. She been call' to Lafayette by her papa done had another—how you call it?— heart attack, him."

"I'm sorry to hear that. I'll see to it that the message is delivered— both messages. Mr. Villac left one for Miss LaBranche, too."

Paula finished the letter she was writing, stamped its envelope and folded it neatly over the top of the typed sheet, and laid it, with precision, on top of the others she had done that morning. Then she sharpened the pencils she had been using when she took dictation, covered her typewriter and rose. As she did so, Wayland Foster, the rough rice buyer, came toward her with a slip of paper in his hand, on which was written the high bid of the rough rice sale which he had attended that morning.

"Here's something Mr. Prosper needs to know," he said, handing it to her. She glanced at the notation, saw that the Claudia had been overbid and handed the paper back.

"I'm afraid we'll have to tell him that tomorrow, Wayland," she said. "Mr. Prosper doesn't expect to return to the mill today. And I've had an urgent message from him that he wants me to give Miss LaBranche in person. I'm starting for Lafayette immediately. I don't know just what time I'll be back."

Prosper, facing his inquisitors along the length of the scarred jury table, mechanically answered the routine questions about his name, age, citizenship and occupation, each of these, to him, represented a form of reprieve, because each delayed, a moment longer, the ones that he knew must follow. Then came another short delay, in the form of the customary assurance that this was not a trial but an investigation—an assurance so carefully worded that he had the impression this was being unnecessarily prolonged, out of mistaken kindness. It would be better to have the whole miserable business over with, to tell how long and how well he had known Titine Dargereux, what he had given her, when and why, the hour at which he had last seen her. It had all taken on something of a nightmarish quality, the only difference being that this was real, all too real, whereas a nightmare was only a phantasy, from which, sooner or later, there was a safe awakening.

"I gave her the gold slippers with rhinestones on the heels Thursday night," he heard himself saying. "She seemed to be very pleased with them. She tried them on to make sure they fitted."

"And you left her as soon as you had made her this generous gift?"

"No."

"When did you leave her?"

He swallowed hard. "It must have been about four o'clock Friday morning. I don't know exactly. It was still dark. But there was a little light in the sky by the time I reached Bayou Warehouse."

"This was *last* Friday morning?"

"Yes."

"But you made a proposal of marriage to Victoria LaBranche Sunday?"

"Yes—no." He *hadn't* proposed to Vicky. She hadn't given him time. But how could he explain her generous and impetuous action to his questioners? "That is, she'd known for a long time I wanted to marry her and—"

"Such a marriage would be very advantageous to you, wouldn't it?"

Prosper's shame was suddenly engulfed in anger. "If you mean I wanted to marry her for her money—"

"She *is* very rich, isn't she? And these last few years haven't been so good for rice."

"I never thought about her being rich. I wanted to marry her because I fell in love with her."

"That statement seems rather at variance with the ones you made a few minutes ago. But we'll let that pass for the moment. She knew you wanted to marry her, whatever your reasons were, and you began to believe she would consent. When was this?"

"Saturday, when she telephoned me, asking me to family dinner Sunday."

"And, apparently, it was Saturday night that Titine Dargereux came to the mill?"

"Apparently."

"It would, of course, have been extremely awkward for you to continue any kind of an association with her if you became engaged to Miss LaBranche."

"Yes, but—"

Some kind of disturbance was taking place in the hall, outside the closed door. Above the indefinable sounds of commotion, a woman's shrill voice rang out clearly.

"But I must talk to those men this instant, before this hearing goes any further. I've got to tell them—"

Without even looking at Landry, much less stopping to speak to him, Bennett sprang up, strode to the door and flung it open, brushing its protesting guardian aside. "Come right in, Aunt Amanda," he said soothingly. "You bet we'll let you have your say. Here, take this chair."

Amanda Eaton, clutching an untidy bundle, sank into the proffered seat. Like her niece, she was usually the personification of neatness, but in her case, this trait was even more marked; with advancing years, she had become more and more prim in appearance, manner and speech. Now her hair and her dress were both in disarray, and she was so distraught that she spoke haltingly, a word or two at a time. "Ever—since—Saturday—night, I've—been—worrying," she gasped. "And—here—it is—Wednesday!"

"Take it easy, Aunt Amanda. You don't have to hurry to tell us what's on your mind. We can wait. Then you can tell us what happened to worry you Saturday night."

"When I went to get Paula," Amanda said at last, "she had a bundle in her hands. I didn't ask her what was in it. We were both tired and it was late and, to tell you the truth, I—I sort of dreaded to ask. I thought maybe it was more of that bootleg gin she's been getting and drinking, over my protests, and I didn't want to start an argument at that hour of the night. But Sunday, in church, I got to thinking about it and I realized it didn't look like the other packages she's been bringing to the house. So, after we got home, I asked her what was in that bundle, and she was cross and said I must be imagining things, she didn't have any bundle. I knew she was lying to me—it wouldn't be the first time—and, as soon as she'd gone to the mill Monday, I started searching. I searched in every place I could think of all that day and all day yesterday, without finding anything. Yesterday night I went out, but not until I'd seen her safely home. I always see her safely home in the evening, Tobe, you know that. It isn't because I think she's a young girl any more, or needs protection at six o'clock. It's because—" She looked pathetically at her nephew. Tobe cleared his throat.

"What Aunt Amanda means," he explained, "is that Paula has hallucinations sometimes. Harmless enough ones, we've always thought. And they didn't interfere at all with her efficiency in her work. You'll bear me out in that, won't you, Prosper?"

"I sure will. No one could ask for a better assistant than she's been to me for years."

"What form did these hallucinations take?" Landry inquired sharply.

Tobe and Amanda exchanged glances.

"Well," Tobe said slowly, "she had some kind of a love affair that she was half ashamed of and half proud of, when she was in France, same as a good many others did. We never heard—I never did, anyway—who the man was, but I've got a pretty strong suspicion now who it may have been, and I think you have, too, Theo. After that, she never had another. But she would have liked to. She even went so far as to pretend she did. She'd get all dolled up when she got home from work and make believe she was waiting for someone. Like I said, we thought that was harmless enough. She didn't indulge in fancies like that during working hours. At least—" He looked across the table at the witness whose questioning had been so abruptly curtailed "—she thought an awful lot of Prosper. I don't mean just as an employer or a friend. She was jealous of every other woman he looked at. I think she had a secret hope that someday he'd be her sweetheart."

"Did she ever give you any such impression, Prosper?" Landry inquired.

"Lord, no!"

"And she never gave you the impression she was jealous of anyone?"

"Lord, no!" Prosper said again. "She did make a disagreeable remark one time, but it didn't sound jealous, just spiteful."

"Well, if you think it has any bearing on this situation, tell us what it was and when."

"It was last Friday. I suddenly remembered that I'd never given her a message which Scholtze had asked me to deliver some time before. I told her I was sorry I hadn't done it sooner and she said it didn't matter at all; then, when I said I didn't realize she knew him, because I'd never seen her at his place, she grew quite sarcastic. She said I'd never seen my sister there, either, or my 'new-found friend Victorine LaBranche.' My retort wasn't very polite and neither was hers, the next time."

"I think that does throw some light on the general situation," Landry said dryly. "I may want more details about your retort and hers later. Right now, I'd like to have Miss Eaton go on with what she was telling us before we learned about her niece's hallucinations."

"I looked and looked," Amanda said pathetically. "And I kept getting more and more upset. I knew I hadn't imagined that bundle and still I didn't see, in a four-room house, where Paula could have hidden it, so that I couldn't find it when I'd ransacked the place all the way from the recess under the front steps to the rooftree and been through the shed and even the trash cans into the bargain. Finally, I decided to take one last look at her closet, and I noticed that the shoe bag on the door—you know, the kind made of chintz—that has a separate pocket for every pair of shoes—looked fuller than usual. Paula keeps her clothes in beautiful order, especially the ones she wears when she's waiting—I mean hoping—for company. Her best dresses—and lounging pajamas—are all bagged in cheesecloth and anything that might tarnish is wrapped in black tissue paper. I'm not naturally a prying woman, I hope you don't think so—"

"No, of course we don't, Miss Eaton. We think you acted very wisely. I gather you noticed that the shoe bag looked uncommonly full; you couldn't remember that your niece had quite so many pairs of slippers that would require protection from tarnish, so you started unwrapping all those done up in black paper and—"

"Yes, yes, that's exactly what I did," Amanda said, her words coming with a rush at last. "And I found a pair of gold slippers with rhinestones on the heels, done up with a pair of shabby old black shoes. I suppose Paula wanted the gold slippers herself, and meant to wear them when I went to church meetings, after the excitement about Titine Dargereux had quieted down, and that she hadn't had a chance to throw away the old black ones, because I'd been watching her so closely. So I wrapped them up together again, as nearly as I could the way they'd been before, and started for the mill. I thought maybe Paula could give me some explanation. Of course, it was just a forlorn hope, but I clung to it. And, when I got there, I found she'd left, that she'd gone to Lafayette. She told Wayland Foster she had some kind of a message for Miss LaBranche from Prosper and that Prosper wanted her to deliver it *in person*."

"I never told her anything of the kind," Prosper interrupted vehemently.

"All right, we'll hear about what you did tell her presently. But let's hear the rest of Miss Eaton's story first."

"I meant to come on here, anyway, to talk to Tobe, and see if Paula couldn't be taken to a medical examiner and put in an institution, before she was charged with—with anything," Amanda went on. "I hurried as fast as I could, but Paula has the car—she took it this morning, the way she always does, because she leaves before I get up. Then she drives back for dinner and, after dinner, I bring her to the mill, so that I can use the car during the afternoon before I call for her at night. But you see today she didn't come home to dinner and I had to get here on foot— that's why it took me so long. But there are the slippers—you can see them for yourselves!"

With a sudden movement, she flung the bundle which she had been clutching onto the table in front of her. Out of it rolled the two pairs of shoes which told the whole story. "By now, Paula must be almost to Lafayette and I'm worried about that message she said she had to deliver in person," the distraught woman said.

Without waiting to see or hear anything further, Prosper leaped up and dashed toward the door. Landry shouted, "Let him through, Joe!" and sprang to his feet while the sheriff reached for the telephone, as Amanda finally finished what she had come to say.

"You know, Tobe, we always carry a gun in the car."

Chapter Twenty-seven

WHEN VICKY TORE UP THE FRONT STEPS, AFTER HER FRANTIC DRIVE FROM the Primeaux farm, she found Dr. Martin waiting for her, with a reassuring smile, in a house that was hushed, but in no way suggestive of sudden tragedy.

"Don't worry, honey, everything's under control and, as far as I can see, likely to remain so," he told her without preamble. "Your father's heart attack was sudden, but I don't believe it's serious and, fortunately, Gifford was able to get hold of me at once. When he took up your father's luncheon tray, he found him leaning over the bathroom basin—Moïse had gone in there to wash his hands—and gasping for breath. I could hear the sound of the gasps myself when Gifford telephoned and I was here inside of five minutes. I saw there wasn't an instant to lose, so I played my trump card—injected morphine directly into a vein. It's a risky process, but there are times when it's worth the risk and this was one of them. Next, I administered digitalis by mouth, before Moïse was too drowsy to take it and, of course, got him right to bed. He doesn't seem to be having any more trouble with his breathing, so I haven't thought it necessary to put him under an oxygen tent, but all the necessary preparations have been made. I shan't leave the house for the present and one of the two nurses I've sent for has already arrived and is sitting in his room."

"May I go in and see him?"

"I'd rather you didn't just yet. By the time the morphine has really taken hold, a slight noise—even a fairly loud one—won't disturb him, because he won't hear it. But I don't want to take any chances yet—I've even had the telephone temporarily shut off and I've told Donovan to keep Levvy with her—as I've said, I don't want to risk disturbance of any kind. You may go into his sitting room and look in on him if you want to—the door's open from there into his bedroom, and I'm going back there myself, now that I've spoken to you, but, of course, he mustn't do any talking tonight. I'll go up with you and let you satisfy yourself that everything's all right. Then I'd like to close the door into the upper hall. Why don't you go to your own sitting room on the other side of the stair well? It wouldn't take but a minute to reach you there, if there's any reason to do so. But I must ask you to believe that the quieter your father's kept, for the next few hours, the better his chances are for a rapid recovery. Also, that I'm telling you the truth when I say I think he *is* going to recover—this time. However, I think the moment has come to let you know that someday, perhaps before very long, he'll have a more severe attack and that will be the end."

Vicky nodded, her eyes filling with tears. "I know," she said steadily. "He never told me so himself, but I realized, from the beginning, that he wanted to come home—to die. And then, he's been in such a hurry to see me married—you don't think that's impossible, do you?"

"Of course I don't. If you were married very quietly, it might even be possible within a week. That is, unless—"

He could not very well say to her "—unless something that comes out in the investigation, which is taking place in Crowley right now, should cause Prosper Villac to be kept in custody on a charge of murder." But she nodded again, and he knew she was facing up to that, also.

"All right, you've told me everything I need to know," she said. "Let's go upstairs, shall we? I would like to look in on Father, since you think that's all right. Then I'll go across the hall to my own quarters and stay there until you tell me I should come back—either because everything's cleared up—or because it hasn't. As you say, it won't take but a minute to get me. And I can have my meals served in my sitting room."

There was nothing disturbing in her long-range view of her father who was, indeed, sleeping quite peacefully, with a white-clad nurse sitting close to his bedside. Without protest, Vicky herself closed the door leading from his sitting room into the hallway and then skirted the great stair well to her own side of the house. Once there, she found it harder to retain her composure. She did not dare completely shed her clothes and take a bath, for fear she might suddenly be called. But she pulled off her rumpled shirt and, before putting on a fresh one, hastily sponged off the upper part of her body. Then she sat down and tried, without much success, to read. If she could only have heard from Prosper and

learned that all was well with him, the wait would not have seemed so
long. But the unbroken silence, without even the comforting presence of
Levvy, was almost unendurable.

Though the dragging minutes seemed like hours, it was actually only
a short time before Donovan knocked and came in. Vicky started up in
alarm. "Come, come, lovey, there's nothing to be afraid of," Donovan
said soothingly. "Your father's sleeping like a baby—the doctor opened
the door and told me so as I went by. He heard my footsteps, quiet as I
thought I'd kept them, but your father won't hear those or anything
else this night and, in the morning, he'll wake up almost his own self
again. But there's a young person downstairs, says she wants to see you.
When Gifford let her in, he thought it was that second nurse we're expecting. But it seems not. It seems she's a Miss Bennett, Mr. Villac's secretary, and that she's come to you with a special message from him."

"Oh, Donovan! I want to see her, quick, quick, quick! I've been hoping
for a message!"

In her eagerness, she started toward the door. Then she remembered
her promise to stay where she could be summoned within a minute, if
necessary. But she went to the threshold of her sitting room and waited
to greet her visitor warmly.

"Miss Bennett, how very kind of you! Do come right in, won't you?"

Paula was looking around her with unabashed curiosity. So this was
the way a girl lived, a rich girl with the world at her feet! In a huge
house, with half a dozen servants running around to do her bidding
and an upstairs sitting room of her own! *She* did not need to run any
risk of discovery if she wanted to take a surreptitious drink or receive
callers privately; *she* was not exposed to the prying gaze of anyone who
chose to ring the front doorbell! And *she* could dress in well-fitted black
breeches and a white shirt open halfway down the front and no one
would think any the worse of her for it! Paula was so absorbed in what
she saw and in the thoughts that these sights evoked, that she did not
instantly answer Vicky's next question.

"You've brought me a message from Prosper, haven't you? Do tell me
what it is—of course, I'm dying to know!"

"Mr. Villac's at the courthouse now."

"But that isn't all you came to tell me, is it?"

"No. He said he couldn't keep an appointment he had with you. He
said I was to tell you so."

"But you didn't need to come all the way to Lafayette to tell me that!
Of course, it was nice of you, but I'm sorry you've been put to so much

trouble. As far as that goes, *I* had to break the appointment—or rather, I had to ask Mrs. Primeaux to do it for me. I had to hurry back to La-fayette because of my father's heart attack. Didn't she tell you that he was very ill?"

"Yes, Mrs. Primeaux told me so. And then that man at the entrance. And then that woman at the head of the stairs." Paula turned and looked out of the sitting room door, which still stood open. "But she's gone now—that woman, I mean."

"Donovan? She was my nurse when I was little and now—well, she's practically my right hand. Would you like me to ring for her to come back? You might enjoy talking to her. She's quite amusing sometimes. And perhaps you'd like tea or something?"

"No, I don't want to talk to her or anyone but you. I don't want tea, either. . . . And so your father's sick, very sick? That means you won't be going on with your plans for getting married."

"Oh, yes, I shall. Father was very anxious to have me married quickly. And Dr. Martin's told me, since I came in, that the heart attack isn't as serious as he feared at first, that he thought possibly I could be mar-ried, very quietly, within a week."

"You won't be married, quietly or any other way, within a week. You won't be married at all."

"You mean something's happened to Prosper you haven't told me about?"

For some moments, the feeling had been growing on Vicky that there was something about her visitor which did not seem quite normal. At first, she thought this must be her own imagination. She knew she was upset and excited, that it would be easy for her to delude herself in such a way. But when Paula, instead of answering, came very close, her face thrust upward and forward, Vicky was convinced that her instinct was not playing her false. She knew she must be on her guard, though against what she still did not feel sure.

"Prosper Villac isn't in love with you," Paula was now hissing at her. "He's in love with me. He has been for a long time, but that dirty little slut, that swampish vampire, lured him away for a while. Well, she's where she won't lead him or anyone else into sin again. And you thought you could steal him from me, with your moneybags and your bold for-eign ways and your sick father to help you out. But you can't. If you'd come to the mill today, the same thing would have happened to you that happened to Titine Dargereux. You'd have been taken up to the top floor to see Prosper, who wasn't there, although you'd have been told that he was, and then you'd have been pushed over into a rice bin; and, this time, there wouldn't have been any telltale slipper sticking out. But you didn't come to the mill. So I came here. And you'll come with me, quietly, out of this house and get into my car with me and we'll ride out into the swamps together. Then I'll ride back alone. The chances are that what's left of you won't ever be found."

Vicky managed to continue looking steadily into the face that was thrust so near her own, and to keep her voice under control as she answered.

"You're mistaken. I'm not going to leave this house. I'm not even going to leave this room."

"Oh, yes, you are. I've got a pistol in my handbag. I can fire it into the floor and explain that it went off accidentally. The sound of the gunshot would kill your father."

"It might, if he could hear it. But he won't hear it, not when he's heavily drugged, and there are two rooms and two closed doors and a large hallway between the place where we are and the place where he's quietly sleeping. On the other hand, the shock would certainly kill him if he found I were missing when he came out of his drugged sleep. And you would be left with the very awkward necessity of explaining why you had a pistol in your handbag when you came to bring a message from your employer to his fiancée, and what became of her after you'd been admitted to her presence in a room she'd promised her father's physician she wouldn't leave. . . . Just a minute," Vicky said imperiously, as Paula attempted to break in. "All this is supposing we could get from here to your car without being seen by Donovan, who's on the alert even if you think she's well out of the way, and Gifford, who's waiting near the front door, to let in a second nurse, not to mention my dog Levvy, who may come bounding in at any moment. She's apt to do that when she's kept away from me too long."

While she was talking, Vicky had gradually retreated, as Paula kept steadily advancing, her face still thrust close to that of her intended victim, her fingers already groping toward the catch of her handbag. When they reached the flat-topped desk, Vicky leaned back against it, her hands plainly visible at her sides, but one foot pressed on the push button underneath the rug, which made no sound in her sitting room, but which rang a bell in the service quarters. It was this signal that Donovan and Levvy always awaited, the signal that Vicky wanted them. Paula was still fumbling at the catch of her bag when the faithful servant and the great dog came rushing together across the room.

The huge house was again hushed and its stillness was one of even greater quietude than when Vicky had dashed up the front steps, with a fast-beating heart, six hours earlier.

This quietude had been disturbed only temporarily and, in the sickroom, the peaceful sleep of the stricken man had been unbroken; he was mercifully unaware of what happened elsewhere. Dr. Martin, from his post on the opposite side of the stair well, had heard the precipitate arrival of Donovan and Levvy and instantly recognized the existence of some emergency; he had reached Vicky's sitting room almost as soon as they did. Levvy, in her joyful leap to greet her mistress, had not injured Paula, but had knocked her over; and Vicky was giving terse orders to both servant and dog, and both were obeying with swift, unquestioning obedience. When the physician strode forward, the dog was standing over the prostrate woman and the maid had wrenched away her handbag; thanks to a hypodermic needle, her screams were quickly silenced, and it required few words of explanation to let the experienced doctor know what had happened. Meanwhile, Captain Bob, whom Tobe had called at the City Hall, even before finding that the LaBranches' telephone had been temporarily shut off, had responded by arriving in person, heading a detachment of city police. Between them, the mayor, and the physician, who was also a city judge, had the situation under control, even before Prosper's car came tearing up the driveway. When Landry and Bennett arrived, ten minutes later, it was to find their work practically done for them, as far as its immediate necessities were concerned.

Vicky was still standing, her back to her desk, when Prosper dashed into the room. She had shaken her head, showing that she did not even want to be spoken to, much less to speak herself, when Donovan began to murmur comforting words, and she gave no sign that she was aware of Levvy's continued presence. She was trembling now, from head to foot, and her face was deadly pale; but she had not once cried out, and when Prosper took her cold hands in his warm ones, and smiled down at her without a word, she looked up at him with eyes of love. The next instant, she had flung her arms around his neck and buried her face in his shoulder.

"You won't be needing me here any more for the present, sir," Donovan said quietly. "And if you should want anything later, you can always ring—thank the good Lord! Come, Levvy!"

The dog looked anxiously toward her mistress, bewildered because Vicky did not issue an order herself. For the first time, Prosper did it in her stead.

"Why not let Levvy stay, Donovan?" he asked. "It can't do any harm, can it? I'm sure she'll just lie down quietly as soon as she sees Miss Vicky doesn't want anything. And you're right, I don't need you at present. But it looks to me as if you and Levvy had come when you were both very much needed, and later on I'd like to thank you properly. I *will* ring, but just now—"

He gathered Vicky into his arms and carried her to the big armchair, where, two nights before, she had sat so contentedly in his lap. *Two nights before*—was that really all it was? In the space of a few days he had lived a lifetime, a lifetime made up mostly of nightmares, or so it had seemed, as he tossed restlessly about in his bed and faced his inquisitors at the jury table. At last the nightmares were over, and what was happening now was not a dream, even a happy dream. It was reality, reality for him and—little as he deserved it—for his love. . . .

Little by little, Vicky stopped trembling and only stirred slightly, from time to time. Then she nestled down again. When she finally spoke, her words were muffled because her face was still half hidden against his shoulder. "I'm beginning to feel like myself," she whispered. "I'm sorry to have acted like such a fool, but—"

"*Acted like such a fool!* You're the bravest girl I ever knew—and the best—and the dearest!"

"We really don't need to argue about it, do we? We've quarreled so many times that I think we ought to have got that out of our systems, by now!"

"If we haven't, we wouldn't deserve all the happiness that's ahead of us. Not that I deserve it, anyhow. But I'm going to have it."

"Then you won't keep on making objections, when I say I'd like to get married right away?"

"What do you think?"

She slid from his knees and went back to her desk, where she pretended to consult a calendar. "This is Wednesday," she announced, as if imparting a startling piece of news. "Dr. Martin says that, if everything goes the way he expects, I'll be able to talk to Father sometime tomorrow and I'll consult him then. That will be Thursday. Do you think that if he and Bedon agree, that by Saturday— Of course, we can't have any honeymoon. . . ."

"Can't we though? You mean we can't go *away* for a honeymoon! But what's the matter with a honeymoon right here? I thought, the first time I came in this room, it was the pleasantest one I'd ever seen in my life. I still think so. I don't see why we need to look for anything better—

in fact, there couldn't be anything better. I'm entitled to a week end off once in a while, even if this is the busy season." To his surprise and hers, he found he could speak almost jestingly. "Maybe I could actually get a few days extra—Mother could look after both mills and she'd be glad to." Fleetingly, he remembered that Paula would not be there to help, as she had been for so many years, and the dreadful reason for this; but he dismissed the thought. "And after we're married, darling," he added, "remember you won't have to send me home nights. I'll never forget the way you said, Monday, that you wished you didn't have to."

"I still wish I didn't have to."

"Well—Wednesday—Thursday—Friday—that's only three more."

"I'll be counting them off, too. And, meanwhile—"

"Yes?"

"Meanwhile, perhaps I could have that multicolored ring."

Sapphira, instead of being hushed like the Great House, echoed to joyous music.

When Dale went home, after his session at the courthouse and his visit to Anne Marie, he stopped his car on the bridge that spanned Bayou Cypremort and looked thoughtfully around him. It was a beautiful bright day, and still the bridge was shadowed by the mossy branches of dead cypress that overhung it, the tangle of muscadine and swamp myrtle; he would put men to work, that very afternoon, cutting all this back, so that, henceforth, light would stream over the bridge. The growth of palmetto on the farther side had also spread beyond all reasonable limits; that space must be cleared completely. Anne Marie would not want an unkempt yard with no other border than this jungle growth; she would want a flower garden. Uprooting, leveling, beautifying must begin at once; there was not a moment to lose.

When he crossed the gallery, Dale flung open the front door and realized that only this simple act was necessary to flood the long central hall with sunshine. Then he went on and on, fastening back the shutters. Everywhere, the result was the same. The house, which for so long had been shrouded in gloom, emerged as a dwelling place of light. When he approached the rear, he stopped at the room which had been his mother's, to do there what he had done in the hall and the parlors. He had thought this never would be used again; it had seemed the very abode of death. Now he visualized its archaic equipment modernized, its dulled draperies renovated, its darkness dispelled, but its essential beauty unchanged. It could be made into a bridal chamber worthy of a fairy princess. . . .

He stepped out into the hall again and walked rapidly through the dining room to the rear gallery, calling as he went, "Tiger! Tiger! Where are you?"

"Heah I is, Mistuh Dale." Tiger, who had not been more than two yards away, answered heartily, looking up from the wood he was chopping.

"Let that go for a while. Get a crew of men to work. I want all those dead branches and tangled vines cut away from the bridge. Just because you're a tiger, married to a lioness, there's no reason why we should live in a jungle. I want the yard cleared, too. I don't mean next month or even next week. I mean right now, today."

"Yessuh, Mistuh Dale." Tiger's ebony countenance revealed surprise, but no reluctance. "You's expectin' company?"

"Yes, a guest for dinner. I'll have a word with Leona. And more company—lots and lots of it, later on."

"Yessuh. We sho' will be proud to see all them fine folks at Sapphira."

Dale went on to the kitchen and frowned as he looked around him. It was bad enough that he had not realized, long before, that the cubicle connecting with his mother's chamber, where he had slept as a child, should have been converted into a bathroom and dressing room; why on earth had he not also realized that the kitchen should be modernized, that the stove and sink and refrigerator should all be white and gleaming, that there should be linoleum instead of rough bricks on the floor? Not that Leona had ever complained or that her cooking had ever left anything to be desired; and the place was impregnated with the fragrance of good food in preparation for the table. But he must not let Anne Marie into this kitchen until everything in it had been torn out and properly replaced. Neither Anne Marie nor Lavinia. He shuddered to think what Lavinia, whose standards for equipment permitted no compromise with the obsolete, would think of this kitchen. . . .

"What are you giving me for dinner, Leona?" he inquired.

She turned from the big black stove, a stocky, turbaned, bright-aproned figure and flashed him a friendly smile, showing beautiful white teeth. "I got you some shrimp," she told him, "just come over, fresh, from the Point this mornin'. Crabs, too, iffen you want 'em. An' a fryer an' mirlitons an' yams an' hot rolls I just finished bakin'. An' a pecan pie. Us can freeze you a peach cream, too, Mistuh Dale."

"It sounds as if there might be plenty without. But let's get a bottle of champagne on ice right away, shall we? And put the best china and glass on the table, as if we were going to have a big party. I'm expecting only one guest today. But I want it to seem like a great occasion. It *is* a great occasion."

Leona watched him out of sight with the same puzzlement her husband had regarded him a few minutes earlier, but with equal good will. Dale's servants were fond of him. Indeed, before he had finished his critical tour of the house, Tiger's first recruits were already hacking away at the palmetto, and Dale could see two men, with axes over their shoulders, trudging off toward the bridge. There had been no question of waiting until the next month or the next week to begin doing what the Boss Man wanted, whether the reason for it were clear or not.

If he had not been so absorbed with inspection and plans, Dale might have wondered why the Professor did not arrive more promptly; as it was, he was unaware of the length of time that had elapsed since they parted at the courthouse. After he had visited every room in the house, he opened a small safe, theoretically concealed in the wall behind his headboard, though, of course, Tiger and Leona knew it was there and were, doubtless, not unfamiliar with its contents. From it, he took, one by one, small boxes covered in faded velvet, with lids which sprang up when a spring was touched. Inside, on satin beddings, printed in gold letters with the names of such famous firms as Tiffany and Cartier, every conceivable kind of old-fashioned jewelry came to light: bracelets, necklaces, earrings, brooches, some in individual designs, some in complete parures which included all the different pieces. His plantation, which had originally been given another name, was rechristened Sapphira because his mother was so fond of sapphires; and these stones, he thought, would be especially becoming to Anne Marie, since they matched her beautiful eyes. There were plenty of them, very fine ones. And, somehow, pearls seemed suitable, too. There were several ropes of those. He wondered whether or not, when he went back to see her the next Sunday, he might take her pearls—one of the smaller strings, perhaps, to begin with. . . .

The sound of the piano, announcing the Professor's arrival, brought him back to the immediate present. He let the pearls slide once more through his fingers, for the mere pleasure of feeling their smoothness, then put them back in the velvet case and returned all the little boxes to their hiding place. When he entered the parlor, the Professor looked up with a smile, but finished the serenade he was playing before he rose to greet his host.

"I hope my tardiness hasn't inconvenienced you, Mr. Fontenot."

"I wasn't even aware that you were tardy. I've been having a look around my house with a view to making a few improvements." As he spoke, Dale noticed that the large Persian rug, which covered most of the floor, was frayed on one side. The damage had not showed when the room was in semidarkness. Now that light was pouring in, it was obvious that he must send the rug away for repairs at once.

The Professor bowed. "Nothing could give it greater distinction than it had already. But, perhaps, you've decided to admit more sunshine."

"Yes, that's the idea."

Dale's glance was already roving about the room. Some flower prints, perhaps, instead of quite so many ancestral portraits. He would keep his mother's picture, of course, over the mantel—his mother, painted by Sargent, in the very dress Anne Marie had worn the night before and wearing the pearls he intended to give his sweetheart. He must have Anne Marie painted, too, and her portrait would go over another mantel, the one in the dining room, perhaps. But surely some of these colonial governors, some of these generals in a series of wars, could be allocated to spaces where they would seem less overpowering than when they were grouped so closely together.

"I was delayed," continued the Professor, who seemed bent on apologies and explanations, "because I stopped at the Tuileries. As I told you, I felt that Mr. Landry and Mr. Bennett, though they accepted my story of the unspent money for the gold slippers, still seemed to believe that I might be withholding information in regard to the accordion, despite the fact that I had told the truth about that, also: I had not seen it from the time poor little Titine left it in my car, a week ago, until it was produced, in a battered condition, during the course of the investigation. I knew that, although the question was in abeyance for the moment, it was not closed. And I felt that, possibly, I might secure some light on the subject at the Tuileries."

"And did you?" Dale inquired, mentally removing another picture ancestor from his place over the parlor sofa and relegating him to the upper hall.

"I did, indeed. Not from Scholtze. Whatever his faults—and I would be the first to acknowledge that these are many—he is not a liar. I knew he had told Landry and Bennett that he had no idea how the accordion came to be found under a trash pile in his back yard and I believed he was telling the truth. But I still felt Baer might be able to tell a different story."

"I hope he could, if it would help to clear Maurice—not that I have anything against Baer or that I think he's guilty. But I don't think Maurice is, either. And the Benoits have been lifelong friends of mine, so, naturally—"

"Well, I gathered the plan was to call Baer for a second questioning, after the interrogation of Mr. Maurice Benoit. Of course, I knew that schedule might be subject to change. But I thought, if I could get to Baer first, and he could or would tell me anything of import, it might not only clarify, but ease the situation all around. And I was fortunate. I found Baer alone. Scholtze had driven into Jeanerette to fill a special order—he has a number of regular patrons there, and of course, after his recent trip to the Gulf, he was in an excellent position to meet their needs. Baer broke down and told me the whole story of his 'stealment,' as he calls it, of Titine's accordion. He had taken it out of my car Saturday night in the hope that she would guess he had done exactly that, and be forced to appeal to him for its return, to make up for the shabby trick she had played him. Then, when he heard she was dead, he was so frightened by the thought that he still had the accordion in his possession that he hid it in the nearest place of concealment which suggested itself to him."

"His uncle's trash pile?"

"Exactly. I persuaded him that he should either go to Landry and tell this story without waiting to be summoned, or that he should let me do so. Obviously, he could not go immediately, himself, since Scholtze had the car. So I offered to take him in mine. But, when we got as far as Lafayette, we found that pleasant and peaceful city in an uproar—"

"You found Lafayette in an uproar! What about?"

Dale was no longer contemplating the frayed rug and the ancestral portraits. He had not been vitally interested in the accordion; it had not seemed to him of primary importance. But what the Professor was at last getting around to tell him was something else again.

"Well, it appears—"

And so the whole story, or most of it, came out. Dinner was a long, leisurely meal. Leona had made the peach ice cream after all. Somehow, she had learned, in that roundabout way which is even more infallible among blacks than among whites, that this was the kind Mr. Dale's sweetheart especially favored; and, though Anne Marie's name had not been mentioned that day, in Leona's hearing, she and Tiger were both convinced that it was at last certain she was to be their new Boss Lady.

The champagne was beautifully iced and the glasses were filled and then refilled over and over again. And finally, Mr. Dale and his guest went back to the parlor, and Tiger took in coffee and, later on, bourbon, and the music man sat at the piano and played and played and played. The sunshine was gone now, but the moonlight that was streaming in was almost as bright. Some folks said there was ghostes at Sapphira, but they didn't have good knowledge. Wasn't no ghostes at Sapphira. Magic, maybe. That was different. The music man, he was making magic right now, on that old piano. And when the new Boss Lady came, she'd make more, of different kinds. They sure was lucky, Tiger and Leona, to live in a place like Sapphira.

Anne Marie was peacefully sleeping in her frilly pink and white room, having told her mother that everything was all right, after all. Dale had been a perfect angel. As far as that went, Didier had been back to see her that afternoon, also, and had apologized for his conduct the night before and begged to be forgiven. But it was too late to do him any good. She had made up her mind at last. Lavinia had said she was glad and Anne Marie had gone blissfully off to bed, prepared for happy dreams.

Now Lavinia was standing by the window in another room: the same window at which she had stood the night her husband Claude had been accidentally shot by his cousin Fleex, who had brought him home to die and then gone forth to kill himself.

She had seen Fleex as he went down the garden walk, for dawn was just breaking, but after that he was swallowed up in the shadow of the trees. However, she had continued to stand at the window, as if she were instinctively waiting for the shot she would not hear, but which she knew would crackle through the still air of the prairie before daylight really came. She had known it from the moment Fleex had said good-by to her, after a last farewell to the dead man in the room beyond—the man he had loved better than anyone in the world, except Lavinia herself.

"I've killed him and ruined your life. I told you once before it was the end. That time, I didn't mean it. This time, I do."

"I know," she said. And then he had left her, and what he had said was true: life had never been the same again.

But, strangely enough, it was not of that night when Claude had died and Fleex had shot himself that she was thinking now. It was of the other time, the first time Fleex had told her this was the end and had not meant it; the time she had thought he did, instead of knowing he did. Everyone had said he was not good enough for her and he had gone away, nobody knew where. And before he came back, never doubting that she would have waited for him, she had yielded to persuasion and married Claude. So Fleex had gone away a second time, and she had been a good wife and a good mother and had made a proud place for herself in the community. Everyone said there was not a finer woman in the state than Lavinia Villac and, for once, everyone was right. But there were many happier women, though this was something that everyone did not know. And if Fleex had only not told her, that first time, this was the end, he was never coming back, he was not good enough for her. . . .

Well, she had done what she could with her life, and she had tried, conscientiously, not to think of what it might have been, if he had not said that, if she had not believed it. She had faced the world with fortitude, she had never been afraid—that is, she had never been afraid until Titine Dargereux had been found dead in the rough rice bin, the night that Prosper had been the last to leave the mill. Then she had been frightened, so frightened she could not believe she had successfully concealed her terror. Not because, for one moment, she believed her son guilty of murder, or ever would believe it, whatever the evidence against him; but because she knew he had been guilty of lust, almost at the moment when love was within his grasp, and she was consumed with fear lest he might lose his love because of his lust. . . .

So she had pled with Prosper. "Vicky has told you, over and over again, that she loves you, even though she knows you're the subject of scandal and perhaps worse. She's told you she loves you, no matter what you've done or what anyone else thinks you've done. Don't tell her you know you're not good enough for her. Don't tell her to put you out of her mind. Tell her instead that you hope to be more worthy of her someday, but that, meanwhile, it means everything in the world to you to have her confidence and her love." He had looked at his mother in amazement, he had not promised to do as she asked; she knew how strong had been the instinct that he should confess his unworthiness to his beloved, then and there, and tell her that he could no longer hope that there could be any place for him in her life. Lavinia's terror had continued until she herself had seen Vicky, until she realized that no matter what Prosper had said or anyone else had said, Vicky would never let him go. He was her man and she knew it. What he confessed and when did not matter; what mattered was not what he had done in the past, but what he would do in the future. He would not even need, ever, to confess his repentance and his shame and his sense of unworthiness for her to recognize them; she understood how he felt, without having it put into words. He had sinned and she would always hate the sin, and recoil from the thought of it. But she would still love the sinner. And she would know that he would not fail her again. He was hers forever, just as she was his forever. . . .

And now the danger was past and Lavinia did not need to be afraid any more. Prosper and Vicky were together, both safe and both happy and, in a few days, they would be man and wife. Lavinia's son would never lose the glory which she had missed. Again, she could face the world with fortitude. She would try to believe that, after all, this was what mattered most in life.

EPILOGUE

September 21, 1927

Rice Carnival Day

A YEAR AFTER THE TRAGIC DEATH OF TITINE DARGEREUX, THIS AND THE events most closely connected with it had receded from the forefront of community consciousness. The Primeaux' family cemetery was still carefully tended and, having given the poor girl her last resting place, they would no more have neglected her grave than any other in the little enclosure; but, since *Toussaint*, it had not been visited by her parents, whom the Professor had brought to it at that time, and he himself had been back only once since then, on this second occasion accompanied by Baer. Paula, after examination by Dr. Davila, had been committed to the East Louisiana State Hospital at Jackson, and Amanda and Tobe paid her periodic visits; but they did not talk about her much, even in the family circle; hers was certainly one of those cases when the less said, the better.

Soon after the new year, the first formal carnival celebration was organized in Lafayette by a lady from New Orleans who missed the seasonal festivities of her native city, and a gala ball was held which became the talk of the town, to the exclusion of grimmer subjects, which were dropped almost completely. During Lent, when there were fewer dances, the younger set drove 'round and 'round Parkerson Avenue—still the only paved street—waving to each other, and went, in gay groups, to the movies. The girls could not decide who gave them the greater thrill—Ronald Colman in *Beau Geste* or Rudolph Valentino in *The Sheik*; the young men were almost unanimous in their admiration for Douglas Fairbanks in *The Black Pirate* and Red Grange in *One Minute to Play*; both men and girls were equally enthusiastic over two operettas—*The Chimes of Normandy* and *Blossomtime* which came to Lafayette. After Easter, evenings there were largely devoted to dancing; the Black Swan Orchestra had achieved tremendous vogue, and *"Allons à Lafayette"* became almost a theme song among the gilded youth of Crowley. They had stopped singing "Valencia" and "The Desert Song" and had begun to sing "Old Man River" and "Mississippi Mud." The latter had caught on with surprising swiftness, considering that it was first sung by an unknown youngster named Bing Crosby; it was a very general favorite; still it did not displace *"Allons à Lafayette."*

In May, the terrible floods which inundated the entire region in and around both Crowley and Lafayette, crowding the latter with thousands of refugees from sections even more affected, and lasting, in varying degrees of damage and disaster, for nearly a month, were naturally the main preoccupation of the countryside and displaced its gaiety with gloom. Even Lindbergh's nonstop flight to Paris, made just as the local outlook was at its worst, failed to rouse the depressed and distressed citizenry to the pitch of excitement which prevailed everywhere else throughout the country. When the waters at last receded, and the grumbling over the alleged mismanagement of the emergency had begun to subside, a fresh grievance arose: in a booklet, issued by the Southern Pacific Lines, Lake Charles, instead of Crowley, had been publicly acclaimed as the birthplace of the rice industry; and though the misstatement was afterward corrected, with apologies, community pride had been cut to the quick. Of course, the floods had been bad for the crops, too; several farmers reported a yield of only eight bags of rice to an acre, instead of the customary ten or eleven. On the whole, however, conditions were not as discouraging as had been feared a few months earlier; one editorial in the *Signal* even lightheartedly defined an expert in the rice business as "a man who can look at a field"—presumably a field that was yielding only eight bags!—"and tell how much gravy it would take to eat that much rice." Brent Winslow's new variety "Princess Victorine" came up to expectations and brought a good price; and, before the end of August, the predominant feeling was no longer one of resentment and discouragement. The major topic of conversation was the coming "Rice Carnival Day." A "Rice King" and a "Rice Queen" would preside over this festival, which would be celebrated in late September, with a flower show and a baby show, a pageant and a parade and a ball, a gala luncheon for distinguished guests, and a "joint political meeting" at which the gubernatorial candidates would deliver addresses, among them that forceful, brilliant, uncouth young lawyer from Winnfield, whose star seemed to be steadily rising, despite his defeat three years earlier—Huey P. Long. That was the man whom everyone really wanted to see and to hear.

It had long been a foregone conclusion that Brent Winslow would be the unanimous choice of the official committee—which, in turn, reflected the unanimous choice of the community—as the king who would reign over this carnival. The feeling was almost equally strong and united in regard to the prospective queen—unquestionably, this should be Winslow's only granddaughter, Anne Marie Villac; but the committee had some difficulty in persuading Brent to accept so public an honor. Despite his growing fame and fortune, he had remained withdrawn and reticent, disparaging his own achievements and generously giving credit for them to both his collaborators and his rivals. Mary, his wife, was equally unassuming and equally reserved, though she had achieved almost as much distinction in horticulture as he had in agronomy; and Lavinia Villac, their only daughter, had never tried to persuade them to abandon their quiet and retiring way of life. It remained for Lavinia's children, aided and abetted by Anne Marie's fiancé and Prosper's young wife, to batter down the elderly gentleman's resistance.

Anne Marie, to be sure, might not have been considered entirely disinterested, if there had been detractors of her merits or even serious rivals for the role. It was well known that she had hoped for this honor, not only because she was Brent Winslow's granddaughter, and for this reason logically entitled to it; but because her wedding day was already fixed and she would never have another chance to reign, since there was an unwritten law that, except for Mystic, Carnival queens, in New Orleans, should be unmarried and Crowley was now setting a precedent for regional festivals. But her sweet and even disposition, which almost no one had ever seen ruffled, had made her a general favorite since her babyhood, and her blond beauty and gracious manners were so patently unequaled that no one thought of disputing her prerogative. However, vanity was not among her faults; and it was on the basis of her relationship to Brent that she wheedled her grandfather.

"Some other girl might get to be queen if you wouldn't be king," she told him, beguilingly. "It's natural for the committee to take kinship into consideration at a time like this. And then I'd never have a chance to wear a crown and wear a beautiful long white train and everything that goes with them."

"From what I hear, you're going to wear a beautiful white train, not to mention a crown, a couple of months from now," Brent told her rather dryly.

"But the crown won't be made of *rice!* It'll be made of *orange blossoms.* And the train won't be a queen's train! It'll be just a bride's train."

"Dale wouldn't thank you for that word 'just' and I wouldn't blame him," Brent said, still dryly. "Well, you'd make a beautiful queen, there's no denying that, just as you'll make a beautiful bride. You take naturally to crowns and silks and satins and that sort of thing. I don't. I'd feel like a fool, all decked out in doublet and knee breeches."

"You might, if you'd got fat like so many men your age," Anne Marie said sweetly. "But you've got a wonderful figure. I don't believe you've gained an ounce since you were twenty-five, and Grandmother's always said you were the best-built man she ever saw, when she married you. Of course, she has a wonderful figure herself, so she's in a position to appreciate yours. And so has Mother—in fact, I think we've *all* got pretty good figures. At least, Dale's forever paying me compliments on mine. Don't you think I'd look nice in royal regalia, Grandfather?"

"Very nice. I've told you that already."

"Well, just think how much more effective *my* outfit would be if I had you, dressed to match, beside me on that first float, with our pages, all in white, too, and my maids and your knights in pastel colors, like a living rainbow."

Anne Marie's voice, like her language, was becoming dreamy with joyful anticipation. Mary, who, so far, had taken no part in the discussion, now interposed a mild comment.

"Anne Marie's right, Brent," she said quietly.

"About what?"

"About everything. It's natural for her to want to be the queen of the first rice carnival and it wouldn't be half so logical for her to be chosen unless you were the king. It's also true that you've got the figure and the bearing to wear the costume which would be suitable for such an occasion—most men your age would look ridiculous in it, just as she said, but you could carry it off. Furthermore, it's true that she'd be seen to much better advantage if she were seated beside you, instead of some fat old man—always provided she'd be on the royal float instead of the fat old man's granddaughter, if you don't listen to reason."

" '*Et tu Brute!*' " Brent said, glancing sideways at his wife, who returned the glance in a startled way. She had never heard him quote Shakespeare before—indeed, she would have said, offhand, that he did not know any to quote, though she had learned, after nearly fifty years of married life, not to be too sure what Brent might or might not know. "Suppose we talk about something else for a while?" he now inquired.

But he did not say it curtly, and Mary knew he was not offended by her championship of Anne Marie or, as far as that went, with anything Anne Marie herself had said. Mary was even hopeful that he might think the matter over, as a result of this conversation, and eventually regard it in a more favorable light. But she did not dare try to hurry him, despite her realization that it would be necessary for the committee to have his final answer within the next few days. With this in mind, she telephoned Vicky and asked if there were any likelihood that Prosper and his wife might be coming out to the farm within the next day or two.

"Why, yes," Vicky responded, without hesitation. "We can come this evening, if you want us to."

"That would be fine. We really haven't heard much about your trip yet, you know. Prosper's grandfather's especially interested in hearing more about the rice paddies in Java. Incidentally . . . you knew he hadn't actually consented to serving as king of the rice carnival, didn't you?"

"No! And I'm sure Prosper didn't, either. We'll be out right after supper—or would you like us to come to supper?"

"I'm sure that would please my husband very much. You haven't been here to a meal, you know, since you came back."

"We're a couple of wretches. But we'll mend our ways, starting tonight."

Mary hung up the receiver with a smile of pleasure—her first favorable impressions of Victorine had been confirmed and strengthened every time she had seen the girl; it would be good to see her again tonight. Having set the wheels in motion for a festive supper, Mary took her sewing and went out to the arbor, overhung with wild grapevine, in the garden where roses bloomed all the year round and other flowers in swift succession. Then, seated at ease, she dwelt with contentment on the successive steps of this ripening acquaintance.

First, there had been that party at Lavinia's when Prosper was under a terrible cloud, and Vicky had won the hearts of everyone by her staunch and gallant refusal to admit that such a cloud existed or could exist, as far as he was concerned. Then there had been the morning she had come out to try the horse Grandpa Jim had given her and had put it gaily and expertly through its paces, before going on to delight the Primeaux with a visit, too—a visit which had ended in her swift recall to her stricken father's side. He had rallied, temporarily, but that same day Vicky's life had been threatened by a maniac, and it was only her own presence of mind in the face of sudden danger which had saved her. Yet she had shown no traces of the shock this shattering experience must have given her when, three days later, she was married to Prosper in the presence of his immediate family. Moïse LaBranche was not even able to rise from the sofa, to which he had been lifted from his bed in the adjoining room, when he gave his daughter away; but, again, Vicky had betrayed no qualms as to her course. She was a grave bride, rather than a gay one, but her gravity became her; Mary would never forget the way she had pronounced her marriage vows, or the way she looked at Prosper as she said, " 'For better, for worse, for richer, for poorer, in sickness and in health, till death do us part.' "

A month later, her father's temporary improvement permitted him to have the wedding feast on the lavish and expansive scale which he had originally planned, and all the relatives, near and far, were present on this festive occasion. That night, Vicky was radiant. It was obvious that, to her, union with her beloved had meant rapture; there had been no doubts, no fears, no reservations of any kind; and because she had given herself with such joyous self-abandonment to her bridegroom, he had been able to make her transition from maidenhood to wifehood one of triumph for them both. Mary's own marriage had been happy, but, almost from the beginning, it had been one of devotion, rather than of passion, and she knew this was true in Lavinia's case, also. For herself, she had no regrets; for her daughter, she had stifled them. Now, in the girl who had chosen Prosper for a mate, she recognized, for the first time, the glory of what she had never previously missed and of which Lavinia had been robbed. . . .

Mary next saw Vicky at the funeral of Moïse LaBranche, only a few weeks later. Throughout the services, the girl was completely composed. That she must have wept, Mary could not doubt; but her countenance was not disfigured with tears in the presence of the hosts who came to pay a final tribute to one of the finest men their state had given to the world; and later, when Mary and Lavinia saw her by themselves, she was still calm and, in a sense, even content.

"He wanted very much to come home," she told them. "I mean, to die. He knew that he did not have long to live and the only dread he expressed about death was that it might overtake him while he was 'amid the alien corn.' That's the way he always spoke of it. So he had his wish. He did get home in time to avoid what, to him, would have been the greatest tragedy. Then he was afraid he might leave me unprotected. He wanted to live long enough to see me happily married. And this wish was fulfilled, too. After that, he was ready to go. He was old and tired and I'm afraid he suffered a great deal. Now he is at peace."

"You don't think it hastened the end—making the effort to have that big family party?" Mary asked solicitously.

Vicky smiled. She had continued to be calm, but this was the first time she had smiled. "I don't think so. But, if it did, that wouldn't matter, either. He wanted very much to have that big family party, to see me among Prosper's kinsfolk, since I didn't have any of my own who could be here. That wasn't such a serious wish as the others, of course, but it was an important one, too. It made him very happy to feel it had been granted. He joked sometimes about a fairy godmother who had said he might make three wishes and that they'd all come true. He said she'd kept her word. But later, toward the end, he didn't talk about fairies. He talked about divine loving-kindness. He said the Eternal Father had been very good to him. I know he felt that way. I know that he wasn't afraid to die, that he believed in immortality. Some Jews don't, you know." She made the pronouncement quite without self-consciousness and went on in the same quiet voice in which she had spoken before. "He quoted something else to me, quite often, just as he did that line about the alien corn. 'The end of birth is death, the end of death is life, and wherefore mournest thou?' That's an inscription on a tombstone in Rock Creek Park Cemetery. He took me to see it, the last time we were in Washington. He told me never to forget what it said. I never shall."

"I'm sure you won't," Lavinia told her warmly. Among the many reasons why Mary rejoiced over Prosper's marriage was the consciousness that his choice had made Lavinia so happy. "But, my dear, isn't this house going to seem very strange and—well, empty to you without your father? Wouldn't it be a good idea, perhaps, for you and Prosper to come and stay with me for a little while?"

"Thank you, Mother." Vicky had called Lavinia Mother from the beginning and had, in fact, addressed all Prosper's relatives as if they were hers, too, which had delighted them. "As a matter of fact, Prosper and I have been talking about what we'd better do next. He was going to talk to you about it, too, himself, but I may as well, since the subject's come up. I'm sure he wouldn't mind. The house does seem a little strange and empty—you're right about that. So we thought, if it wouldn't mean too much work for you to handle both mills—if you wouldn't feel we were imposing on you—we might take a trip around the world. He reminded me you'd wanted him to have one, after he graduated from college—he'd told Father and me about this plan the very first time he came to see us and I knew things hadn't come just right for it then; but they do seem to be just right for it now and we thought you might like to have us go together, on a wedding journey. I think it's bothered Prosper a little, not on his account, but on mine, because he felt I was missing something I was entitled to when we couldn't have one as soon as we were married. It shouldn't have. I've been traveling most of my life and I was glad enough to stay in one place for a while; anyway, all I wanted was Prosper. He's still all I need to make me happy. But I'll be glad to go anywhere with him, just as I'm glad to stay anywhere with him. So, if you approve—"

"My dear, of course I approve. That is, unless—"

"Unless what, Mother?"

"Unless you're expecting a baby. You haven't said you were and I'm not trying to force your confidence, but I'd be sorry to have you take any chances. You see I—I miscarried the first time I was pregnant. I've never spoken about it much. I think most people believe it wasn't a great blow to me. But they're mistaken. I wouldn't want you to have a tragic loss like that."

Mary looked at her daughter in amazement. More than thirty years had passed since the mishap to which Lavinia had just referred and she had never mentioned it before; as she had just said, everyone, even her mother, had assumed it had not been a severe blow. Lavinia certainly knew how to keep secret anything she did not choose to reveal. But now she had chosen to disclose a sorrow which, all this time, had been locked in her heart, because she hoped that no such calamity would be risked again. Vicky looked intently at her husband's mother and spoke in the same grave way that had so impressed Mary when the girl pronounced her marriage vows.

"I'm terribly sorry," she said. "No one ever told me about that before. I promise, Mother, that I'll be very careful when I'm expecting a baby. But I'm not, yet. In a way, I'd have been glad if it had happened right off. It must be wonderful when it does, when a girl feels that the man she loves has given her a child at the same time that she's given herself to him—conception has a double meaning then, doesn't it? I don't mind telling you I've been a little disappointed, because I'd have loved to have that double meaning a part of my marriage. And then, of course, it would have meant a lot to Father to know . . . but, perhaps, it's better this way. Because Prosper really has his heart set on that trip, and now I know it would have worried you to have me take it and why, if I were pregnant, I wouldn't have gone."

"Thank you, darling," Lavinia said in a hushed voice. Then, speaking more naturally, she continued, "Of course, I'll be glad to take charge of both mills. You and Prosper should be on your way as soon as possible."

Vicky nodded. "Before I do get pregnant," she said and smiled again. "But please don't worry, Mother. I promise, if it happens while we're gone, I'll be very, very careful and even come straight home if you'd feel any better about it. When we do. . . ." She hesitated a moment and then plunged ahead. "We thought perhaps it would be better if we came to Crowley to live. Of course, this isn't far off. But the commuting does add up to a long day for Prosper, especially when he's kept late at the mill and, besides, if we were in Crowley, we'd have that much more time together. I haven't any special sentiment about this house, now that Father's dead. It was his pride and joy and I'm glad to have lived here with him for that reason. But it isn't the kind I'd build myself, if I had my choice, and I'm pretty sure Prosper feels the same way, though he hasn't said so—he wouldn't, of course, so soon, for fear of hurting my feelings. But we'd both like one more like yours and nearer you."

It was not often that Mary had seen tears in her daughter's eyes. But she saw them then, as Lavinia rose and walked over to Vicky and put her arms around her son's wife.

So Vicky and Prosper had started off on their trip, leaving the great house and the great dog in charge of Donovan and, periodically, letters came back, addressed to first one member of the family and then to another, telling about the wonderful things they were seeing and the wonderful things they were doing. These letters were shared by their recipients, so Mary had seen them all. Prosper and Vicky were in Hollywood, making the rounds of the studios. They were in Hawaii, bathing from the beach at Waikiki. They were in Japan, overawed by the Daibutsu. They were in Hong Kong, buying silks and riding in rickshas. They were in Java, staying at a tea plantation. They were in Colombo, going crazy over the jewels that were poured out like so many grains of rice for them to choose among. They were in Egypt, going on camel back to see the Sphinx. They were in Athens, spending the night of the full moon on the Acropolis. They were in Venice, floating down the Grand Canal in a gondola. They were in Paris, reveling in the opera. They were in Strasbourg, visiting the Zweigs. They were in London, bidden to a Royal Garden Party. . . .

"And now," Vicky had written Lavinia, "we're coming home. It's been simply grand, every moment of it, and I hope you all enjoyed reading our letters. But here's the *really* big piece of news. Last week, I started losing my breakfast, and the first two or three times I thought it was just the English food. (Coffee you wouldn't even recognize as such, toast served on silver racks so it will be nice and cold, rice relegated to pasty puddings, horrid little fish called plaice.) But a night or so ago, I passed out cold—no, I hadn't had too much to drink, I just fainted. So our ambassador got me an appointment with one of those topflight Harley Street specialists, and the pompous old boy said there wasn't the slightest doubt. . . . We've got passage on the *Leviathan* and we'll be home in August, early enough for Prosper to help with the worst of the rush season and you and Grandma and I can start right in making baby clothes!"

Lavinia had brought the letter straight out to the farm and she and Mary had read it and reread it together. And now, so opportunely that it seemed to Mary providential, Vicky and Prosper were back again and could be counted on to aid and abet Anne Marie and Dale in urging Brent Winslow to serve as king on Rice Carnival Day. . . . Why, that must be the young couple driving into the *passage* this very minute! Mary folded her sewing and rose, taking the flower-bordered walk that led from the arbor toward the house, as she went forward to greet them.

Prosper no longer drove a dilapidated Oldsmobile. (For that matter, neither did Anne Marie. Dale had insisted on giving her a new car for one of her engagement presents and had made sure that it was neither the same make nor the same model as the one belonging to his future brother-in-law, or even the same color.) The jade-green Chrysler convertible, equipped with a French horn the travelers had brought back with them, was the last word in chic and had been affectionately nick-named "The Green Apple"; from this, they alighted at the *passage* gate which led to the flower garden. Prosper held out his hand to Vicky and she took it, descending with deliberation, instead of leaping lightly from the car as she once would have done; but, except for the slightly rounded and very becoming contours which had displaced her extreme slender-ness, her figure showed no change and her face glowed with health. She threw her arms around Mary and then stood back to spread out the newspaper she had hitherto kept folded in one hand.

"Where's Grandfather?" she inquired eagerly. "I've got to get hold of him right away! He hasn't seen this, has he? Well, there's something in it I've got to show him!"

Brent, as usual, was in his workroom. Vicky invaded it without a qualm and the others followed her. She embraced him in the same joyous way that she had Mary and then laid the evening paper before him.

"Look at that!" she said excitedly, pointing to an editorial with the heading, "Perennial Gratitude." Then, slowly and expressively, she read aloud the article that appeared beneath these words:

" 'To attempt to set a value on Brent Winslow's contribution to the rice industry and Southwest Louisiana would be like putting a price mark on the soil, the sunshine or the elements that go into a crop; for the rices he has developed have been brought out at a time when old varieties seemed to have worn out and when the very condition of the business called for remedy.

" 'Every market report, every warehouse receipt book and every article on rice carries words that are in themselves testimonials to the importance of the man. His perseverance and his determination have demonstrated the effectiveness of his method of approaching his labors and undertaking his quest for something better.

" 'His achievements will be perpetuated each year when the fields turn green, then bend for the harvest.' "

"You see what people think of you, Grandfather!" she said happily. "Prosper and I are so proud of you we're nearly bursting."

Brent removed the strong glasses which he had begun to use for work, in addition to a microscope, during the past few years, and wiped them carefully; somehow, they had gathered moisture. "That's young Will Duson's writing," he said. "His father was always a good friend of mine —one of my first, when I came here, and it's been a friendship that's lasted into the next generation. I'd expect my family to be pleased, even if Will did exaggerate some. But that's not saying everyone—"

"Father always said a man wouldn't be worth his salt if he didn't make a few enemies, along with a host of friends," Vicky said swiftly. "Someone's always going to be jealous, someone's always going to be mean, someone's always going to be crooked. But you wouldn't give one or two spiteful, envious persons the satisfaction of seeing you disappoint thousands, would you—the thousands Mr. Duson's speaking for when he writes about 'Perennial Gratitude'? That wouldn't be reasonable, Grandfather, it wouldn't even be fair. It isn't just your family to whom this means a lot—it's the neighborhood, the town, the parish, the state—in a way, the whole country. What Mr. Duson says is true—to try to set a value on your contribution would be like trying to put a price mark on soil and sunshine."

"If it is true—I'm not saying whether it is or not—it wouldn't be any truer just because I went in for play acting."

"It wouldn't be play acting! It would be interpreting the truth, so that everyone who still doesn't understand what it means to say you're the Rice King would know it! It would be making those who do know it happy to see that you appreciate their understanding and their affection! They're offering you the greatest honor they know how to bestow—even if you don't like the form it's taking, you must realize that. You can't be so ungracious as to spurn their offering."

Brent sat very still for a moment and then he put his glasses on again and reread the editorial quietly to himself. Vicky did not speak while he was doing so and neither did the others; they all remained very still.

" 'Every year when the fields turn green and then bend to the harvest,' " Brent said at last. "*That's* the greatest tribute I could ask for. If people think of me at those seasons, after I'm gone, their memory will be the monument I'd want, above all others. And it does a man good, every now and then, to have such words spoken while he can still hear them. You're right, Vicky, I can't be so ungracious and seem so ungrateful as not to do what's asked of me. With all of you to help me, I guess I can see it through."

After that, there was no more hesitation; preparations for the great event went buoyantly forward. The king and the queen were to ride in a float at the head of the parade in which the rice industry, all the way from seed propagation to consumption, would be fittingly represented. It was to be the most ambitious display of its kind ever undertaken in Southwest Louisiana and the floats were to be followed by private passenger cars, similarly decorated. All this involved endless activity on the part of the committee and the prospective participants. Dale grumbled that he could never snatch an uninterrupted moment with Anne Marie; she was either endlessly talking on the telephone or she was endlessly trying on clothes. Brent Winslow came into town as regularly and mingled with as many people as Grandfather Jim, and the nonagenarian insisted this was the first time his son-in-law ever got around. From now on, Garland insisted, there would be a change; Brent had learned how to have a good time and the next thing they knew, he would be playing dominoes! Lavinia and Prosper were both overworked. After all, the season was in full swing; they could not stop superintending operations at the Monrovia and the Claudia because of the carnival, and yet, they must do their share in making that a success. Vicky offered to move over to Crowley for the time being; it would save Prosper the fatigue of commuting. But both he and Lavinia vetoed the suggestion. Her visit should come afterward, when things had quieted down; meanwhile, she must save her strength for the great day.

Privately, Vicky thought she had strength to spare, but she did not argue about it. She was very happy and she saw no reason why she should add to the burdens of her husband and his mother by causing them anxiety, however unnecessarily. It had now definitely been decided that, after the baby was born, she and Prosper would build a house of their own near Crowley, about halfway between Lavinia's and the farm, so that they would be equally accessible to both. The land was family property and architectural drawings had already been made. During the daytime, Vicky pored over these, so that she would be able to discuss possible changes for the better with Prosper when he came home at night. Captain Bob had been consulted about the landscape gardening and plans for that were also under way; Vicky had no idea of trying to rival either Mary Winslow or Anne Marie in her flower garden, but she did want something that would seem adequate and suitable to these experts. The LaBranche house was to be converted into a museum, which would perpetuate the memory of Moïse, and the grounds would be used for a park which would be open to the public. Some of the servants, who had never been really contented in Lafayette, though they had not deserted their posts, would be dismissed with good references and substantial farewell gifts of money; some would remain in the museum and park as caretakers; Donovan, who was delighted at the prospect of being a Nannie again, and at least two others would move to Crowley with the young couple. The reorganization of all these lives was not without its problems and they could not be solved hastily; but none of them involved hard feelings or financial difficulties. Vicky settled down contentedly to dealing with them. She would enjoy the great day when it arrived, but she did not share Anne Marie's impatience for it, any more than she had Lavinia's feeling that she would be thankful when it was over.

It finally dawned, bright and clear and warm. The streets were festooned with the carnival colors, pennants floated from the wires suspended across the avenue and all the pillars were wrapped in gay bunting. Crowds from the neighboring towns and surrounding countryside milled about, mingling jovially with the citizenry which was out in full force and which was expressing itself with gusto. "My daddy's tractor's gonna pull the float the king and queen ride on. . . ." "Wish the stores was open. I'd buy something for my kids that was too young to bring along. Maybe there'll be a chance after the parade. . . ." "Did you know Pathe News was taking pictures? I tell you it won't be long before the whole country knows this is its rice capital. . . ." "It don't look a hell of a lot like six years ago when rice that cost us more'n three dollars a pocket to plant had to be sold for less'n a dollar and a half. . . ." "Long'll sweep the state, you'll see; he damn near did it four years ago." All the shops had gone in for special displays, many of them ingenious, symbolic or really beautiful. The largest crowd was gathered around Brandt's Furniture Store, where an enormous plate-glass window revealed a bed of snowy rice, on which Brent Winslow's name, captioned with the words, A GREAT MAN, had been traced in golden grains. Standing sheaves of rice formed the lower part of the background for this base and, above them, a central portrait of Brent was flanked on either side with the names he had given the varieties of rice for which he was responsible. To make this display even more convincing and complete were two placards, one at the lower left and the other at the lower right. The former was inscribed:

75% OF THE 1927
U.S. RICE CROP
WAS GROWN TO GRAIN DEVELOPED BY
BRENT WINSLOW
50% BLUE CAMELLIA
15% PRINCESS MARY
10% LADY LAVINIA
IT IS CONFIDENTLY EXPECTED
PRINCESS VICTORINE
WILL BRING THE TOTAL TO 80%

The right-hand placard was inscribed:

"BURBANK OF THE
RICE INDUSTRY"
BRENT WINSLOW
"HIS ACHIEVEMENTS WILL BE PERPETUATED
EACH YEAR WHEN THE FIELDS TURN GREEN,
THEN BEND FOR THE HARVEST."
—THE *Signal*

This window also called forth its quota of conversation: "Neat, I call it. . . ." "No more'n he deserves, him. Say, look at the picture, will you? That's made of rice, too. . . ." "I'll be thinking about that piece from the *Signal* and about Brent Winslow both whenever I harvest my crops. . . ."

More and more people stopped before this display, more and more voiced their enthusiasm for it; meanwhile, the milling throngs kept on increasing in volume. By noon, the streets were already so crowded that it was hard to clear the way for the distinguished guests who were to attend the luncheon at the Egan Hotel; as it was strictly "stag," Lavinia and Vicky and Anne Marie had to get their impression of it through their menfolk, and Anne Marie was not much interested, anyhow. She was preoccupied with her beautiful white dress and her rice crown and her long train, and Lavinia, who would gladly have heard an account of the speeches, was kept busy helping her. But Vicky listened with absorption to the details Prosper brought them.

"That's enough for now," he said at last, "we must get going or they'll think we're not coming and someone else will steal the seats that have been saved for us."

They were not actually late in taking their appointed places; on the other hand, they certainly had no time to spare. The music of the approaching band could already be heard, and the mayor, the city clerk—who was acting as grand marshal—and the chief of police, all mounted on fine spirited horses, were swinging into sight with their escort. Next came the royal float, surmounted by the throne. Vicky leaned forward eagerly to get an immediate view of it; then she felt impelled to glance back at her husband and his mother and grandmother and found it was their faces that she wanted to watch, even more than the two regal figures. For this was their great day, too; Mary's pride in her husband, Prosper's in his sister, Lavinia's in her daughter, illumined their countenances. Vicky had seen exultation in Prosper's expression before, but she was seeing it for the first time in the expression of the others. It held her fascinated and a little awed at its underlying meaning, different in each case, but, in each, equally strong, equally moving. Mary, she knew, was thinking that this celebration was a symbol of the goal to which the hardships of pioneering, the discouragements of futile experimentation, the hopes long delayed before fulfillment had, all the time, been leading. Prosper was forgetting that Anne Marie had lacked strength and faith in a crisis, he was telling himself that he had expected too much of her and that their temporary friction had been all his fault.

He was beginning to understand that, if she had possessed their mother's
fortitude, she would have lacked something of her infinite appeal; he
was remembering that he had adored her from the day of her birth and
was convinced that the adulation she was now receiving was only her
just due. And Lavinia? It was tenderness, rather than pride, that she
felt for her daughter. Perhaps she, like Vicky, recognized Anne Marie's
limitations better than Prosper did; perhaps she loved the girl more because she knew that, all her life, Anne Marie must be shielded and
cherished, and was rejoicing because she knew marriage with Dale
would assure such shielding and such cherishing. The pride, Vicky decided, was not in Anne Marie, but in Brent Winslow. Lavinia, like
Mary, had shared his struggle and, even more actively than Mary, the
fruits of his success. He and she had harvested these together. Now,
she, too, was having her special reward.

"Don't look at us, honey, look at the float," Vicky heard Prosper saying
and, obediently, she turned in its direction. It was almost opposite them
now; this was, indeed, the moment when she would see it to best
advantage. The throne was placed high, in order to permit grouping the
ladies-in-waiting, the knights and pages on the steps leading up to it;
their rainbow-colored costumes formed a radiant contrast to the dazzling
white worn by the king and queen, as Anne Marie had predicted. Also,
according to prediction, Brent wore his royal robes well; he had, indeed,
the figure and bearing which permitted him to carry them with dignity,
even with distinction. However, he took his honors seriously; he bowed
responsibly to the cheering multitude, and when the float halted briefly
opposite the place where his family was stationed, he looked straight at
his wife and gave her a grave personal salute. For him, this was a
momentous, rather than a festive, occasion; like Mary, he saw in it the
symbol of the goal they had so long striven to reach and, like her, he
felt that its meaning was fraught with solemnity. It was Anne Marie
who dimpled and smiled, who threw kisses to her family and friends,
who, every now and then, laughed softly in response to a gay greeting.
The farther the float progressed, the louder grew the applause; she had
captured the hearts of everyone in the milling crowds; she was their
sweetheart, their darling, their treasure.

On and on came the other floats. One, dominated by a beaming
farmer, carried specimens of everything he might hope to raise in the
region—not only rice, but cotton, corn, sugar, fruits, dairy products.
Another bore a wagon loaded with rice in the shock, surrounded by
colored laborers carrying their pitchforks, as if ready for work. Still an-

other was surmounted by a miniature field of rice with some land under cultivation and scattered models of tractors made to scale; the effect of active farming operations which this produced was very realistic. Vicky, clapping her hands, announced she was sure this would be the prize winner.

"I think you're probably right," Prosper told her. The last of the floats was in sight now and the private pleasure cars, almost covered with sheaves, were following in its wake. "Look, when the way's clear, what do you say we go back to Mother's?" he continued. "If you're bound and determined to go to the ball tonight, I think you ought to have a little rest first."

"I'm not bound and determined to go to the ball. You're the one that's really hankering to do that. You know you wouldn't miss feasting your eyes again on Anne Marie in all her glory. I'm perfectly willing to go back to the house and rest, if you want me to. However, why don't you say right out, meanwhile, you'd like to go to that political meeting that's going to be held under the shade trees on the east lawn of the courthouse, right after the parade, and that you'll feel easier about me if you see me tucked into bed first? I know you're dying to hear Huey Long talk some more and light into the other candidates, which he couldn't do at luncheon."

Prosper laughed. "All right, I do want to see Anne Marie again in all her glory and I would like to hear Huey Long talk again. No use trying to fool you, honey. Just the same, even if I didn't and even if I weren't, I think you ought to rest. So be a good girl and come along. The 'Green Apple's' parked right around the corner. What about you, Mother? Are you ready to leave, too, or do you want to stay a little longer?"

"I guess we're all ready to leave. We've seen what we really came for."

When they reached Lavinia's house, they found that the entire court and most of the family had reached there before them. The living room was full of merrymakers. Anne Marie and Brent Winslow were standing in front of the fireplace, receiving congratulations, Dale was hovering near by, and Callie and Verna were serving sandwiches and something that looked suspiciously like champagne. Lavinia seemed pleased, rather than otherwise, that the others had not waited for her in order to begin this celebration. Nevertheless, she immediately took over, guiding her mother to a seat on the most comfortable sofa and whispering to Vicky that she need not stay in such a crowd any longer than she felt like it.

Vicky was enjoying the crowd and she had never thought of such a thing as a daytime rest until it had been foisted upon her; but, because that would give Prosper a chance to slip out to the political meeting, she good-naturedly agreed that, perhaps, she would go upstairs for a while.

"I never would have thought, a year ago last spring, that you'd be so tractable," he told her, when they had reached their room and she had taken off her dress and was reaching for a negligee.

"I am entirely cowed by my husband and his family," she replied demurely. "Besides, I thought that possibly—just possibly—if I came up here, you might find time for a little love-making, which I confess I should enjoy, between the political meeting and the ball."

"You young devil! You know perfectly well that, if I start making love to you, I won't get to the political meeting at all and, possibly, not to the ball."

"Oh, you'd get to the ball! Mother and Anne Marie would see to that. They'd come and pound on the door if we lost track of the time. I'd want them to. After all, this is Anne Marie's great day—hers and your grandfather's. We mustn't forget that or begrudge it to them. Because all *our* days are great days—aren't they, darling?"

He came and put his arms around her, suddenly grave. "Yes. And they always will be. 'As long as fields turn green and bend for the harvest.' That goes for us as well as for Grandfather. And you can't put a value on the way we feel about each other, either, any more than you can on the sun and the soil. It's as priceless as they are."

For a moment, they stood still, enfolded in each other's embrace. Then, as Prosper's arm tightened around her waist and she felt the rising tide of his desire, Vicky gently freed herself and shook her head.

"If I didn't believe that was true, I'd keep you here now," she said. "I'd snatch at every moment I could have with you, because I'd be afraid there couldn't be enough of them. But I know there will be. So I want you to go, to take your place with other men, to do your share in the things they're doing—and then come back to me. I know you always will. Good-by, darling."